A SET MARGINS' PUBLICATION

DOING CREATIVE WORK FROM YOUR POLITICAL BODY

A Guide and Process for Practice-led Research

Myriam D. Diatta

CONTENTS

PART TWO

PART THREE

ACKNOWLEDGMENTS

Between 2018 and 2025, the work for this project was supported by many people, and I wish to extend my gratitude here. In addition to the first version of the acknowledgments I wrote in 2021, I have added an acknowledgment written at the end of Summer 2025.

Acknowledgments: 2025
Thank you to Lisa Grocott for enabling me to first start shaping the concept of "materializing" and teaching me about reflective practice in your design research course at Parsons in 2012. Thank you for supporting me through independent study, research assistantships, design jobs and collaborations, intercontinental travel, a spa visit, and an invitation to pursue a doctorate. I am grateful to Stacy Holman Jones for introducing me to the notion of *doing theory*, on which much of the content of this book is built. Thank you to Jamer Hunt for writing me an email with the subject heading, "Next level..." in which you strongly encouraged me to turn my dissertation into the book you now have in your hands. I am grateful to Freek Lomme of Set Margins' for making this book tangible and accessible and to Toni Wagner for our collaboration. Thank you to Doug Lebsack for proofreading. Thank you to each interview participant for generously contributing your experience to the Interlude chapter. Thank you to all the new friends of Nordic Otherwise for supporting this newcomer.

Acknowledgments: 2021
First, I begin by acknowledging and thanking you, the person who has opened this book. The time you spend reading and thinking with this work gives meaning to the years-long endeavor.

If you are reading this on a screen, these words are reaching you because of the physical hardware that connects the digital device you have acquired and mine. The hardware between us runs underground through territorial waters and stolen land, made from minerals extracted using forced Black, Congolese labor under

Belgian colonization through Chinese distributions. I acknowledge the Bunurong and Wurundjeri people of the Kulin nation and the land that has never been ceded to colonizers. It is through the institution of Monash University, located in what is also known as Melbourne, Australia, that the PhD research was done. I acknowledge the Muscogee (Creek) Nation and what is now also known as Roswell, Georgia, where I wrote the majority of the contents of this document. I acknowledge the American chattel slavery that built the wealth of the city of Roswell and the country I benefit from living in today. This work is built on Black American scholarship. I am grateful to have had the company of theories and hardy offerings from the Black American thinkers and scholars found throughout this work. Thank you for messing with me and urging me to appreciate how it feels to be affected by theory. Thank you to Seren Sensei, Moya Bailey, Tiffany Lethabo King, and Tapji Garba, whose work has influenced the crafting of this acknowledgment.

To my research community, I first thank Lisa Grocott for encouraging me to pursue a doctorate and for your affirming influence, mentorship, and support since 2012. I thank my supervisors, Lisa Grocott and Gene Bawden, for guiding me through the research journey and allowing for the many inflections of this work along the way. Thank you to Stacy Holman Jones for your influences found throughout this book. Thank you to my milestone panelists, Shanti Sumartojo and Brian Martin. Thank you to Shana Agid and Yoko Akama for your grounding pointers for approaching academic research. Thank you to my doctoral examiners, Maarit Mäkelä and Licho Lopez, for your affirming and thoughtful feedback. Thanks to each of you in the WonderLab community for the Zoom calls, meals, walks, and international sleepovers. Thank you to Lina Patel, who never fails to make the subtlest of gestures that have meant the most to me. Finally, thank you to Sonali Ojha—"infinite blessings to you," as you say.

Thank you to Akeema, Ace, and Azar for opening up your homes to me and sharing your wisdom. Thank you to the Nordic Design Research Society's 2019 doctoral consortium at Aalto University and the connections made there: our conversations encouraged portions of the research. Thank you to the participants of the Design Research Society workshop in 2020. Thank you to Ricardo Dutra Gonçalves, Lisa Grocott, Stacy Holman Jones, and Kate McEntee for collaborating on our writing projects and co-authored papers. I have been lucky to have Francis Tseng's company to develop the website portion of this exegesis. Thank you to Katherine for proofreading this document and to David Venema for editing the references and citations. Thank you to Kate McEntee and Lillian Tong for reading and offering notes on this exegesis.

Thank you to the artists and collectives in New York who inspired this work in the first place. Thank you to Karen B. Hanna, whose sharp article, "Living Beyond Survival: 11 Tips for Women of Color in Academia," and our email exchanges deeply informed how I have navigated this academic endeavor since day one. Thank you to Ejoe Wilson, whose work I learned about through watching countless videos online, who is as an example of mastery in embodying movement, politics, history, and spirit—in one step.

•

Lastly, thank you to Sean, my friends, and family.

INTRODUCTION

This book emerges from specific histories and origins. This introduction is intended to provide you, the reader, with insight into the contexts behind this book.

Many of us have learned about oppressive systems and structures around us, but not by reading books or being taught about them by school teachers. We first knew them through feeling them in our bones, guts, or flesh. On the street. While at the produce market. Through whispers between those whom we believed were friends. Where we call home. Or, on the job. And they stick with us on restless, sleepless nights. If we're not privileged enough to be nurtured by family and community that show us that we can resist this violence and operate in other ways in our youth, we're especially vulnerable to decentering and betraying what we know firsthand about the world around us. You then may go to design school, architecture school, music school, art school, theater school, or self-study because you muster up some hope that, compared to conventional studies, there's potential and spaciousness to build on or move past your incoherent experiences.

However, the dissonance can persist in these formal environments. Being is separated from knowing. Practice is separated from theory. You go to the studio or rehearsal space to make things and then go to the lecture hall across campus to study from books and presentation slide decks—back and forth, day after day, year after year. These separated spaces have often worked for me when I was a design student. The repeated movement back and forth, along with the space between, was crucial in my studies as I attempted to connect the two.

Typically, this work of bridging what we learn in theory and what we make in practice is done tacitly without formal guidance or dedicated exploration. For those of us who have first come to know the politics of the world through being in our racialized, gendered, disabled, classed, and politicized bodies, how can we create a space dedicated to what happens between theory and practice? How do we foster that space for the purpose of honoring our particular ways of knowing the world?

Doing creative work from your political body involves using your personal experience, your creative skill set and materials, and your understanding of the social and political world around you. This book was written to affirm what you already know about the world through your experience. My hope is that if you are experiencing isolation as a professional or student among harsh, dismissive, corporate, state, or institutional contexts, this book will become a trusted companion as you navigate, contribute to, abolish, leverage, refuse, and subvert these spaces.

WHO IS THIS BOOK FOR?

This book is for anyone interested in being politically engaged. It is for anyone drawn to making creative interventions—at any scale. Alternatively, you may be an onlooker curious about the inner workings behind these kinds of practices.

You may have picked this book up because you are a creative practitioner—designer, musician, architect, dancer, writer, filmmaker, computational artist, photographer, sculptor, or beyond, who is looking to incorporate more of your own experience into your professional practice. You may be a student, from doctoral to master's level, seeking out ways to work with and write with theory that feel relevant and honest to you.

You may have a long personal history of taking action on the front lines of a particular political lineage. You may want to braid together the action you take and the politics you believe in. Or, you may be seeking out ways to incorporate these political ideas into the things you make and do. You may do political work for which you want to interweave and turn up the creative aspects of what you do in meaningful ways.

You may be an educator seeking methodologies and approaches to better support your students and the everyday political conditions they navigate. You may want to encourage a more integrated, transformative pedagogy. You may be a theorist or historian who teaches practitioners and is looking for frameworks to reposition how you approach your role to support them.

WHAT YOU'LL GAIN FROM THIS BOOK

When you pick up a book at your favorite political bookstore and read it, what happens to the political ideas you were touched by? How do the theories make their way into what you perform, build, or facilitate? When you work in your studio or rehearsal space, how does the time you spend making come to shape your politics and worldview? Where and when does the shaping happen, precisely? How do you discern which aspects of your practice need nurturing? How does it all come together toward your intentions or aims?

Using the guide and process presented here, the practitioner can learn four robust skills that, when used together, can be used to study and advance their own practice. As a result, the practitioner can precisely pinpoint where and articulate how they engage with socio-political issues and theories. They can move with more accountability and radical conviction as they grow in their political and creative maturity. This means they can build a kind of self-awareness that is action-oriented, calibrating to each concern at hand. Thus, the practitioner can deepen their creative work's engagement with socio-political issues while boosting the meaning their work generates about everyday life.

The art and design theorist can also gain insights into a framework that prioritizes practice. This book aims to reposition the historian, critic, curator, and theorist's gaze on and relation with the creative practices on which they write and teach. This book also offers the educator a comprehensive package that connects the often disparate-seeming dots that students are often left to traverse on their own: the gap between theory and practice.

TERMS AND CONCEPTS

Here, I define the references, common understandings, and misconceptions associated with some of the concepts in the book. More terms are defined in Chapter 1.

Theory and Practice

I use multiple phrases interchangeably to describe a pairing of things that are abstract and things that are concrete: theory and practice, thinking and doing, knowing and being, values and actions, and politicized commitments and everyday life.

The relationships between theory and practice remain fluid and fragmented throughout this book. At times, I work with the reality that theory and practice can be two separate entities. Sometimes, I treat them as one thing, fundamentally inseparable. In other instances, I work with the premise that they are distinct yet mutually influential. Sometimes theory refers to things that are text-based, like a book or essay, while sometimes, I refer to it as knowledge far beyond the limits of academic knowledge production. At times, I have angst toward theory—troubled by the hegemonic ivory tower from which it is disseminated—and also have gratitude toward theory—centering the Black, queer, southern, and creative theorists I relate most with who have written and produced it.

While the term *praxis* may seem appropriate to use to describe the work we do with theory and practice, I have not found the term useful as it is used liberally and imprecisely—sometimes in place of "practice" simply because it sounds sexier. It has specific uses within spiritual, medical, and pedagogical contexts. It can connote a unidirectional action of applying theory to practice. Most notably, the term itself comes with a complex, philosophical, European can of worms that is not appropriate for the interests of this book.

Creative Work

In this book, the term "creative work" is inclusive. The term "creative" concerns modes of operation not limited to architecture, dance, sculpture, jazz, lighting design, poetry, coding, filmmaking, fashion design, and beyond. "Work" refers to the concrete act of making things and the technical skills and conceptual thinking involved in doing it, whether in professional practice or in the preparation of students for professional work.

The approach in this book stems from design, which has been extrapolated to support all kinds of creative work. When I use the term "design," I primarily refer to a professional commercial practice in which designers design functional things, ranging from hearing aids, bicycles, packaging, apps, and dinnerware to hospital wings and user experiences with public services. I derived the process and methods detailed in Part 2 of this book from the ineffable, tacit sensibilities and skill sets designers develop over time. The years I have spent studying, training, and working as a designer has informed how I handle others' experiences, develop ideas, make the ideas usable, and take the process of "making" seriously.

Political Body

The term "body" can refer to flesh, bones, and selfhood. Here, it suggests that the body is a site of inquiry or point of departure. This guide, process, and framework pair the terms "political" and "body" to suggest the two are entangled. Throughout the six chapters, this relation is further deconstructed, defined, and practiced.

I initially developed the approach described in this book to house multiple things at once: my creative work, my personal politics at the time, and the realities of being in fragmented states of consciousness, dissociation, and dysmorphia. This book offers an approach for reckoning with incoherent, fragmented, violent, unstable, impossible, and irresolvable political conditions.

Knowledge and Expertise

Formalized knowledge is presented as written theory published by an academic journal or publisher. Traditionally, to be a "good" student, author, or academic, you must master and demonstrate expertise *over* schools of thought. The effort to know and establish familiarity with existing work is approached through a systematic review of ideas published in academic papers, dissertations, and books. In this book, I do not attempt to demonstrate my expertise by identifying problematized gaps in knowledge, exercise rigor by asserting my mastery over others' work, enhance the replicability of the outcomes, or imagine carrying out an objective, unbiased review of an established field. This book aims to be unsystematic and approaches others' work by way of acknowledgment and intimacy.

There is temporality in knowing things. I write about the creative work I did between 2018 and 2021. The first pieces of content from this book were first written in 2019. Then revisited in 2024. Then finalized in 2025. With this temporality, much of the content in the book has remained unchanged since 2019, despite developments in my practice and changes in my beliefs since then. Some content has been edited or newly added to reflect changes over time. Further, I fully intend for my ideas to have changed and transformed by the time this reaches your hands, years or decades from now.

The area of expertise from which I write is professional practice. Secondarily, I use theory to argue for the epistemic depths of critical creative practice. Where, in Part 1, there may be theoretical arguments and concepts that appear, especially to the traditional theorist, thin or incomplete, in Part 2, I double down on my epistemic stance by rounding out the same theoretical inquiries through the doing of concrete practice rather than continuing via the single mode of theoretical abstraction. I model how practice can speak back to theory.

HOW TO USE THIS BOOK

This book can be read in two modes. It can be read as a theoretical text for you to think with, to find language to describe your creative work, to use as a reference for refining your research or teaching approach, or to keep close as an affirming companion as you navigate a prickly academic program you're enrolled in.

Alternatively, you can use the second half of this book as a practical, hands-on guide for doing creative work from your political body. You can regularly crack the book open in your studio space, take notes in it, and actively use it alongside what you're making.

This book also serves as a demonstration of the shape a book can take—one that not only produces ideas on a topic or theorizes about creative practice by observing, thinking, imagining, reading, discussing, and writing, but itself theorizes *through* actual making and doing—through practice.

Approach

The theoretical chapters of the book, including Chapters 1 through 3, serve as scaffolding. The work I write about in this book started with doing actual creative work. As a result I built the theoretical framework to name what went on in practice. The approach can be shared, challenged, and used to argue for what you do as a practitioner.

This approach, where practice leads the inquiry, stems from the field of "practice-led research." The term "practice" in "practice-led research" refers to professional practice. "Research" refers to questions, studies, and knowledge produced by doing research in academic institutions. Rather than conducting research through surveys, interviews, observation, literature reviews, or comparison to explore a question, practice-led research repurposes professional practice and its competencies as the means of exploring research questions.

Methods
In Chapter 3, you will find the methods I used for studying what happens between theory and practice. You can refer to Chapter 4 for a detailed demonstration and examples of the methods in use. Chapter 6 teaches you to use the methods, step by step. These sections of the book are especially suited for politically engaged practitioners who work with creative mediums, for instance, clay for the ceramicist, code for the internet-based artist, paper models for the architect, or one's own body for the dancer. Secondarily, the methods can be used by anyone who works with social and political contexts.

Footnotes and Citations
On nearly every page, you'll find footnotes that point to other folks' writing, films, YouTube videos, personal stories, and more. You can use the footnotes as much as you like, skip most of them, or follow what draws your attention. They elaborate on the ideas in the main body of the page and bring into conversation the ideas, troubles, people, affirmations, and lineages that inform what's on the page. Sometimes, I expose details of how I came to know a reference or who shared it with me. Other times, I do not. Sometimes, the footnotes will take up a large portion of the page, symbolizing the pieces and forms of knowledge that are on the periphery, made illegible to others, and happen elsewhere.

Through my critical citation practice,[1] I am intimate with what I reference and cite. I read what feeds or challenges what I am seeking. I include content that touches me. Messes with me. I refuse the

1 Myriam Diatta, "Undisciplining Who We Bring to the Academic Table: Practical Tactics to Accompany Critical Creative Inquiry," *Parse*, no. 17 (2023), https://parsejournal.com/article/ undisciplining-who-we-bring-to-the-academic-table/

gaze and the bluffing that the paranoid reader does:[2] "You haven't read her book?!" "You don't know this author? What?!"[3] Instead, I deliberately reveal precisely how we are personally in relation with others' ideas, creative work, lineages, and schools of thought over time. I approach my authorship and investigations as always unfinished, temporal, relational, interpersonal, malleable, and unsystematic. I reject the notion that an author exposing that they are piecing together others' thoughts is a sign of a lack of original expertise. The ideas in this book are in progress before, during, and after its writing.

Reader–Author Relationship

Throughout the book, the relationships between the book itself, you, the reader, and me, the author, shift. Sometimes, I refer to a collective "we." This may refer to creative practitioners as a whole, to those of us who are racialized, or to everyone and anyone. Sometimes, I refer to you—speaking directly to you or signaling tacitly that I am not referring to you, positioning you as an onlooker while I direct my message to a specific audience. This asks the reader to pay attention to and be accountable to the relationships between theory, the author of the ideas, and the reader's relative positionality.

I also introduce ways to approach theory and practice; the reader becomes a participant, being prompted to use the methods and exercises to reflect on their own critical and creative practice. When I switch to writing in first person, I peel back the curtain and reveal what goes on behind the scenes for doing practice-led research.

2 Eve Kosofsky Sedgwick, Michelle Alna Barale, Jonathan Goldberg, and Michael Moon, "Paranoid Reading and Reparative Reading, or, You're so Paranoid, You Probably Think This Essay is About You," in *Touching Feeling* (Duke University Press, 2002), 123-51.

3 Esperanza Spalding, "I'm Not the 'Musical Prodigy' I've Been Made Out to Be." Guy Raz, September 10, 2024, 29:42, https://www.youtube.com/watch?v=uw7piG9vRic&t=2s

A Special Note for the Doctoral Student

This book, in its earliest form, was originally a doctoral dissertation in the field of design research. Since then, I have taken sections of chapters and moved them to another chapter, removed most mentions of terms like "methodology," "epistemology," "ontology," "dissertation," "exegesis," etc., and lastly, inserted a new interlude, and added the hands-on guide at the end of the book. If you are seeking precedents for how to deal with the traditional expectations of writing a dissertation, you can use this book as one way of doing practice-led research. In addition to the critical citation practice and authorship style I discussed above, I have modeled an alternative to (1) the literature review, (2) methodology, and (3) contributions.

You can find what was originally the literature review in Chapter 2, Section 2, in the Extended Acknowledgments. A traditional review of literature was not possible because I could not find adjacent academic research that would be authentically relevant to the research I did through my design practice. One day, I came up with and decided to play with the concept of an Extended Acknowledgments that would be a continuation of the acknowledgments section, usually at the beginning of a dissertation. Instead of thanking professors, family, and friends in the literature review, I acknowledged and gathered the professional practitioners whose practices—some academic, others not—made a relevant home for my research project. This was my review of the literature.

What would traditionally be the methodology chapter is now found in Chapter 2, Section 3. I did not pick a theoretical framework "off the shelf," so to speak. While it may have been possible to pick an existing and established methodology from anthropology or literary studies and then begin the practice portion of the research, I was doing practice-led doctoral studies. For me, practice-led research, distinct from practice-based research, means starting with actually doing professional creative practice, letting questions emerge about creative work at the *epistemic* level—not only about a new topic, method, or technique—and then building a framework around the questions that then allow for that inquiry to be discussed and examined. In this book, I use the term "framework" to refer to the methodology.

The contributions section of my dissertation can be found in Chapter 5. Through my research community of critical friends and supervisors in WonderLab at Monash University in Melbourne, Australia, I was taught that "new" and "original" contributions are what are traditionally expected in research, and this was neither possible nor desired in our community. Research in our lab aimed to acknowledge the lineages we build on and problematized the notion of the "new" knowledge. A professor and critical friend of the lab, Yoko Akama, advised me once on a walk through her neighborhood in Melbourne that as PhD students, we were contributing one small brick to a larger house. We could critique the premise of the house, but I took that to mean that I could choose the house to which I would contribute a brick, as well as whether that brick was being launched from the other side of a gate or congruently laid, among others. The contribution I made was to fellow critical creative practitioners and practitioner-researchers. In Chapter 5, I lay out how I matured my professional practice, how the epistemic questions about it were explored through practice, as well as the greater socio-political implications of this contribution.

CONTEXT AND BIRTHPLACE

I finished the first version of this book in September 2021. At the time, I was a designer, facilitator, and doctoral student who was reading about and working on politically-engaged projects. That early version of the book was a result of a very personal search to understand the inner workings of my own creative, personal, and political practice starting in 2018. This was important to me because, as many people do in their careers, I hit a point where

I needed a pause. In my case, I needed to reconcile more than a decade of design training and experience on the one hand with the increasingly political and liberation-oriented life I was living on the weekends and evenings. 2018 marked the start of a project to build up a library of ideas for reference, create actual methods I could turn to and use, and conceptual frameworks I could rely on and keep me centered on my creative upbringing and political aims. This book is a result of what I drew together through that project.

My education and training led me from the spatial and commercial foundations of interior design and industrial design to the formal study of transdisciplinary design. The latter concentrates on the social and system orientations of design—designing how a patient interfaces with the services provided by a hospital, designing ways for school teachers to incorporate new cognitive science research into the way they teach their students, or reimagining city infrastructure for its residents' preparedness in the case of an environmental disaster. From there, I ran a design consulting studio in New York City with two graduate school classmates for a few years. When I first began my endeavors in design as a high school intern at an architecture firm for two years, my interests were in how material things and spaces could support our internal emotional well-being. At the time, while I believed design may be the way to go about that kind of inquiry, my attraction had less to do with becoming a "professional designer."

I began a PhD with that same pressing interest in mind. As a low-residency student, I found myself in a research culture in an Australian university. Personally and academically, the nature of this space urged me to articulate the tangle of anti-Blackness, anti-Indigeneity, and whiteness in which I was to do the research. I began the research process in 2018 as an inquiry into the everyday coping tools folks use in their living rooms, bedrooms, and kitchens. I set out to study the interiority of the lives of those of us who press up against dominating imaginations and structures. I had set out for that project to be a way for my education in interior design and industrial design to intersect with my growing understanding of my own politicization in the world. Quickly, though, doing three-hour interviews with friends and friends of friends in their private spaces while I reported on my time with them became unsettling. It was unsettling because I was investigating the coping objects and the intimate conversations between us, not exclusively by us and for us as intended, but in an institutional research setting. Because of this, I shifted the boundaries of what is appropriate to bring into that space. I turned my focus to studying, writing about, and being accountable for how I show up in my own practice.

I became more real with myself about the formal, extremely specific values that come with doing work in this setting, so I came to understand that much of the work is about attending to the boundaries and shifts between private and public. I turned to focus on my relationship with whiteness, drawing on what I personally know to be true, as well as theory about that relationship: namely, W. E. B. Du Bois' notion of double consciousness. I explore the concept in the second half of this book, but what I highlight here is how this work depends on the scholarship of descendants of American chattel slavery.

I am a Black and Asian researcher born in Dakar, Sénégal, who was raised in a Japanese household in the periphery of Atlanta, Georgia in the US. I am not a descendant of American chattel slavery; I am a first-generation immigrant from a French-colonial context. Black American scholarship is often auto-theoretical, meaning it comes from firsthand ways of knowing. Through this book, I aim to stay in conversation with scholarship about Blackness and engage with it—not topically or casually—but as ways of knowing. I remain concentrated on our interiorities: Black interiority. The conviction and curiosity about the potential of material things and how we make things, with which I started, remain.

•

When I think about community members, designers, artists, and scholars whose work and ways of showing up I look up to, I spend a lot of time thinking about how they got there. Sometimes, these thoughts consume my conversations with friends and colleagues. We wonder what kinds of things they pay attention to on an average day, how they spend their time, who is in their mind's eye as they do their work, whom they look up to, and how that affects what they do. It is the work they do behind the thinking, methodology, projects, or words they outwardly present that I look for. You may also find yourself digging around the haze, looking for answers as you read their work or listen to talks, interviews, and conversations in which they are a part. I have experienced rare moments in which they have revealed a piece of it in their work, or I have gotten a glimpse of it when I have had an opportunity to ask them in person.

There are, also, the kinds of community members, designers, artists, and scholars who are confident, open, and generous in the sense of explicitly sharing these things they do behind the work: they not only mention how they do what they do here and there but intentionally pay attention to and compose the deeply inner, messy, vulnerable parts of their work to share with us. They expose much of what it takes for them to show up in the way they do. I see their transparent offerings as invitations for more of us to interrogate how we do what we do—breaking down the separation put up between the expertise of one person and that of those working to make their own ways through the haze. Informed by this, the methods, my explorations of what happened in each context, and the framework I built have all aimed to make things visible. It makes visible what I pay attention to, who is in my mind's eye, the tables where I have a seat, and how that affects what I do. This book has been my effort to carefully craft the deeply inner, messy parts of the much larger project of unmaking the worlds we live in.[4]

This work is tailored for the designer and artist who explores socio-political contexts—from Blackness and Indigeneity to queerness and disability. While the theoretical essays and books that you read about these contexts are a core part of your practice, this book is an invitation to consider the relationships between these texts you read, the things you make as a creative practitioner, and your everyday experience in these socio-political contexts. My hope is for this book to affirm the way you already work and help you make decisions about how you cut, glue, code, weave, dye, rhyme, read, and weld to make and unmake our contemporary realities.

4 Diatta, "Undisciplining Who We Bring to the Academic Table."

PART ONE

CHAPTER ONE

This book is dedicated to a single matter: the space between theory and practice.

At the heart of this book lies an inquiry into theory and practice.[1] This is executed in cumulatively morphing forms throughout the book: *first*, in the form of a framework that languages what the space between theory and practice entails; *second*, in the form of everyday stories of practitioners working between; *third*, in the form of a special process for investigating the space between; *fourth*, in the form of a demonstration of this process being used; and *finally*, in the form of a hands-on workbook for you to learn to use the process.

Although it is the task of this book to animate "the between," the following opening establishes what the space between is, why it's worth investigating, and defines the core concepts underpinning the book.

1
WHAT IS AT STAKE?

In every political act lies a relationship between what is done in practice and what is valued in theory. The ways we show up in a meeting, for a friend, fund a project, or respond to an emergency may be in tension with the politicized commitments with which we may associate. You may happen to believe in the power of communal living, but at home, you neglect the agreement you made to do your dishes, leaving the labor to your exasperated housemates.[2] When I was teaching, I was committed to subverting the university system in theory, but in the classroom, I didn't account for the shared responsibility of students' broader learning environment, judged

1 See Introduction: Terms and Concepts for how theory and practice are defined for the purposes of this book.

2 A misalignment noted by Mia Mingus, abolitionist, disability justice, and transformative justice organizer, in "What Is Accountability?," Barnard Center for Research on Women, July 26, 2019, https://www.youtube.com/watch?v=LjRbj57vBvA.

students' individual performance, and gave out grades.[3] You may ideologically value mutual aid, but you have not introduced yourself to your neighbors who have lived to the left and right of you for years.[4] You may be a well-renowned professional known for your philosophy and politics, but your hiring practices perpetuate the realities you warn against.[5] These misalignments have personal and societal implications that range from inconvenience to true harm. It is a personal endeavor to recognize where we are aligned and misaligned with what we may personally care about. If we take this vantage point on politicized work, it can be seen that we constantly move between everyday actions in practice and commitments made in theory.

Each individual's capacity to recognize and act on rifts between what's valued and what's actually done is also constituted by societal forces at play that enforce the binary separation. Drawing from the previous examples, what makes it so challenging for you to open up to your neighbors? Could it be related to your experience with a xenophobic stranger who violated your autonomy and personal space? How did the neoliberal conditions of my already precarious employment as a part-time teacher living in one of the world's most expensive cities prevent me from acting on what I believed about universities? Holding oneself to one's own values is a malleable and multi-scalar endeavor. This can be challenging and even physically dangerous to align theory and practice. Collaborating with others

3 A misalignment noted by Stefano Harney in a conversation organized by StrikeMOMA Working Group of the International Imagination of Anti-National Anti-Imperialist Feelings (IIAAF). "A Conversation with Sandy Grande, Stefano Harney, Fred Moten, Jasbir Puar, and Dylan Rodriguez," Strike MoMA, May 28, 2021, https://www.youtube.com/watch?v=V2vzhwnjy4s.

4 A misalignment noted by Ambar in a conversation titled, "Anarchism and Black Struggle: A Panel Discussion," organized by Rosa Negra–Anarchist Federation (2020).

5 A misalignment disclosed to me by a friend in 2017.

and noticing the doings of folks around us is an ever-changing undertaking.

Whatever principles we follow become aligned with our actions in multiple ways. You may pick up a different manner of working from the communities in which you surround yourself. Your actions may slowly come to reflect your commitments through disorienting, dread-filled private moments of introspection. It may happen through an intimate conversation with another person. You may go out of your way to seek mentorship to become more consistent and accountable to what is important to you. While reading a socio-political book, you may come to validate and reify your past experiences. You may rarely think about your values because you've wholly embodied them in your mannerisms, grammar, and spirit thanks to your friends and family traditions. You may have improvised your approach to a hard conversation with a neighbor one evening and later gone online to find resources created by folks who have more experience with conflict resolution. You may suddenly be hit with a story a grandparent used to tell you while you're in the middle of a meeting at work, causing you to immediately center your demeanor. You may read a poem before bed that changes you completely.

While we are affected by others' actions and their ideas, the inner workings of precisely *how* we do the aligning are harder to pinpoint. Exactly how did the ideas in your favorite book affect what you ended up making in your studio? How did the intimate conversation you had with someone change how you show up? How did the challenging conflict with your neighbor shape your abstract political ideals?

This book exposes the relationships between theory and practice, defines ways of making the relationships visible, and equips you with ways to bring the two closer and closer together in your own practice. I do so through an approach developed and led not by abstract theorizing but by practice. You are invited to do this investigation through practice while simultaneously speaking back to textual theory. A practice-led approach can give continuity between creative practice and the written theories that inform a practitioner's politics.[6]

This book does not imagine it possible to eliminate misalignments between theory and practice. Nor does it care for exposing the misalignments of others. This book aims to productively tug on each of our own internal unrest as we consider the ways we show up in the world. I intend this work to offer not only abstract frames of thinking and anecdotes but also practical methods for you to observe how you traverse between your concrete work and your abstract work. I aim to demystify the breadth and depth of working between which often emerges tacitly, by chance, or is disciplined out of us. By doing so, I open up multiple possibilities for investigating the implicit relationships between theory and practice.

For the politicized practitioner dedicated to collective action with others, this work brings attention to and honors the hum of private, interior reflections and experience that goes on moment to moment. For the critical scholar, this work brings the theoretical negotiations and debates into conversation with actual practice, not only to apply theory to practice but to illustrate how theory and the theorist may be shaped by practice and the practitioner.

Getting to know what happens when we oscillate between what is concrete and what is abstract means we can move between them more deliberately and approach our work with more self-awareness in contemporary socio-political contexts with others.

6 See the Introduction chapter for more on practice-led research.

2
CORE CONCEPTS

This section of the introduction defines the basic concepts on which this work is built: *politics, practice, theory,* and *knowledge production*. This establishes the frames of reference on which the concepts, approaches, and tools of this book are based. First, I take the boundless landscape of political takes on oppressive systems and name the specific scope of interest for this book. I follow that with notes about (creative) practice, (critical) theory, and (practice-led) knowledge production. While the following section begins to detail the terms one by one, it solely serves to introduce you to each relevant core concept. The concepts are incorporated and expanded on in the following chapters.

In this book, the term *politics* refers to experiences, activities, and worldviews concerning power. When analyzing and participating in political contexts, what is readily evident are the systems, complexes, matrices, pillars, structures, products, and overt actions done by people.[7] These are resisted in the public domain: on the streets, in forests, at geopolitical borders, in institutions, and online. What is less evident—but loaded with material consequences—are the conversations had behind your back, how "that woman expected

7 Kimberlé Crenshaw, Patricia Hill Collins, Angela Davis, and Andrea Smith inform this understanding of the systems we navigate. They are Black and indigenous scholars. See Kimberlé Crenshaw, "Demarginalizing the Intersection of Race and Sex: A Black Feminist Critique of Antidiscrimination Doctrine, Feminist Theory and Antiracist Politics," *University of Chicago Legal Forum*, no. 1 (1989): 139-67; Patricia Hill Collins, *Black Feminist Thought: Knowledge, Consciousness, and the Politics of Empowerment*, Unwin Hyman, 1990; Angela Y. Davis, *Are Prisons Obsolete? Seven Stories Press*, 2003; Andrea Smith, "Heteropatriarchy and the Three Pillars of White Supremacy," In *Color of Violence: The INCITE! Anthology*, ed. INCITE! Women of Color Against Violence (Duke University Press, 2016), 66-73.

something from me,"[8] or the slick replacements made at your expense.[9] Oppression and violence also happen in covert, whispery ways, and I concentrate the efforts of this book at this register.

In the 15th century, long before the ships set sail southward and westward, there were first private conversations being had and insinuations being made in the Mediterranean and what is now Europe.[10] These conversations and insinuations were full of deadly imagination.[11] It is the same elusiveness that has us watching our backs today. In a supermarket parking lot, for instance, it is not only the woman's words or tone of voice toward you that are disturbing. It is the erotic behind her expecting you to move for her that makes up the intimate dimensions of domination.[12] It reaches into how you are depended on. It is in the humidity of sitting in the classroom, reading the textbooks that begin with "shakespeare. ... keats. ... austen" that is so scalding.[13] As poet Nayyirah Waheed offers, the dead authors crash "into our young houses. making us islands. easy isolations."[14] In this book, I stick to these understandings of what

8 Sharon P. Holland, *The Erotic Life of Racism* (Duke University Press, 2012), 3.

9 Nayyirah Waheed, *Nejma* (CreateSpace Independent Publishing Platform, 2014).

10 Hortense J. Spillers, "Changing the Letter: The Yokes, the Jokes of Discourse, or, Mrs. Stowe, Mr. Reed." In *Black, White, and in Color: Essays on American Literature and Culture* (University of Chicago Press, 2003), 176-202; Tapji Garba and Sara-Maria Sorentino, "Slavery Is a Metaphor: A Critical Commentary on Eve Tuck and K. Wayne Yang's 'Decolonization Is Not a Metaphor,'" *Antipode* 52, no. 3 (2020): 764-82, https://doi.org/10.1111/anti.12615.

11 Toni Morrison, *Playing in the Dark: Whiteness and the Literary Imagination*, Harvard University Press, 1992; Saidiya V. Hartman, *Scenes of Subjection: Terror, Slavery, and Self-Making in Nineteenth-Century America*, Oxford University Press, 1997.

12 Sharon P. Holland, *The Erotic Life of Racism* (Duke University Press, 2012).

13 A book of poetry given to me by one of my oldest, dearest friends, Azar (Waheed, *Nejma*, 36-37).

14 Waheed, *Nejma*, 36.

we are up against. Neither the individuals nor the ideologies that make up the dominating conversations, white imaginations, intimacies, and humidity are centered in this book. However, I have briefly introduced them here to assert that we need inner investigations that can hold up against these dimensions of domination.

We gain some insight into what inner investigations and approaches may look like if we imagine what we do behind closed doors when we go home or shut the car door and sit at the wheel to counteract that incident in the supermarket. Or what intimate face-to-face education we arm ourselves with, despite the humid conditions of the classroom. Or the affirmations we repeat to ourselves in bed in the dark on sleepless nights. It is at this scale—in our private spaces—that we can resist the whispery kinds of advances made on us and explore, despite them, what it entails to work with the theory we know about, the history we experience, and the creative practice we think with. There is a politics to the inner dimensions of social life.

For instance, bell hooks suggests the goings-on and significance of interiorities by stating, "To enter black homes in my childhood was to enter a world that valued the visual, that asserted our collective will to participate in a noninstitutionalized curatorial process."[15] There is a connection between the "noninstitutionalized process" that hooks hints toward and a story about James Baldwin, a beloved American literary figure. When he fled the US to write in Switzerland, Baldwin "had to bring his records with him in the fifties, like a secret stash of medicine ... to keep him connected to a Harlem of the spirit."[16] The interiorities behind this story about Baldwin are not limited to the physical interior space of his living room in Switzerland, but are about the "quality of being inward": a

15 bell hooks, "In Our Glory: Photography and Black Life," in *Art on My Mind: Visual Politics* (The Free Press, 1995), 61.

16 Teju Cole, "Black Body: Rereading James Baldwin's 'Stranger in the Village,'" *The New Yorker*, August 19, 2014, https://www.newyorker.com/books/page-turner/black-body-rereading-james-baldwins-stranger-village.

"reservoir" of inner experience.[17] So, hooks brings forth that there are deliberate decisions, a curation that goes on in terms of what is brought in and kept out of our interiorities. Black culture and literary scholar, Kevin Quashie marks the significance of interiorities in the context of political resistance by revealing that "the interior can inform a way of being in the world that is not consumed by publicness but that is expressive and dynamic nonetheless."[18] These notions of interiority are the point of focus of this book's politics.[19]

The work of this book is led by personal experience. The entirety of this work is done at a scale like that of being behind closed doors. First-person accounts of everyday social life form the basis of this book. I spot the tactics I use in the everyday to navigate oppressive insinuations. Through the concepts I detail in theory and the actual methods and exercises you'll engage with in this book, I advocate for what we already know and do in the face of the whispery forms of oppression inflicted on us and double down on this register to intensify how we navigate it. I situate this work between arguments that reject the outside gaze and arguments that resist it head-on. The politics of this book are not optimistic, not looking to make amends, spiritually bypass, or brush off everyday oppressive systems. This would be a dangerous endeavor (both conceptually and physically). Nor is it consumed by constantly and only speaking back and dismantling those systems and imaginations—an essential endeavor that proves to be exhausting without places for us to

17 Kevin Everod Quashie, *The Sovereignty of Quiet Beyond Resistance in Black Culture* (Rutgers University Press, 2012), 21.

18 Quashie, *The Sovereignty of Quiet*, 52.

19 This section introduces the notion of interiorities. Throughout this book, I repeat, build, and elaborate on interiorities: inner ways of knowing and the interior structure of creative work in Chapter 2, and working in the interiorities in Chapter 3.

hide.[20] This work is based on upholding spaces in which to center oneself, re-arm, and create our own safety and sustainability.

I use the concept of *practice* to describe the repeated, informed application of an idea or method that happens while doing professional practice. The term can also imply a close association with an established field of academic study. The sort of practice this book focuses on is creative practice. It is designed to support practices including design, architecture, performance, music, writing, digital media, visual art, and more. There are many lineages, value judgments, and distinctions drawn between what is produced by each respective creative practice, its functions, and the skillsets of the practitioners who enact them.[21] Much less interested in the discipline-specific paradigms around designerly, performative, and artistic practice, I use the term to highlight the knowledge that professional creative practitioners develop through the materials with which they work. A highly repetitive, methodical, years-long interaction with physical materials amounts to informed sensibilities toward them that is only possible through this kind of repeated interaction.[22]

We can appreciate the nuances of these sensibilities if we think of the knowing behind the movements a seasoned dancer makes with their body, an architect's negotiation of conceptual and spatial considerations of a city block, or the knowing behind a skilled potter responding to the chemistry of their glazes and plasticity of

20 E. Jane, "I Am Not an Identity Artist Just Because I Am a Black Artist with Multiple Selves." Tumblr, November 1, 2015, https://www.e-janestudio.tumblr.com/post/132335744305/i-am-not-an-identity-artist-just-because-i-am-a.

21 Grace Lees-Maffei and Linda Sandino, "Dangerous Liaisons: Relationships between Design, Craft and Art," *Journal of Design History* 17 (2004), https://doi.org/10.1093/jdh/17.3.207.

22 Riika Latva-Somppi, Maarit Mäkelä, and Ozgu Gündeşlioğlu, "Traces from the Anthropocene: Working with Soil," *RUUKKU Studies in Artistic Research* 14 (2020): 1-26, https://doi.org/ 10.22501/ruu.697190.

the clay with which they work. I work with the understanding that, as my mentor and design researcher, Lisa Grocott wrote about more than 15 years ago, there is thinking involved in making[23] and I take an interest in the ineffable goings on when visual, material things are made. When I use the term practice throughout this book, I not only refer to a profession or physical actions but emphasize the conceptual negotiations and making tangible that creative practitioners do amid producing a made thing. What is of interest here is what making can do in combination with everyday social life and socio-political theory.

> Interviewer: You said somewhere that making abstract art can be just as political as making art with representation. What do you mean by that? How can abstract art be political?
> Sam Gilliam: It messes with you.
>
> —An interview with Sam Gilliam, Black American painter[24]

The conversation quoted above brings attention to the relationship between material things and abstract things. In the context of the academic institution, when the term *theory* is used, it traditionally refers to abstract ideas, arguments, propositions, and worldviews that are thought about, discussed, written, reviewed, and published in academic publications like journals and books. Here, the concept of theory takes on various forms. Sometimes the term does refer to theory that is formal, academic, institutional, and text-based. Many times, the term will be used to unsystematically describe things we know about social life and can take the form of a story, a conversation between friends, a song, a memory, a film, a novel,

23 Lisa Grocott, "Design Research & Reflective Practice: The Facility of Design-Oriented Research to Translate Practitioner Insights into New Understandings of Design," PhD thesis, RMIT University, 2010.

24 b. 1933; Louisiana Channel, "Sam Gilliam Interview: Artists Are Supposed to Change," May 28, 2020, 06:00, https://www.youtube.com/watch?v=ciN6ZPDMJV4.

a proverb, an observation made in childhood, a poem, and much more. Throughout the past two or three decades, Black Studies has made use of "critical theory" to critique its (European) lineages and magnify arguments about social life and death.[25] I use what Black Studies[26] produces as an apparatus for critiquing material and immaterial violence—rife with potential for messing with our worldviews.

Formal theories and worldviews belong to various schools of thought and lineages. Whether you have taken a traditional academic path by enrolling in an art academy, design, performance, or architecture school, are self-taught, or developed your education through a series of apprenticeships and residencies, we are surrounded by established borders that define what we produce. These delineations mark the worldviews and lineages we are and are not a part of. These borders can be maintained by design studios, clients, cultural institutions, professors, online platforms, publishers, curators, educators, peers, and funding bodies. For critical, politicized practitioners, our processes and what we produce veer across, beyond, and against these borders. As we work, we produce not only things and experiences, but we also produce ideas and knowledge about the worlds we navigate.

> "Despite knowing otherwise, we are often disciplined into thinking through and along the lines that reinscribe our own annihilation."[27] ... This is why, as it is for black philosophers like Moten, Hartman,

25 Patrice Douglass and Frank Wilderson, "The Violence of Presence: Metaphysics in a Blackened World," *Black Scholar* 43, no. 4 (2013): 117, https://doi.org/10.1080/00064246. 2013.11413674.

26 See the Acknowledgments for more.

27 Christina Sharpe, *In the Wake: On Blackness and Being* (Duke University Press, 2016), 13; cited in Axelle Karera, "Blackness and the Pitfalls of Anthropocene Ethics," *Critical Philosophy of Race* 7, no. 1 (2019): 32-56. https://doi.org/10.5325/critphilrace.7.1.0032.

> Jackson, Sexton, Warren, and many others, to be black and critical is necessarily to engage in disorderly conduct, to become "undisciplined" as Sharpe herself puts it.
>
> —Axelle Karera in "Blackness and the Pitfalls of Anthropocene Ethics"[28]

Knowledge production, in this book, is anti-disciplinary and led by practice. The task of producing knowledge traditionally involves surveying all the relevant literature published in a particular school of thought. Then, you identify a gap in the academic literature and fill it with new knowledge you produce. However, I did not develop the methods and concepts I establish in this book by identifying a gap in the academic literature. What I did in my creative practice and the questions that arose from it led the inquiry.[29] As a result, neither the politicized interests nor the explorations are about the discipline in which I am trained (i.e., Design).[30] One reaction to this may be to attempt to fit the knowledge back into the "orders and borders"[31] of a domain of knowledge production. Emerging professional practitioners, students, or early-career researchers may be inclined or instructed to do so. This would make the work possible and legible to disciplinary ways of knowing.[32] However, in the making of this book, I took on a problem-oriented approach to research by understanding it as disciplinary imperialism and

28 Karera, "Blackness and the Pitfalls," 32-56.

29 See Introduction: Knowledge and Expertise for more. Also see Irit Rogoff, "Practicing Research: Singularising Knowledge," *MAkuZine* 9 (2010): 37-42; Linda Candy and Ernest Edmonds, "Practice-Based Research in the Creative Arts: Foundations and Futures from the Front Line." *Leonardo* 51, no. 1 (2018): 63-69, https://doi.org/10.1162/ LEON_a_01471.

30 See the Introduction: Creative Work or Context and Birthplace for more.

31 Wendelin Küpers, "4/29 - Between Non- and Post-Disciplinarity ?!" *Integral Leadership Review* 14, no. 2 (2014), http://integralleadershipreview.com/11426-non-postdisciplininarity/.

32 Messer-Davidow et al. 1993, cited in Küpers, "4/29."

cognitive capitalism.[33] I bring forward a call to action from Fred Moten and Stefano Harney in *The Undercommons: Fugitive Planning & Black Study* about refusals. They put forth,

> After all, the subversive intellectual came under false pretenses, with bad documents, out of love. Her labor is as necessary as it is unwelcome. The university needs what she bears but cannot bear what she brings. And on top of all that, she disappears. She disappears... into the undercommons of enlightenment, where the work gets done, where the work gets subverted, where the revolution is still black, still strong.[34]

Moten and Harney write about a place "paved with refusal"[35] and invested in the project of world-ending. This book draws on the concept of "anti-disciplinary knowledge production" to mean a rejection of "disciplinary regimes and practices in order to develop creative research (questions, ideas, and approaches)."[36] The creative qualities of the book do not serve as institutional bridges: "using all 'faculties' creatively."[37] Instead, this book centers the unauthorized and experiential knowing[38] of creative practitioners. While this research is not a direct investigation of anti-disciplinarity, the practice and the activities of this book itself are ruptures in the

33 Küpers, "4/29"; Rogoff, "Practicing Research."

34 Stefano Harney and Fred Moten, *The Undercommons: Fugitive Planning & Black Study* (AK Press, 2013), 26.

35 Jack Haberstam, "The Wild Beyond: With and For the Undercommons." In *The Undercommons: Fugitive Planning & Black Study*, ed. Stefano Harney and Fred Moten (AK Press, 2013), 2-13.

36 Küpers, "4/29."

37 Küpers, "4/29."

38 Dominique Johnson, "Beyond Bare Life: Onto-Epistemic Archives, Precarity, and the Praxis of Being Human," PhD thesis, University of Pittsburgh, 2017.

institutional borders[39] that are maintained through knowledge production. Therefore, the contributions of this book are not to disciplines. The practice-led approach to the knowledge produced here encourages the work to speak back to both practice and theory, consistent with these anti-disciplinary understandings.

This chapter introduced the basic concerns of this book as they relate to politics, practice, theory, and the production of knowledge. What creative practice offers at the juncture with critical theory is the possibility of working with theory in visual, material ways. In this book, ideas are explored at the scale of the practitioner arranging, writing, and hand-making things about inner, past experiences, which allows for a politicized exploration that stays with our interiorities.

This work is a provocation that appreciates the potential that artistic, conceptual approaches have toward the task of aligning values and actions, which typically takes on a pedagogic and instrumentalized angle. It trusts the knowing we already have from living politicized lives in racialized bodies. It is an exploration, fitting for those of us whose ways of being in the world are politicized and necessarily critical. This work is inspired by the precious, intimate time we spend reading critical theories about our own lives and what it means to be affected by them in the everyday. It looks to close the loop, allowing what we know from living life to speak back to theory and circulate.

39 Gloria Anzaldúa, *Borderlands: The New Mestiza = La Frontera*, Spinsters/Aunt Lute, 1987.

CHAPTER TWO

Theory is commonly written and thought about. Practice is often done and experienced elsewhere. This chapter messes with that separation by introducing the notion of a *parallel practice* and defining the framework, *doing theory, thinking practice*.

Rather than exclusively thinking, reading, and discussing theory, the concept of *doing theory*[1] acknowledges that we have firsthand lived experiences[2] and that it is possible to theorize through those embodied experiences. Knowing and being are already mutually influential; the binary separation of theory and practice is already being messed with in daily life.

Chapter 2 pulls together threads across time and disciplines to weave together a conceptual framework. The framework serves as the theoretical background for understanding and naming the relationships of theory and practice.

1 Della Pollock, "Performance Trouble," ed. D. Soyini Madison and Judith Hamera (Sage Publications, 2005), 1-8.

2 By using the phrase "lived experience" or "embodied experience," I delineate between knowing about something—for instance, knowing about the US as a country or watching someone raise a child—and a different way of knowing one has from experiencing something such firsthand—such as actually living a life in the US or raising one's own child.

1
"DOING THEORY" IN THE EVERYDAY

In this section, I outline how theory and practice are already being messed with in daily life by centering cases of unauthorized and experiential knowing.

The first case of messing with theory and daily life I present here is demonstrated in an essay by La Marr Jurelle Bruce.[3] He makes evident that the physical, everyday act of loitering is, for Black queer folk, teeming with critical theorizing. Loitering is a refusal to comply with policed, patrolled movements—whether it be waiting for friends by a football field, in a trap house, or hanging out on school grounds. In the same essay, Bruce describes twirling or the sensation of remaining in dynamic motion as an act, for Black queer folk, of flinging the haters away, casting one's gaze all around. This is "a mode of self-making and praxis of resistance."[4] The Black queer child who twirls or loiters need not source and read theoretical texts about twirling and loitering or read about "mandates for proper movement"[5] to know them well, analyze them, critique them, and possibly make dissenting moves accordingly. It is in the acts of loitering or twirling where critical constructs, conceptualizations, and theorizations are first known and made. We know the enforcements of the outside gaze, linearity, and "proper" movement that make loitering and twirling defiant. Another instance of *doing theory* is found in Maya Angelou's televised reading of her poem,

3 La Marr Jurelle Bruce, "Mad Is a Place," *American Quarterly* 69, no. 2 (2017): 303-8, https://doi.org/10.1353/aq.2017.0024.

4 Bruce, "Mad Is a Place," 360.

5 Bruce, "Mad Is a Place," 353.

"The Mask."[6] In this reading, she makes apparent her understanding of her own laugh, her grin. Angelou performs her theorizations in the poetry reading, exposing how her grin is inextricable from death and whiteness. Her critical articulations about grinning are known through her chronic, embodied experience with it. An analogous argument is made in an essay titled, "'Quare' Studies, or (Almost) Everything I Know About Queer Studies I Learned From My Grandmother." In this essay, scholar and artist E. Patrick Johnson succinctly states, "Although people of color may not have theorized our lives in Foucault's terms, we have used discourse in subversive ways because it was necessary for our survival."[7] The chronic, incoherent state of surviving in one's own Black body is how he initially knows the "imperialism of power"[8] to the depths that he does. It is not by didactic study or by reading abstract theorizations written by Foucault, a white French philosopher. André Carrington discusses the same lived-in knowing in his essay, "Mike Brown's Body: New Materialism and Black Form." There, he critiques white feminist calls for the creation of an anti-racist praxis. These calls to start or invent a praxis presuppose a lack of one, and furthermore, they overlook how "living Black human beings take such action by demanding to go on living."[9]

The constituted conditions surrounding Black loitering, twirling, grinning, surviving, and going-on-living[10] are first known, conceptualized, and acted upon through lived experience. I do not

6 Maya Angelou, "The Mask," Thames Television, London, 1987.

7 E. Patrick Johnson, "'Quare' Studies, or (Almost) Everything I Know About Queer Studies I Learned from My Grandmother," *Text and Performance Quarterly* 21, no. 1 (2001): 1-25. https://doi.org/10.1080/10462930128119. 12.

8 Johnson, "Quare' Studies," 21.

9 André Carrington, "Mike Brown's Body: New Materialism and Black Form," *ASAP Journal* 2, no. 2 (2017): 279, https://doi.org/10.1353/asa.2017.0025.

10 Throughout this book, I refer to loitering, twirling, grinning, and going-on-living as shorthand for the ways of knowing discussed in this chapter.

go so far as to put the onus on the agency of one's subjectivity to transcend constructs. Instead, I stick to the point that some theorizations, namely critical ones, are not sourced first from outside observation made by an anthropological "other" but from necessary, firsthand ways of knowing. This book argues against universalized feminist premises that "we" must not be objective, outside observers, as these claims subsume those of us who are not constituted to think of ourselves as outside observers in the first place.

Bruce, Johnson, Angelou, and Carrington precisely describe ways of knowing that are lived-in and necessary for survival and resistance. Here, I briefly bring in Black feminist, Womanist, feminist, African Indigenous, Afropessimist, queer, and disability scholarship, as they allow for a meta-theoretical take on the same point. In simple terms, the embodied and necessary ways of knowing I reviewed resist the separation of epistemology and ontology.[11] Across scholarship, critiques of this separation are sometimes termed "onto-epistemology." This analysis through theory is not necessarily a step to take or something to apply but part of and grounded in politicized ways of being. One way that onto-epistemologies are understood is as Indigenous knowledge systems whose lineages predate colonization and that, when centered, are "a rebuttal of ontological hegemony" and go "beyond concepts and seeing ontology as reality representation."[12] In other schools of thought, onto-epistemology is a universalized "way to think about the kind of understandings that are needed

11 "Ontology" defines what exists, such as society, people, and physical objects and spaces. "Epistemology" defines how we know things.

12 Maximus Monaheng Sefotho, "Basotho Ontology of Disability: An Afrocentric Onto-Epistemology." *Heliyon* 7, no. 3 (2021): 3, https://doi.org/10.1016/j.heliyon.2021.e06540.

to come to terms with how specific intra-actions matter."[13] They are for "dismantling the existing strategies for knowing."[14] Beyond the term as a conceptual tool, some conceive of it as a descriptor for the Black American (queer) femme "conditions constituting a praxis of being human."[15] This school of thought gets us much closer to the specifics involved in the way of knowing found in Black loitering, grinning, surviving, and going-on-living. It brings attention to "the multiplicity of authorized (traditional, scholarly, institutional) and unauthorized (cultural, experiential, precarious) knowledges deployed in the production of social life."[16] This practice of going-on-living under ontological suffering brings attention to traditional theory and what is experiential, with emphasis on the latter. Furthermore, Denise Ferreira Da Silva puts forth that "grounds of Category of Blackness" [17] do have an onto-epistemology of their own. It is grounded in "a multiple consciousness, ... part of the analysis process itself."[18]

Spending time with these written theorizations allowed a much-needed deepening of my understanding of my personal experience and proved to be life-affirming. Watching that grainy video of Angelou's poetry reading uploaded onto the internet was affirming. Carrington's essay articulated suspicions and grievances that

13 Karen Barad, "Posthumanist Performativity: Toward an Understanding of How Matter Comes to Matter," *Signs: Journal of Women in Culture and Society* 28, no. 3 (2003): 829. https://doi.org/10.1086/345321.

14 Denise Ferreira Da Silva. "Toward a Black Feminist Poethics: The Quest(Ion) of Blackness Toward the End of the World." *Black Scholar* 44, no. 2 (2014): 82. https://doi.org/10.1080/ 00064246.2014.11413690.

15 Johnson, "Beyond Bare Life," 10.

16 Johnson, "Beyond Bare Life," 10.

17 Da Silva, "Toward a Black Feminist Poethics," 82.

18 Venus Evans-Winters, *Black Feminism in Qualitative Inquiry: A Mosaic for Writing Our Daughter's Body* (Routledge, 2019), 5.

were growing in me. The references I collected over time kept me company as I formed my own arguments. Through them, I have gathered the theoretical grounds for understanding my embodied knowing. I arrived at some profound stability in the embodied point from which my deepest personal concerns depart. At its premise, *doing theory* upholds politicized, lived-in ways of knowing. We have the possibility to produce knowledge about contemporary contexts through our bodies.

2
"DOING THEORY" IN THE STUDIO

Although we may already organically be *doing theory* in the everyday, it is possible to intentionally mature and thicken the way we do theory. This can be done in a manner that does not value thinking and discussing over being and experiencing. In this section of this chapter, I remain committed to our embodied, private, interior ways of knowing. The aim in politicized work may be to do theory in real time—in a meeting, in an emergency, with neighbors. However, aligning one's actions and values requires some time and space to develop. The space and time I refer to isn't one that is idle. Nor do I imagine that development to be inevitable. This time and space requires deliberate activation.

In *doing theory* in the everyday, we have the bodies and flesh we live in as points of intervention—we can grin, twirl, loiter, and go-on-living. When turning to *doing theory* deliberately and in the context of creative practice, the materials and the proficiency that critical creative practitioners already have in using their materials become a fundamental component. In this section, I link everyday cases of embodied criticality investigated in the previous section with their conceptual potential in the creative studio.[19] A creative practitioner can purposefully develop the way they *do theory* by enacting a space and time in parallel to their existing practice. This parallel space is a specific genre of practice that deserves a clear definition.

DEMARCATING "PARALLEL PRACTICE"

Over a period of four years starting in 2018, I developed a process that allowed me to work in parallel and in tandem with my pre-existing design practice.[20] The purpose of a *parallel practice*, as I call it, was to lift the hood and mature my understandings of the relationships of theory and practice in my professional practice to deepen my political commitments. Chapter 6 is a hands-on guide for you to start building your own *parallel practice*.

A *parallel practice* has several characteristics that distinguish it from other forms of inquiry and creative practice. This is also illustrated in Fig. 1.

1. A *parallel practice* is an investigation that is done in sync and parallel to one's practice. It can be practiced as a break in the middle of the workday or as a designated period of time, separated from the practitioner's professional work week.

2. The primary intention of this time and space is to make intimate meta-investigations of one's own practice. It is a space dedicated to aligning one's politicized commitments and everyday actions.

19 The "studio" is not understood as a delineated space in the design, performance, architecture, or art school or work space, but as an expansive site where the creative practitioner engages in deliberate processes of thinking and making.

20 See the Introduction: Context and Birthplace for more.

3. A *parallel practice* is grounded in approaches that allow the relationships of what is abstract and what is concrete to be understood and studied.

4. The active components of a *parallel practice* include:
   a. Oneself and one's own body
   b. Creative mediums and the practitioner's proficiency in using them
   c. Reflexivity: Taking account of one's experience and interactions with the greater contexts

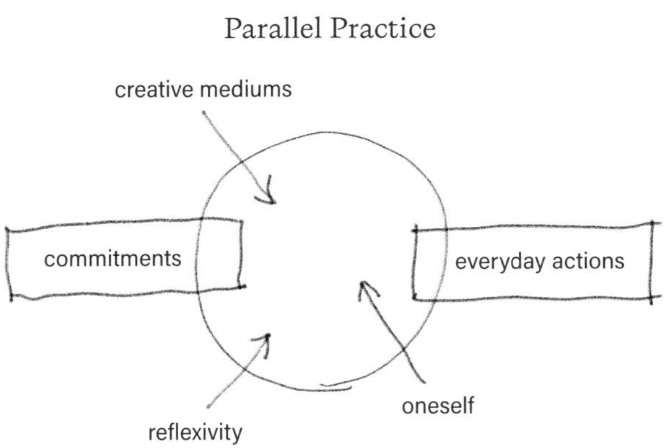

Fig. 1. Characteristics and components of a *parallel practice*.

Taking a few steps back, I note that *parallel practices* sit within a larger landscape of practices dedicated to aligning values and actions. This broader landscape is conveyed in Fig. 2.

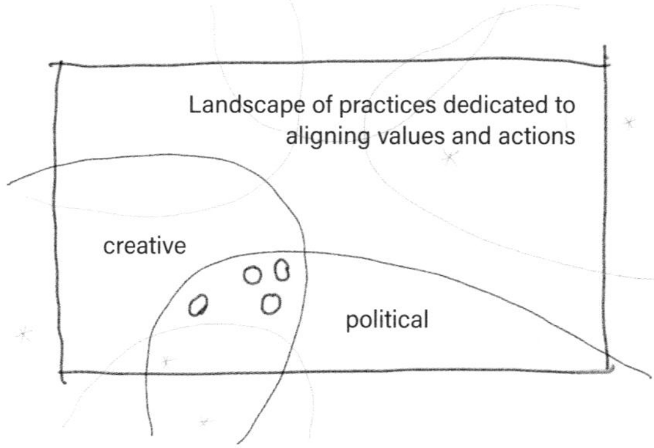

Fig. 2. The surrounding context of a *parallel practice*. The four small circles in the center of the diagram represent *parallel practices* as defined above. The light gray curves suggest other types of related but distinct practices.

The sketch above shows part of the landscape, which brings attention to a concentrated area between practices that are creative and those that are political. Of course, there are extensive demonstrations and discourse surrounding designers, musicians, painters, and dancers (to name a few) whose practices are political and personal. Furthermore, there are creative, political practitioners who, importantly, produce instructive content, teaching tools, and professional development to encourage other practitioners to reflect on their values and skillsets. However, a *parallel practice* proposes a different set of moves: it asks the practitioner to deliberately investigate themselves in politicized, poetic, and material ways.

EXTENDED ACKNOWLEDGMENTS

To further demonstrate what a *parallel practice* entails, I bring together the work of three practitioners for the first time: Daria Garina's Accountability Mapping practice toward abolition; Robin M. Boylorn's blackgirl autoethnography practice, which interlinks with "blackgirlhood"; and Torkwase Dyson's practice of Black Compositional Thought toward environmental liberation. I introduce each of their distinct practices to show how a performance artist, writer, and an interdisciplinary painter, respectively, have developed what I would characterize as *parallel practices*. To share their work with you, I take the approach of acknowledgment, meaning that I make a gesture to the importance and qualities of others' work.[21] I dedicate brief sections to introducing the work of Dyson, Boylorn, and Garina in turn. Across the descriptions, I highlight how they use visual and material methods to attend to theory and practice. The process defined in this book does not combine or adopt their practices. I bring these fellow practitioners into conversation with one another to retroactively conceive a relevant home for the framework I establish in this book. What I propose through this book is that by bringing together the approaches and sensitivities of each of these practitioners—who otherwise are not in direct conversation—it becomes possible to demarcate a distinct genre of creative, politicized work.

A Parallel Practice: Through The Body

> And from inside this place, see if you can call into your center and into your lower dantian, what you deeply care about, what deeply matters to you, what you deeply long for. Letting that fill you and your entire energetic body, letting what you care about live at the very center of you, this place that you can continually check in with, for guidance, for clarity, for grounding.
>
> —Daria Garina, Accountability Mapping Course[22]

21 See the Introduction: Knowledge and Expertise, for more.

22 Daria Garina, "The Centered Accountability Course," Accountability Mapping. https://www.accountabilitymapping.thinkific.com.

Daria Garina offers a practice for aligning values and actions through Qi Gong, a somatic practice rooted in ancient East Asian cosmological traditions. In his practice, self-accountability is not invested in attaining a perfect image of oneself[23] or expecting that of others. He builds on the provocation of his early mentor, Mia Mingus, that "taking care of ourselves is how we are accountable in this world."[24] Garina's practice, Accountability Mapping, uses breathing, sitting, and movement to find one's center and to clear energy. Our relationship with ourselves is attended to in these intimate, embodied ways. Garina offers an approach for mapping default responses to stressors on any given day. He gives us a structure that can reflect back to us when our values and actions are not aligned. He offers five-element approaches, three energetic centers of the body, and other energetic anatomies[25] for mapping retaliative, manipulative, overactive, and shut-down ways of processing everyday interactions. It is a practice focused on "locating and experiencing centered accountability through the body."

The politicized aims of Accountability Mapping are deeply tied to an anti-capitalist, anti-imperialist, radical, community-based drug detoxification program, which was organized by the Black Panther Party and The Young Lords in the South Bronx, New York City, in the 1970s.[26] The program used acupuncture techniques, in particular, a practice adopted from a doctor in Hong Kong. Today, as Garina informs us, the practice is "professionalized, commodified,

23 Barnard Center for Research on Women, "What Is Accountability?" July 26, 2019, https://www.youtube.com/watch?v=LjRbj57vBvA.

24 Statement made in 2019 to an audience at Barnard Center for Research on Women's National Gathering on Transforming Harm. Garina's work is part of transformative justice, an abolitionist framework.

25 Garina cites his experience with the Acupuncture & Integrative Medicine College, Berkeley (AIMC) as a source of his knowledge.

26 Ellinor R. Mitchell, „The Lincoln Story," National Acupuncture Detoxification Association, https://www.acudetox.com/the-lincoln-story.

and regulated by white people through the state for their own power and profit that the simple ... 5-point ear detox protocol is illegal for non-state licensed acupuncturists to practice." These conditions begin to highlight the significance of Garina's practice. It is part of the radical traditions in the United States that use Eastern technologies toward non-institutionalized and abolitionist aims. His practice offers ways of centering personal, intimate, energetic dimensions of larger, collective work. It offers techniques for being better able to participate in accountable communities.

A Parallel Practice: Through Prose

> I see blackgirl and black (space) girl as distinct and not the same, so I merge the words to make them touch on paper the way they touch in my everyday existence. ... In the context of my life, my feminism, my politics, my lived experience, my autoethnography, I put the two words together so that when you see them, hear them, think about them, read them, and write them, you see the connectedness of those pieces of me, of those pieces in me, and my story.
>
> —Robin M. Boylorn in "On Being at Home with Myself: Blackgirl Autoethnography as Research Praxis"[27]

Part of Robin Boylorn's practice is in an academic setting. This work involves being an associate professor in a white-dominated institution in the Southern United States. Her autoethnography practice is an approach to keep herself accountable to "home" while navigating the white gaze. It involves writing first-person narratives to study and analyze culture. Boylorn does not describe her work as self-accountability, but her practice does center her body as the site of her research. In "On Being at Home with Myself," she describes home as not "where my mama lives, or the home I have made for myself. ... [it] is centered and grounded in my own self." Boylorn

27 Robin Boylorn, "On Being at Home with Myself: Blackgirl Autoethnography as Research Praxis," *International Review of Qualitative Research* 9, no. 1 (2016): 44-58.

uses the first-person, reflexive qualities of autoethnography as performative and critical practice grounds.[28] She writes about the lives of Black women. The autoethnographic writing process is, in her own words, a medium to "merge the words" and to "make them touch on paper the way they touch in my everyday existence."[29] Boylorn's blackgirl writing practice is an approach to merge "our public/private selves."[30] It is a refusal to compartmentalize herself. Boylorn uses critical blackgirl autoethnography to investigate her "body/home." There were times in her past fiction writing[31] where she separated herself and the story and separated her Blackness and her girlhood because she was in "a stranger's house (the academy), a white stranger's house, trying to tell [her] blackgirl truth."[32] Her practice has become one that refuses "renting-to-own [her] home, living in somebody else's mess, and losing [her]self in the process."[33]

The politicized aims of Boylorn's autoethnographic practice are toward an endarkened feminist epistemology and Black feminist thought. She works with intersectional representations of social life for Black women, especially as a blackgirl with roots in the rural southern United States. Through the lens of marginalization, she refuses the margin, seeks agency through personal narrative about identity, and pushes understandings of cultural experience. There are multiple implications of aligning with "home." On a personal and interpersonal level, Boylorn offers blackgirl autoethnography as

28 Robin Boylorn, "'Sit With Your Legs Closed!' And Other Sayin's from My Childhood," (Left Coast Press, 2013), 173-85.

29 Robin Boylorn and Mark P. Orbe, eds., *Critical Autoethnography: Intersecting Cultural Identities in Everyday Life* (Taylor & Francis, 2016).

30 Boylorn, "On Being at Home with Myself," 55.

31 Robin Boylorn, *Sweetwater: Black Women and Narratives of Resilience* (Peter Lang, 2013).

32 Boylorn and Orbe, *Critical Autoethnography*, 47.

33 Boylorn and Orbe, *Critical Autoethnography*, 47.

"a way of owning who I am, expressing being at home in my skin, avoiding the pause, accepting the contradictions, fucking with the grays."[34] At a systemic level, it is a technique to disrupt traditional tenets of knowledge production and works with theory as a site for communal recovery and self-recovery.

A Parallel Practice: Through Visual Composition

> These shapes ... were my equation. And that is the curve. That is the rectangle. And that is the irregular triangle.
>
> —Torkwase Dyson in conversation with Christina Sharpe[35]

Torkwase Dyson is a painter trained formally in fine arts, working with multiple media. She uses a drawing and mark-making process to engage at once with the past, her present, and theory. The marks she makes are not representations of places or people. Instead, Dyson uses her process as a way to "inform black people self; using space to self-liberate."[36] Dyson uses the shapes and the drawing process for what she describes as self-liberation. The theories she reads and brings into her creative process bring her closer to her "best geographical self."[37] The rigor of her work is in the compositions she creates.

The shapes in Dyson's compositions are not representational.

34 Boylorn, "On Being at Home with Myself," 50.

35 Graham Foundation, "Christina Sharpe and Torkwase Dyson in Conversation," June 13, 2018, 09:46, https://www.youtube.com/watch?v=BmmVQxz2HEg.

36 Torkwase Dyson, "Torkwase Dyson: Black Compositional Thought and Systems of Spatial Navigation," Columbia University Graduate School of Architecture, Planning and Preservation, 2019, https://www.arch.columbia.edu/media-archive/podcasts/171-black-compositional-thought-and-systems-of-spatial-navigation.

37 Graham Foundation, "Dionne Brand: The Shape of Language," July 21, 2018, 05:36, https://www.youtube.com/watch?v=r_HdOZIFElO.

They are ways of thinking through narratives. Drawing is how she stays with the pressure, composing the geographic shapes constituted on Black life. The embodied process of mark-making and drawing is how Dyson comes to feel, see, and understand strategies for Black spatial, environmental liberation. Dyson reveals there are things she hesitates to say, but still makes the mark on paper.[38] This act is a refusal of whatever is behind not wanting to say something and making a visible, private, illegible, shared, discursive, propositional mark anyway.

What is at stake in her practice is a personal and collective matter. It is concerned with, for instance, housing dozens of friends and family in her home while the U.S. government devised a disaster in the wake of Hurricane Katrina. Or the significance of a Black teenager building a raft and riding it off the shores of a beach,[39] or a fugitive slave shipping himself in a small wooden crate and later becoming an abolitionist and magician.[40] Dyson describes her own experience in her Atlanta home years ago; that of Eugene Williams floating into territorial waters at a Chicago beach in July of 1919; that of Henry Box Brown surviving a 300-mile shipping route from Virginia to Pennsylvania in 1849; and those enslaved in the holds of ships out at sea plotting their escape as architectural, material spaces composed and navigated by Black folk. Under these spatial, "geographical conditions of terror," material space and energetic space are composed. Her works are studies of anti-Black systems, forced migration, and climate change, asking how one may study them to inform and understand one's own movements.

38 Graham Foundation, "Christina Sharpe and Torkwase Dyson in Conversation."

39 Dyson, "Torkwase Dyson: Black Compositional Thought."

40 Henry B. Brown, *Narrative of the Life Of Henry Box Brown* (Lee and Glynn, 1851).

Looking at the practices of Boylorn, Dyson, and Garina, it is evident that their practices are each rooted in different politicized histories, informed by specific traditions, and using various mediums. For Dyson, the rigor behind her drawings offers her ways of imagining her own movements and spatial decisions. Boylorn uses her performative, critical process of ethnographic writing as a form of refusal and to find her ways home. For Garina, his own body is a medium for tuning into everyday misalignments with his values. The columns in Fig. 3 summarize what make up the distinct practices of each of the three practitioners.

	Accountability Mapping	Blackgirl Autoethnography	Black Compositional Thought
Practitioner	Daria Garina	Robin M. Boylorn	Torkwase Dyson
Mediums	body	writing	drawing
Framework	energetic anatomies, qi gong	critical autoethnography	black critical thought
Politicized Direction	abolition	blackgirlhood	environmental liberation

Fig. 3. Examples of relevant practices and their characteristics.

We can begin to trace the overlaps between these approaches when they are brought together. In the table above, I surface the key characteristics that show how practices like Black Compositional Thought, blackgirl autoethnography, and Accountability Mapping make up a particular kind of self-reflexive, creative, politicized work—a *parallel practice*. The significance of bringing these examples together under one term for the first time is that it affords creative fields to develop frameworks for reflection and accountability. In commercial architecture, post-occupancy evaluations are used to assess a building's performance. The social sciences have developed autoethnography for researchers who study other people to also study themselves. Corporations and institutions offer management coaching for their employees. Manufacturing and pharmaceutical industries have quality assurance procedures to bridge the micro and macro. These examples are mechanisms for reflexivity inherently built into and standardized in these respective fields. Colonial research fields and capitalist industries are not to be centered, and to some, the degree of implications that come with a building collapsing, perpetuating colonial study of people, or distributing faulty medicine may appear to be irrelevant to creative practices. In the project of world-ending and liberation, design, art, and performance have the potential to play a crucial role alongside direct action, schooling, rebellion, spiritual practices, medicine, engineering, public health, planning, philosophy, and scholarly research. Creative practitioners whose practices are both conceptual and political have the unique possibility to contribute a distinct skillset: to negotiate concepts and speculate in concrete, visible ways—enabling us to imagine otherwise. This book re-examines what is personally and socially at stake with critical creative practice and, in turn, takes the task of iterative feedback loops, accountability, and alignment of practice and values seriously.

3
A FRAMEWORK FOR "DOING THEORY" IN THE STUDIO

The previous section in this chapter outlined a particular genre of creative practice dedicated to the relationships of theory and practice—*parallel practice*. To do this kind of practice, a framework is needed. This half of the chapter serves to reveal the invisible mechanics of the approach I establish in this book.

To deliberately study one's critical creative practice, one's own past experiences and actions, one's own body, the creative mediums of one's own practice, and one's political commitments all need to be recruited at once.

The framework I introduce here hinges on revisiting past moments in professional practice. From practicing and teaching this, I have come to know that the distance between a past event and the present can be considered a space that is interstitial—revisited thoughtfully, this space offers room to reflect and create differently. This margin affords the possibility not only to actively pause and reflect but also to make and study our relationships with socio-political theory. The point at which past events and socio-political theories are intentionally brought together is where self-awareness and reflexivity can begin to emerge. Revisiting a past moment over time allows it to expand, giving more space to work with. By figuratively placing one's own body in the past and checking the physical environment surrounding oneself, the nuanced details of the past moment can be named. Those details can then be made visible by the creative practitioner in embodied, material, and spatial ways.

From that spacious, decompressed, and material condition,

the past moment in practice and critical theory can be tuned and calibrated to each other—and consequently circulate through one another. This is possible because the theories about our contemporary realities, which are predominantly presented and consumed in the written form of a book, article, or essay, are often first known through the book author's own politicized body; more specifically, the relationship between firsthand experience and theory can be seen in how Black experience informs Black critical thought, being disabled informs disability studies, queer experience informs queer theory, and surviving environmental racism informs Black ecofeminism.

Like a piano tuner uses both their technical and tacit knowledge to finely tune the strings of an acoustic piano in relation with each other and with a theoretical standard, the task of deliberately *doing theory* requires similar sensibilities. A double calibration takes place. For one, the embodied knowledge of the practitioner using the framework and the embodied knowledge of the author who wrote about a theory can be tuned to each other. At the same time, the abstract, metaphorical language often used in theory and the abstract, metaphorical things the practitioner physically makes through this process are calibrated to each other. Once theory and practice are in circulation together, a new and different reading on the present—through theory—can be made.

In Part 2, I will continue this argument through modelling it several times over in practice. In Part 3, I break it down step by step in the hands-on guide. Here, I continue with describing the goings-on behind the scenes of the framework.

TRACING A LINEAGE

I came to an understanding of the affordances of revisiting a past moment by working in my *parallel practice*. Aiming to name the invisible mechanics behind what went on in my *parallel practice*, I also read and dug through reference lists in the appendices of essays rooted in cultural theory, performance studies, and queer theory. In 2020, I eventually came to trace a 15-year lineage that begins with the scholarship of Stuart Hall and is extended by Della Pollock and Stacy Holman Jones, respectively. In this section, so you may follow it, I preserve and leave exposed my encounters and train of thought alongside these scholars' theories. The texts I pull from them successively build, revise, and extend Hall's articulations of theory and social life. This unfolding serves to deepen the same inquiry rather than to launch into a sprawling survey of methodologies and disciplines. Drawing together a red thread of ideas and terminology, I introduce what the framework of this book entails: *doing theory, thinking practice*.

To highlight the through line of *doing theory* in the context of professional practice, I make the connection that Hall engages in *doing theory* through the mode of the *archive*; Pollock, with *performance*; and Jones, with *story*. I do not set out to adopt their approaches. Nor do I aim to collage the work of Hall, Pollock, Jones, and others together, as they are each based in a wide array of schools of thought and histories. Instead, I do the work of pulling a single methodological through line from inquiries like theirs. Later in this chapter, I introduce my own practice stemming from design: *doing theory, thinking* form.

DOING THEORY, THINKING STORY

In her 2016 essay, "Living Bodies of Thought," Jones uses first-person autoethnographic writing as a practice in which queer theory and her written personal narratives are intentionally interlinked. The notion of theory is not understood as fixed, as a standalone, or as a supplement to a written story. Jones offers that critical theory participates as the reflexive, active agent. She clearly highlights the relationship between critical theory and her personal queer narratives of autoethnography: they are "mutually influential" and "focused on engaging with the world."[41] She creates the phrase "doing theory, thinking story"[42] to describe how theory and story are interrelated in critical autoethnographic practice. For critical theory, distinct from other theories, it is the criticality of the theory that is enacted, making it matter in the story. Jones specifies that committing to the ethics and collaboration between theory and story is what makes critical autoethnographic inquiry a way of embodying change.

DOING THEORY, THINKING PERFORMANCE

Jones' 2016 essay expresses the relationship between theory and social life through story—namely, critical autoethnography. Jones builds the title of her essay and one of its main ideas, "doing theory, thinking story," from Della Pollock's work published a decade earlier. In the context of performance studies, written theory is understood as a collaborator and reflexive participant with what is actually done and lived. It is a thing to think with. It is here that Pollock uses the phrasing "doing theory and thinking performance,"[43] on which Jones later riffed and bridged to her critical autoethnographic practice. Pollock specifies, "Performance won't stand still long enough for theory to wrap it up nicely. It moves in time and space

41 Stacy Holman Jones, "Living Bodies of Thought: The 'Critical' in Critical Autoethnography," *Qualitative Inquiry* 22, no. 4 (2016): 229, 235, https://doi.org/10.1177/1077800415622509.

42 Jones, "Living Bodies of Thought," 231.

43 Pollock, "Performance Trouble," 1.

through restless bodies."[44] Revisiting the past story or moment can be taken as a "detour through theory."[45] Pollock points to the temporal, material quality of the way in which modes of inquiry can work to bring movement to theory.

DOING THEORY, THINKING ARCHIVE

If we again trace the lineage of ideas, this time in Pollock's essay, we find ourselves at the work of Stuart Hall. It is Hall's 2003 essay, "Marx's Notes on Method: A 'Reading' of the 1859 Introduction," on which Pollock builds her initial argument and which would later underpin those of Jones (directly or indirectly).

Hall's notes on theory and history (our concrete and material social lives) are framed by a Marxist reading. It is a critique that "the history of man" is an abstraction if it is built on a premise that history and theory are separate and autonomous. Jones' rejection of the idea that theory stands alone may be felt as an echo emanating from this very foundational premise. While what's concrete "cannot be the point of departure for a theoretical demonstration, [the concrete] is the absolute precondition for all theoretical construction."[46] It is the basis for our observations and conceptions. Hall, via Marx, argues that social life and theory are non-linear and are simultaneously and "mutually articulated upon one another."[47] We may deduce that Pollock's nuanced take on theory as a temporalization, a remembering, and a repeating is a reverberation coming from this non-linear, relational, co-determining, complex take on

44 Pollock, "Performance Trouble," 1.

45 Pollock, "Performance Trouble," 1.

46 Stuart Hall, "Marx's Notes on Method: A 'Reading' of the '1857 Introduction,'" *Cultural Studies* 17, no. 2 (2003): 89, 129, https://doi.org/10.1080/0950238032000114868.

47 Hall, "Marx's Notes on Method," 131.

theory and social life. It is from this way of knowing that Pollock and many other scholars build revisions and expansions to investigate the relationships between theory and social life.

Stuart Hall's body of work also engages in theoretical inquiries about practice—to name one, archiving practice. In 2001, his call for attention to the archive was published in a text titled "Constituting an Archive." It is in this earlier essay that Hall critiques the traditional understanding of an archive as an inert collection of works.[48] In this lineage on which Jones and Pollock build their arguments, Hall's text importantly lets me return to and be accountable to Black scholarship. His critique pays tribute to the pre-history of each and any archive that involves personal work done by those who do the constituting and securing of the works, catalogs, and exhibitions of the Black and Asian diaspora. He makes the case that the moment an archive is constituted, the moment a concept or title is named, the moment slides of the work are collected and texts about it are written, is a moment in which one's perception of a collection of works as relatively random comes to an end. It shifts and ruptures the "apparatus of 'a history'"[49] and offers a new reading. Archiving is the method—likened to methods of performance or story—that breaks the separation between theory and social life. For Hall, it breaks the separation between the concept of the institutionalized collection and the social contexts and producers of the individual pieces in the eventual archive. Hall emphasizes the living archive by asserting that a multiplicity "of criticism, history and theory, of personal story, anecdote and biography, are the 'texts' which make the archive live."[50]

48 Stuart Hall, "Constituting an Archive," *Third Text* 15, no. 54 (2001): 89-92, https://doi.org/10.1080/09528820108576903.

49 Hall, "Marx's Notes on Method," 89.

50 Hall, "Constituting an Archive," 92.

Here, I extend Pollock's phrases, *doing theory* and *thinking* performance, which is in reference to Hall's essay, and I take Jones' adaptation, *doing theory, thinking* story, in reference to Pollock, to loop back to Hall's ideas. I take on the task of labeling the kind of archival practice Hall calls for: *doing theory, thinking* archive.

DOING THEORY, THINKING PRACTICE

To translate the various inflections and mechanics of doing theory I presented above into an applicable framework, I refer to the overarching framework as doing theory, thinking practice. The three modes of archiving, performing, and storying, respectively, can each retroactively be understood as modes of enacting the theoretical framework, doing theory, thinking practice. They each have their own histories and disciplinary approaches. Through this book, I stitch this lineage together to propose that as critical creative practitioners, we can take the modes with which we're already fluent and repurpose them to investigate our own practices.

Criticality, temporality, and conditions of the past are important to *doing theory, thinking practice*. Critical theory's criticality makes theory matter in these modes of practice; The temporalities of remembering—of first, second, never, again, and before[51]—is a contributor to becoming different; and historical conditions interpenetrate the present through reflexive practice. The practical modes offer a new reading of an event in social life. Criticality, social conditions, and temporality actuate the framework in practice. Ultimately, the meaning and aim are to commit to the ethics and collaboration of theory and social life.[52] *Doing theory, thinking practice*

51 Pollock, "Performance Trouble," 4.

52 Jones, "Living Bodies of Thought."

aims for "the self-conscious overthrow"[53] of relations in dominating modes of production.

The following section of this chapter takes the framework laid out so far and bridges it to my own *parallel practice* so that you may, in the second half of this book, relate and adapt the framework to your own critical creative practice.

DOING THEORY, THINKING FORM

In my own *parallel practice*, I work with visual, material things to engage with past events and critical theory. Drawing from my field—design—I introduce a fourth mode: visual, material *form*. I use the term "form" and its descriptors "visual and material" broadly to suggest abstract shapes; to connote layouts or arrangements of things on a surface, as on the page of an essay, sheet music, on a canvas, or an architectural drawing; and to suggest the material qualities of a body, like that of a living being's body or an area of space. As story, archive, and performance operate for Jones, Hall, and Pollock, form is the thing that enables me to do theory deliberately. My practice employs the process of form-making to bring together theory and practice. For the purpose of building the framework in this chapter, I lay out the inner workings behind form-making—in theory.

What goes on when people make things? What goes on between things and people? As we are in the process of making a thing, with some attentiveness, we may look into what precisely goes on in the act of making. As we make, matters are negotiated, concretized, reflected on, speculated, destroyed, made visible, externalized, repaired, undone, reified, and more. I assert that these matters illustrate the much wider implications of investigations made about

53 Hall, "Marx's Notes on Method," 137.

and through visual, material form. An exploration done through the mode of visual, material form can be understood as a method of making interiorities visible. At the beginning of my design education, I read theorist Elaine Scarry's work and her premise of "turning the body inside-out."[54] This notion, combined with what I know as a designer, can explain what goes on while I am actually making. The resulting forms or things I make from *doing theory, thinking practice* can be explained as materializations of my interiorities.

On Making and Unmaking

There are many philosophical discussions and updated redirections about the universal relationships between things and humans.[55] I remain focused on the particulars surrounding how practitioners make to stay accountable to the implications of this specific action. Cultural, social, cognitive, and ecological perspectives have allowed us to come to understand the premise that we make objects and that there are various types of making processes. We have vast categories

54 Elaine Scarry, *The Body in Pain: The Making and Unmaking of The World* (Oxford University Press, 1985), 284. Reading Scarry's book for the first time ten years ago was life-affirming, without exaggeration. I was handed a copy of her book from a theorist during my time as a student. The book was written four decades ago. I've come to learn to challenge the erasure in her arguments thanks to Black Studies. I briefly write more about the issues in this section. Aligned with how I aim to demonstrate my relationships with theory in this book, I leave in that ongoing living relationship with theory and relationships—quote after quote, line after line, refusing the impulse to delete and subsume the dynamic.

55 Diana Leong, "The Mattering of Black Lives: Octavia Butler's Hyperempathy and the Promise of the New Materialisms," *Catalyst* 2 no. 2 (2016): 1-35, https://doi.org/10.28968/ cftt.v2i2.28799; Carrington, "Mike Brown's Body," 276-283; Bronwyn Davies, "Ethics and the New Materialism: A Brief Genealogy of the 'Post' Philosophies in the Social Sciences," *Discourse* 39, no. 1 (2018): 113-127, https://doi.org/10.1080/01596306.2016.1234682; Karera, "Blackness and the Pitfalls," 32-56; Christopher N. Gamble, Joshua S. Hanan, and Thomas Nail, "What Is New Materialism?" *Angelaki: Journal of Theoretical Humanities* 24, no. 6 (2019): 111-134, https://doi.org/10.1080/0969725X.2019.1684704.

of made things and understandings of their meanings, uses, and implications. What is less readily understood is precisely *how* we make. It is not a question of the procedural steps for making a thing, but rather the ineffable attributes behind the act of making.

Here, I focus on how we make. To limitedly explore this in theory, I look to Elaine Scarry's 1985 book, *The Body in Pain: The Making and Unmaking of the World*,[56] and its fifth and final chapter, "The Interior Structure of the Artifact." It is here that she attends to the "much more elementary task of identifying, descriptively, what it is that is taking place"[57] while we make. By exploring the interior workings of what is taking place, it is possible to expose how form-making can be appropriated for *doing theory*. For Scarry, several attributes belong to "making." One is the premise that we project interiorities onto objects when we make. We take what we know through our bodies and materialize it in artifacts. Our understanding of our own skin is substituted by a gauze bandage when the skin is broken, and we project the womb in the shelters we build.[58] Moreover, "the shape of the chair is not the shape of the skeleton, the shape of body weight, nor even the shape of pain-perceived, but the shape of perceived-pain-wished-gone."[59]

We make based on the embodied things we know through our bodies. We then can make the connection between what we know about our bodies and acts of grinning, twirling, or loitering. For the critical visual artist, the potential of Scarry's articulations about how we make lies in how our embodied knowing can be made in visible, material form.

56 In *The Body in Pain*, Scarry refers to physical torture, offering a structural analysis of torture, pain, and the body. It is based on research through institutes, universities, and organizations who hold international records and accounts of state-sanctioned interrogation tactics and their victims.

57 Scarry, *The Body in Pain*, 278.

58 Scarry, *The Body in Pain*, 282.

59 Scarry, *The Body in Pain*, 290.

In addition to an exploration of how we make, the study of the resulting form or artifact itself is also integral. An investigation through form is an endeavor worth taking on, as the made thing "is sentient awareness materialized into a freestanding design."[60] By examining one of these freestanding made objects, it is possible to identify its interior structures and find in it attributes of the human condition. Attending to the materialized form would mean accessing the "material record"[61] of the interior.

I take that "The Interior Structure of the Artifact" is the final chapter in Elaine Scarry's *The Body in Pain* because it marks a threshold or a limitation between, one, her philosophical ideas about the body, pain, and making things and, two, actually committing to the act of making things or proceeding in worldmaking. The framework in this book answers to her invitation that we "make ourselves (and the originally interior facts of sentience) available to one another through verbal and material artifacts."[62]

However, I revise this almost optimistic sentiment of making ourselves available to one another. The broader approach I propose here is not invested in using the framework for accessing each other's interiorities. It is grounded in the dangers of exposure under the outside gaze.[63] The theoretical framework I have assembled supports inquiries through visual, material form as it affirms how interior structures and inner conditions of social life can be made visible for the purpose of engaging in a reflexive study of one's own embodied, intersubjective relationships in social life with others.

A visual, material practice requires poetic conceptualizations and lateral approaches. This is crucial, as the live body, pain, its projection, and its reifications do not involve two separate processes:

60 Scarry, *The Body in Pain*, 290.

61 Scarry, *The Body in Pain*, 306.

62 Scarry, *The Body in Pain*, 22.

63 For more on the gaze, see *politics* in Chapter 1.

first, experience in social life, and second, ideating, desiring, or imagining otherwise that can be addressed with literal and rational precision. Consistent with the previous arguments in this book, it "is a single percipient event in which the reality of pain and the unreality of imagining are already conflated."[64] These articulations of the body, making, and pain are yet another way of describing the inner workings of *doing theory, thinking practice*.

Further Troubling Making

As much as *doing theory, thinking* form is interpreted by theorizations about the body, pain, and making, this does not adequately cover the bases necessary for engaging with what is specific to the concerns of this book. Through this book, I engage with racialization as ontological, epistemological concerns: matters of Blackness. Within approaches to materiality in the humanities, the silence, erasure, and unthought of these matters may be commonplace, yet this easily perpetuates material violence. It cannot possibly "guarantee ... that the world we could inhabit ... would be de facto be non-racist,"[65] so it rather "anticipates a ... 'recalibration' of anti-black racist practice."[66] Elaine Scarry briefly acknowledges how "the vocabulary of creating, inventing, making, imagining, ... is usually described as an ethically neutral or amoral phenomenon" but is "in fact laden with ethical consequence."[67] Informed by contemporary Black political theorists Douglass and Wilderson, I take this mention from Scarry and engage with it further.

In "The Violence of Presence," Patrice Douglass and Frank B. Wilderson III[68] mark where Scarry's line of thinking is, in fact,

64 Scarry, *The Body in Pain*.

65 Karera, "Blackness and the Pitfalls," 34.

66 Karera, "Blackness and the Pitfalls," 34.

67 Scarry, *The Body in Pain*, 22.

68 Douglass and Wilderson, "The Violence of Presence," 117.

linear and risks ensuing an "unthought dynamic"[69] with Blackness. We can recognize a problematic scenario where "Scarry's torture victim has the luxury of a narrative progression from equilibrium to disequilibrium,"[70] meaning Scarry organizes the phenomenon surrounding the recipient of the pain, first, as intact, with a voice, and with a capacity for relationality. They then suffer this pain, which is the point at which language is made inadequate and questions of unmaking and making come to surface. Then the tortured's voice is eventually restored.

So, how does this linear framing have implications for the kind of making with which this framework is concerned? I bring this to light by looking at the many contexts in which "making-real" one's material reality in pain matters. The implications of making-real one's pain—or the impossibility of doing so—can be understood if it is pictured in the hands of a jury in a courtroom, in the hands of a physician in a doctor's office, or in the hands of an artist making a painting. However, I press that the impossibility of the initial and then restored voice and relational capacity of the Black patient,[71] defendant,[72] or art subject[73] pushes the conditions of pain and making into a fuller understanding that "disequilibrium constitutes

69 Douglass and Wilderson, "The Violence of Presence," 188.

70 Douglass and Wilderson, "The Violence of Presence," 121.

71 A reference to anti-Blackness and the medical industrial complex. See Jennifer C. Nash's "The Political Life of Black Motherhood," *Feminist Studies* 44, no. 3 (2018): 699-712, https://doi.org/10.15767/feministstudies.44.3.0699; Kimania Paul-Emile's "Blackness as Disability?", The Georgetown Law Journal 106, no. 2 (2018): 293-364.

72 A reference to the prison industrial complex and the present-day slavery loophole that is the 13th Amendment of the U.S. Constitution. See Davis, *Are Prisons Obsolete?*

73 A reference to our precious 14-year-old Emmett Till and the violence inflicted by Dana Shutz, Carilyn Bryant, and the Whitney Museum 2017 Biennial: "What's Haunting Black Feminism: A Haunting We Can See," 2020.

being"[74] for Black life. I underline that the disequilibrium of pain is not one point or phase in a linear narrative toward recovery.

The dangers behind narrative progression[75] are given weight when the deceptively coherent nature of narrative is understood. The insinuations, evasions, and discourse that make up narrative are not as intangible as they may seem: they "contain our demise."[76] Narrative is just as material as physical pain inflicted and just as material as the political and economic[77] world. The white imagination[78] and discourse about Blackness that was occurring in the Mediterranean at the very inception of the New World, before the ships first took sail,[79] is what reified and made real Blackness in the first place.[80] Discourse and narrative have made possible the violent, infinite constitutions of Blackness up to today. This point about discourse is why troubling narrative and linearities in theorizations and practical processes of world-making and unmaking are important.

Troubling it would mean engaging making through disequilibrium, instability, fragmentation, immateriality, and the "figurative capacities of Blackness."[81] Dealing with this—rather than relegating it to the position of unthought—would triangulate making and unmaking with the instability of loitering, the disequilibrium of

74 Douglass and Wilderson, "The Violence of Presence."

75 Douglass and Wilderson, "The Violence of Presence," 121.

76 Graham Foundation, "Christina Sharpe and Torkwase Dyson," 28:25.

77 Spillers, "Changing the Letter," 176-202.

78 Morrison, *Playing in the Dark*.

79 Garba and Sorentino, "Slavery Is a Metaphor," 774.

80 Hartman, Scenes of Subjection; Jared Sexton, "The Vel of Slavery: Tracking the Figure of the Unsovereign," *Critical Sociology* 42, no. 4-5 (2014): 583-97; Adam Bledsoe and Willie Jamaal Wright, "The Anti-Blackness of Global Capital," *Environment and Planning. D: Society & Space* 37, no. 1 (2019): 8-26.

81 Hartman, *Scenes of Subjection*.

grinning, the irresolvability of doubleness, and the precariousness of going-on-living.

This portion of the framework started with the question, *What goes on when people make things?* It unpacked the interiorities of making. It discussed the implications of making visible what is invisible. This was then, in one move, both deepened and troubled with heavy-hitting notions about linear conceptions of "making." The shape that the relationship of critical theory and social life takes is interpenetrating, mutually articulating, lived-in, and temporal.

Uniquely, the interiority, incoherence, instability, irresolvability, fragmentation, and immateriality discussed here can possibly be cared for and supported by the hands-on approach defined in Part 2 of this book.

INTERLUDE

In this interlude, I share portions of interviews I did with multiple politically-engaged creative practitioners. I use this liminal space in this book to illustrate real-world snapshots of practitioners as they organically oscillate between creative practice and socio-political theory.

In the beginning of Chapter 1, I asked: "Exactly how did the ideas in your favorite book affect what you ended up making in your studio? How did an intimate conversation you had with someone change how you show up? How did the challenging conflict with your neighbor shape your abstract political ideals?" In westernized contexts, socio-political theory is dominantly thought, written about, and published, and practice is made, done, and lived elsewhere. The practical framework in this book is designed to support the limitless configurations of theory and practice that the critical creative practitioner navigates under these conditions.

In the eight interviews I conducted for this interlude, theory appeared in multiple registers: as academic books, as ineffable or tacit knowing, as ancestral know-how, as the memory of a sibling, as a proverb, and as firsthand encounters. I've lifted 30 of these various configurations of theory and practice. They are set out at the end of each interview. Some of them are orientations that start in practice and move toward theory. Others are oriented from theory toward practice, practice as theory, theory as practice, or—in several special cases—orientations otherwise. From them, themes have emerged. I have dotted and highlighted these points throughout this interlude, importantly maintaining them in the complex contexts of each practitioner's story. Grounded in the practitioner's position, I use this interlude as a transition between Part 1, which is a theoretical take on what happens in the everyday and the studio, with Part 2, which dives deep into hands-on methods for deliberately deepening the relationships of theory and practice in one's own practice.

The format of this interlude is documentary-style; voice-forward and non-linear, yet thematic. This interlude is written as a conversation space. Each practitioner speaks for themselves. I keep their rhythms and contemplations intact, editing only for clarity. I've laid each of the interviewees' accounts side by side without forcing them into agreement. Across eight interviews, I asked the same fifteen or so questions in the same order, making it possible to rearrange the contents into four parts.

First, I open each account with the practitioner, introducing the things they make, the themes in their work, and their personal backgrounds. This is followed by sections titled "Thinking and Reading Theory," in which they describe abstract concepts in their work, and "Making and Doing in Practice," where they specify what practice actually involves for them. These contextual sections culminate in the concluding section, "Between Theory and Practice," which makes explicit how each practitioner understands how what they think about and what they make are in relation. I assembled the final section by pulling spontaneous statements made throughout the interviews and bringing them together to make visible each interviewee's take on what happens between.

The practitioners were invited to be interviewed unsystematically. I invited them after a serendipitous encounter, after years of following their work online, or after reconnecting after losing touch. The interviews took place between February and June 2025, near the end of the book's writing, with this chapter being the final one to be completed. The conversations ranged from a single one-hour call to two meetings weeks apart, some totaling three hours. Each practitioner's account marks a paused season in their practice, a moment in time. By the time you read this, their approaches and reflections may have shifted entirely. My aim was to unsystematically bring together the accounts of critical creative practitioners to pay tribute to whatever would emerge in our conversation and make concrete the infinite configurations between theory and practice in their various forms. The interviewees include the following critical creative practitioners. The descriptions below include their name and a hint from my conversation with them that suggests their take on what happens between practice and theory.

Heesoo Kwon

BETWEEN THEORY AND PRACTICE:
I imagine some kind of magic because I'm getting the input and really reflecting the energy to my world.

Jelsen Lee Innocent

BETWEEN THEORY AND PRACTICE:
They're extensions of each other—an immediate extension. I can't imagine a separation.

Zakiya Collier

BETWEEN THEORY AND PRACTICE:
I would be on the train reading, getting my life, getting mobilized. What I read was integrated into my mind and the way I work going forward.

Baseera Khan

BETWEEN THEORY AND PRACTICE:
I never could figure out how to make a visual from reading, thinking, and annotating. It can take 10 years to arrive at a place where I can make something from that.

Rain Embuscado

BETWEEN THEORY AND PRACTICE:
I've internalized so much of those readings. I spend 90% of the time there. One out of ten times, I will separate theory and practice and reflect on what that's doing.

AK Wane

BETWEEN THEORY AND PRACTICE:
It's like riding a bus. You're looking out the window and experiencing this passage of time and society. Of course, you can make your own theory. But it does feel like theory exists outside for me.

Fei Liu

BETWEEN THEORY AND PRACTICE:
Once I start to name the theory, I start to create this distance from my work. It starts to create this rubric. This rubric and the practical, material things that I'm trying to do don't go naturally together.

Linda Dounia

BETWEEN THEORY AND PRACTICE:
Sometimes theory has a direct translation that can be made with the hands. Sometimes it's indirect and percolates. Sometimes you see something that becomes a corpus of theory.

Each of these interviewees is at a different stage of their relationship with political work and critical thought; they come from various continents, generations, and entry points into making, formal and informal. They have different levels of experience in being interviewed and fielding questions about their work. I let the interviewees' reputable academic backgrounds, portfolios, teaching experience, professional titles, ages, day jobs, and the like fall into the backdrop. Instead, I push to the foreground what is interior—what they know about how they make and unmake in the world. The details of their locations and personal backgrounds surface organically throughout each account. This includes the absence and important refusal to disclose some of this information due to a range of concerns, like the complexities of the outside gaze on the contents of their story.

Within each conversation, there are several more things not present on the page but live in the paragraph breaks and spaces between words: shared laughs, my set of questions, silences, snack breaks, a teenage son politely interrupting to ask for permission to go out, sweet humming while grabbing a book off the shelf to show me, mutual gratitude, genuine pauses to consider something about their work for the first time, a walk across a university campus, the top of an enormous poodle's head peeking into frame on a video call, a wise offering about being perceived as much younger and more inexperienced than you actually are, passionate bonding about ramen or notebook systems, private matters omitted, and more.

Heesoo Kwon[1]

BETWEEN THEORY AND PRACTICE:

"I imagine some kind of magic because I'm getting the input and really reflecting the energy to my world."

•

Leymusoom is the name of the autobiographical feminist religion I initiated in 2017.[2] When I first started Leymusoom, I thought my experience was so specific. I thought, *Nobody will understand me*. I'm from Korea. I majored in business. My family used to practice Catholicism, now my mom is really into Korean shamanism, and my upbringing was living with all the female ancestors. I thought putting this kind of narrative to my work was too much. And I didn't know how to embody that in my visual work. But as I was working with the converters, the community members, it really changed my perspective because we were from all different places, like from Japan, from Korea. There were Mexicans, Filipinos, and different ages. Everyone was from different cultures, but we shared the universe. Or sharing some experience, like patriarchy. When we were talking about our ancestors' lives, everyone could feel each other and deeply, deeply relate to each other. So it was a really

1 heesookwon.com

2 Heesoo has created more than 50 cumulative projects under the umbrella of *Leymusoom* ranging from gatherings with converters—of which there are more than 100 as of 2024—to ceramic sculptures and large installations to 3D animation and using artificial intelligence technologies. Throughout her narrative here, she refers to three of these projects that contribute to the *Leymusoom* genesis and universe: *Leymusoom Firefly* (2023), *Mago Leymusoom* (2022), and *Bodurinao's Shrine* (2018).

eye-opening experience. And that's when I started to put my own narrative, and that's when I started to feel: *This is the autobiographical part. I really need to bring my own family, and I need to talk about that. I need to work on that.*

I kept my perspective as the artist, like hanging out with people, working with people, and seeing how they see my work. When I first framed it as a religion, it had so many different, diverse layers. I had six very close people who are very active practitioners. We did a lot of collaboration and work together, and became really good friends. I wrote a paper, *How to Become a Founder of Feminist Religion* in 2018 about how they see our time together. And this interview and the answers were very interesting. One of them said, like, *Oh, we're close best friends*. Like, they think we are really hanging out. One of them said, *We are starting a new, emerging feminist movement! I'm part of the active movement.* And some other person said, *We are a religious group*. So the interpretation was very important.

In the spring semester of 2018, one of my mentors from UC Berkeley at the time was giving me a ride back to campus from the studio at Richmond Field Station. It's like a 15-minute drive from campus, and I didn't drive at the time, so I asked for a ride. She said she had a dream of me, and there were people in line waiting in front of my studio, like a shrine. All the dots got connected. Another mentor, even before I wrote the genesis for *Leymusoom*, said, "What you're saying is a religion. You're talking about the vision, the people, and what you're dreaming of. What you're describing is a religion." That's how I first decided the direction of the concept.

Most recently, I'm interested in navigating the possibility of working with AI to address my limits in practice. I started the *Leymusoom Firefly* series in 2023, an ongoing photographic series. Firefly is a generative AI function. I brought my family photos to the center of the blank canvas in Firefly and extended the viewpoint. I asked the AI to extend the border and show me more than the original borderline of the image, so that I can eventually complete the holistic viewpoint of the childhood home I really miss.

The AI tried to create some women figures, and I imagine the AI recognized the baby and the father in the photograph, and in the conventional family photos they have in their database, they always have mom, dad, and the baby. So, I imagine AI tried to bring the woman as the mother figure. So it's so fascinating to see how it's bringing some social norm, because it's based on other people's databases, too, and like reading my family's ethnicity and trying to engage with the situation. I know who this is; it's not an unclear memory for me—this is my mom. And I have other photos of her giving me the bath from a different angle, so I have reference photos, but just completing this Asian grandma's face, or connecting my mom's body, just gave me some really interesting, special reaction. It felt really warm, and it really made me think about my grandmother, too, even though I know it's not my grandmother.

So my first intention was that I found many of my family photos from around 1990 to 1996 were taken in this house. It's an apartment unit we used to live in Irwon-dong in South Korea. I think I was 1 to 6 or 7 years old. When we were living here, and because I was too little, too short, I didn't have a holistic viewpoint of the house.

I was always looking down, on the floor playing, you know? So I have a very vivid memory about the lower part of the house, but I don't remember the layout of the house or the upper part of the house. So I wished, and I felt each of the family photos was some kind of puzzle part, and so there were some gaps between them.

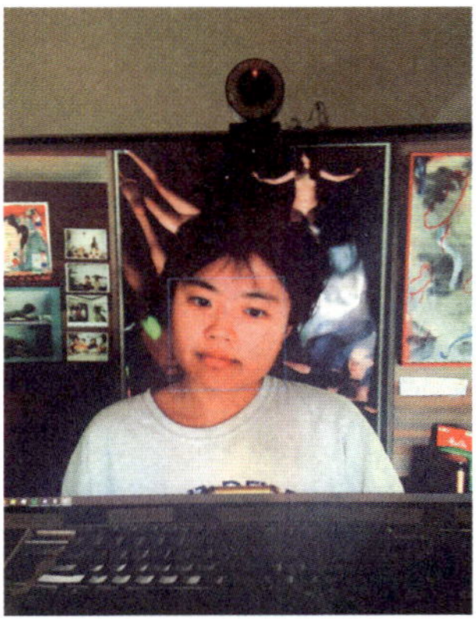

Images captured at Heesoo's San Francisco studio while *Mago Leymusoom* (2002) was in production. Images courtesy of the artist.

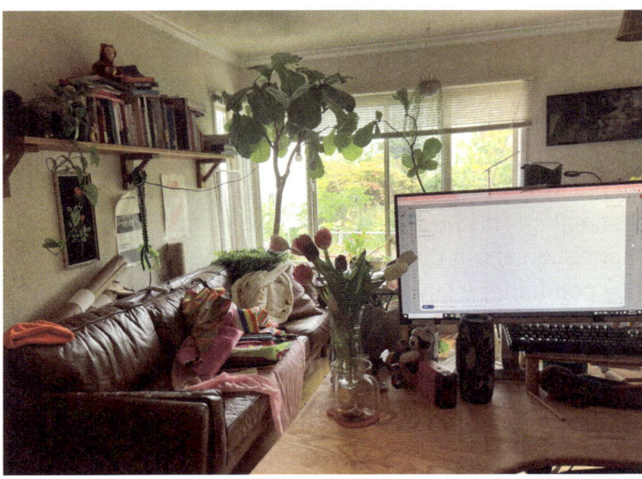

THINKING AND READING THEORY

Before I moved to this new apartment that is quite small, I used to read while I was taking a bath. A really fluffy bubble bath. I had candle lights, played some fun music, and added some Epsom salt. Or I brought books to the park. Sometimes, my partner and I used to go to Dolores Park a lot in San Francisco. Sometimes I was doing gardening really passionately every morning for two to three hours. I grew some Korean herbs from the seeds my mom sent from Korea. Every morning, I had some reading, wrote some journal, and started gardening. That used to be my routine. I used to love going to work at cafes too. When I need to save some money, I play the coffee music at home, make the coffee, and even clean and reuse the plastic cup. And recently, I've been reading in my bed a lot.

Whenever I go to Korea and visit my family or for any research, I try to visit Korean shaman shrines and do some research and interviews. One of the shamans gave me this book: 신들의 세계: 해동 무속총서 [1] (*World of Gods: Haedong Shamanism Collection [1]*). And in Korean shamanism, they say there are 10,000 kinds of gods, and the shamans are called 만신 (*mansin*), which is the same meaning 10,000 gods. They are channeling all different ancestors and their god spirits they're serving and channeling. This book has all the theory and important information about the structure of their world and how they conduct the code and everything.

The book, *Braiding Sweetgrass,* has been really important when I worked on the *Leymusoom Garden* (2023) project, connecting my grandparents' garden in South Korea and my studio at the time in San Francisco.

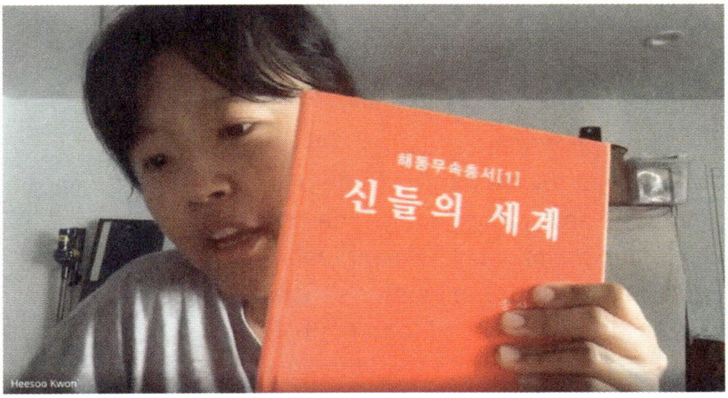

Image taken during the interview between Heesoo and Myriam.

I 3D-scanned the garden and my studio, and combined them together. I wanted to invite all my ancestors and my community members. And this book helped me to understand where I'm located, as an immigrant, how my body is related to the land, and how my ancestors found the new land to settle down after the Korean War, how they cultivated their life and family, and how, seeing myself as a new seed, flying from Korea and settling down.

I got this book, *Surrealism*, from the Pompidou Center. I was really inspired by the Surréalisme exhibition. I didn't take any art history class, but I took some art theory classes when I was in school, like in undergrad. Whenever I revisit art history or theory, I just continue my work. Whenever something comes up, I just revisit the specific topic or artist or theory, and this is where I'm really looking into now. I never identified myself as a photographer because I don't take photos. But now I'm doing a lot of photographic exhibitions, and had a chance to show this piece from the *Leymusoom Firefly* series. In the exhibition, whenever I go to a different wall, I could see how they understand frames like photos and paintings. I was interested in the materials they chose, like the frame materials and the scale of the photos, and how they handle works.

A Korean women's history class moved my life. It transformed my life. I have some papers I collected about patriarchy and misogyny, like the article by Jonghyun Lee, *Shamanism and Its Emancipatory Power for Korean Women*. In the Korean women's history class was my first time to learn about the Mago myth. Mago is the giant goddess appearing in one of the very important Korean Genesis myths, and she started the whole universe. Through the Korean patriarchal history, they didn't want to allow the woman creator story to be believed. And so I was so interested in that theory and how it was degraded, and she became some kind of monster living in the small mountain or in the town. And it's showing how the Korean woman's social status and their life became like that too.

MAKING AND DOING IN PRACTICE

Everything has a vision. I always find inspiration in my everyday life. In Korean shamanism, they see everything has some energy of the universe, guiding my environment and situation around me, there's energy like *gi*, the flow. I really focus on my desk and where I'm at. So it doesn't really make sense to separate my life and studio. I don't want to commute, and I just love being surrounded by what I'm working on.

When I first just came from Korea in 2017, I went to my friend's friend's house for Thanksgiving in Washington, DC. I joined the invitation, and we went to several museums one day. There was the Museum of the Bible.

And one of the pieces I saw there was somebody's self-made shrine. They brought the whole shed from that person's backyard. They were a government worker during the daytime, so nobody knew that he had this kind of hobby, making kind of weird, self-made, mythical creatures and things like that. But after they passed away, somebody found it in their backyard. I saw the whole shed and the altars in the shed. There also was a working desk inside there where he was making things for this ritual space.

Before seeing this shrine or making this *Leymusoom* genesis, I didn't plan to start a religion, but I was taking a tourism anthropology class and wanted to explore, *What's the definition of genesis? What is Catholicism? What is creation? Shamanism?* And so the inspiration from Washington, DC, and the comments I got from the anthropology classes that I was taking, everything kind of combined together, and I made *Bodurinao's Shrine* (2018). *Bodurinao's Shrine* was my first time to think about an altar and room for practice, room for making. Then, I was working closely with the community members, and my shrine and altar were my studio on campus. It was the church. Everyone gathered there, and it became more elaborate. After the pandemic and after graduating from school, my friends left and went back to their own country. Then I also didn't have a studio space.

Now, I'm a traveling body. My body is not located in one specific place, and I don't have family at home. I'm some kind of, like, star. Moving around, trying to locate myself in the big universe kind of feeling, and where I make the *Leymusoom* work is always changing too.

What's important is just myself and my where my body and my spiritual energy exist. And sometimes, even though my body is located in some specific place in San Francisco, all my energy and spiritual energies are in Korea. Sometimes, I find myself in the past, too. I can't afford my own body—how can I move all those sculptures and delicate ceramics? It's so luxury. I can't take that much. Being obsessed with the material and the space doesn't work for me.

When I first started *Leymusoom Firefly* (2023), I didn't even have a deadline for it because I didn't start it as art. It was my research. So I remember I was at the kitchen dining table, eating some food. The whole house was dark because it was 9 p.m. I was quite hungry, so I cooked a rice and veggie salmon bowl and was waiting with my computer for it to cook in my air fryer. There's one light on above my dining table, and I just had so much fun working on it. I made 30 images within one month. I felt it was so intimate. It almost reminds me of hypnosis therapy I'm doing. I imagine the AI has somebody in the dark room, and we are having very intimate conversations. I'm saying, "Oh, this part of memory I'm missing. Can you help me?"

I think about art and making art as a tool to express my thoughts. I always had some conceptual idea or direction first. Because I don't have any training to learn how to make art related to the medium choices, I'm very fluid. I find the best mediums to visualize and realize the conceptual direction. The idea or direction goes first. The conceptual direction or the conceptual theory I'm interested in goes first. I try to find the right medium. That's a really important part of my work.

Magic Between Theory and Practice

In the *Mago Leymusoom* (2022) video, in a 3D scene, I'm sitting in front of my desk, and my mom is behind me, supporting me. *Mago Leymusoom* was inspired by an invitation to be part of the exhibition of sister cities, a collaboration between San Francisco and Seoul, Korea, and the theme was ecofeminism. I decided to think about my mom as Mago, the giant creator, and in my home studio at the time, my living room space, she's giving me birth in my living room—giving birth to *Leymusoom*. The whole studio is a womb. I was reading a lot and researching a lot of papers about Korean ecofeminism, like an

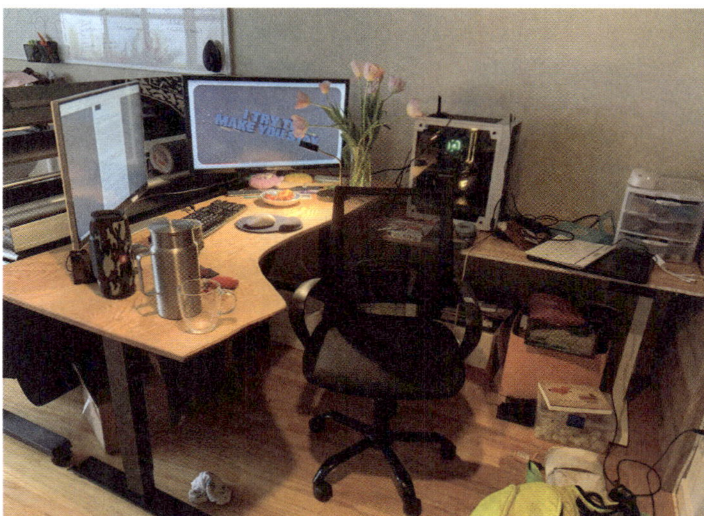

Heesoo's desk and monitors. Image courtesy of the artist.

essay published by the Sunhak Peace Prize and scholars writing about ecofeminism in Korea and Korean culture.

I have two monitors at my desk. I built the 3D scene on the right side and the left monitor for research, theory, or some references. I'm getting the input between what I read and the 3D work and really reflecting the energy to my world. Between the research and the 3D scene, I imagine some kind of magic. I exist at my desk. At the same time, it is where the virtual world is based on, and I see my avatar there, too.

Original Intention Between Theory and Practice

Art making and conceptual ideas are really important things for me as an artist and as a teacher. I'm a tenure-track faculty member teaching animation. I never imagined I would be a teacher teaching animation because I didn't learn how to animate from school. But my approach and my teaching philosophy as an artist and as an art teacher is that mediums nowadays, at the current moment, offer so many resources, so everything is so accessible. You can learn 3D software and animation, and all the methods online for free on YouTube.

But what is hard to learn outside of school, just on your own, is how to understand if your conceptual idea and your visual languages are working or not. My approach to students and also for my art is I'm trying to see what I'm talking and what I'm thinking is actually conveyed well with my visual language. And like, if there are any references that I couldn't consider, or if there's any aspect that's not working, or it's rather working in some opposite direction. I love talking to my curator friends and writer friends, and whenever I make a new piece, I share with them how they see it and try to understand if there is any interesting perspective that I haven't recognized, and trying to fill the gap between my original intention and how the work is existing. That's how I develop and complete the body of work.

Jelsen Lee Innocent[3]

BETWEEN THEORY AND PRACTICE:
"They're extensions of each other—an immediate extension. I can't imagine a separation."

•

The intellectual history of Haiti is scholarship I've been drowning in, happily. Exploring its rich history has been an anchor in my developing work, politics, and overall worldview—that's really important. Digging into peoples of a new and isolated state that has yet to be fully actualized, producing a new, post-colonial society without contemporary examples. How did they navigate this new world as individuals, as scholars, as peasants, as mothers, as fathers? I've really delved into this. I'm finding some type of solace and inspiration. And I'm also wrestling with the current social and political realities of the West in the Caribbean through these different infrastructures of power and how they've been ultimately sustained the last 500 years; reinterpreted as modern manifestations. These are the power dynamics through space and time.

That leads to how I approach material, as far as physical tactility and installations. How do I want people and audiences to engage with the work? How do I—what I call—invite curiosity? With the materials, if you're questioning what it is, then maybe that allows for an opening to question: What kind of world do we live in? You know, that question of your own biases and how you're implicated in the things that the work is concerned with. And that's the world I'm playing in right now.

My work has shifted significantly since I first started.

3 jelsenjelsenjelsen.com

Just like any fledgling artist, initially, it's autobiographical, right? *I like looking at art, and so I'm gonna make art-looking things!* Now it's that I'm intending for it to be in dialogue with multiple things beyond my own instincts. I still rely on my instincts, which I think is still important, but it doesn't start and stop there. You know, I eventually opened a book. I opened a book that didn't have photos in it, and I had to highlight entire paragraphs at a time. When I read Derrick Bell's *Faces at the Bottom of the Well*, it truly struck me. It was also while *Critical Race Theory* was popping off in the mainstream media, and Derrick Bell so happens to be the attorney, the professor who was integral to coining that phrase. Initially, I had bought a vintage copy of it solely because the cover design is so strong, the title is crazy, but it wasn't until years later, maybe 2012 or 2013, that I got to reading it. It was in my accumulating library of books I would eventually read, and then I eventually read it. I was like, *Look at me, ancestors!* Reading this book and understanding or being introduced to these concepts that are far beyond my academic trajectory leading up to that, and just how plainly he broke down the world that I experienced. It's not like I was reading it, removed from the way I was situated as a Black person in America.

Reading that book marked a significant shift in my expression and criticism of racism, and why I eventually named a sculpture after that title, *Faces at the Bottom of the Well* (2016), where I produced this floor piece that took up a whole lot of exhibition space. The piece was an extension of my reflections on how matter-of-factly he phrased the state of race relations in the US. That was a one-to-one: this book was really having an impact while I was producing a work that's inspired by it.

I feel I'm so early into my practice to be able to confidently say, *This is a method I have when approaching institutions,* or *This is the type of relationship or kind of engagement that shows itself consistently*. Honestly, I've been kind of sporadic. My journey from undergrad to graduate school is a 20-year path of starting and stopping and trying different things out. So, I really haven't had an anchoring relationship with any institution at that level. The institution of "just be professional" definitely drove me. Especially as a freelancer, as a corporate creative in New York, where employment is frequent, you can hop around. You stay someplace for a year or so, then move on to the next thing—even right next door. But your role, your experiences, and your capabilities need to transfer directly. Being able to be in different spaces while still producing at the capacity that was intended and expected was important. I started that when I was 21, more than 20 years ago.

My dad's a minister, and I grew up Seventh Day Adventist, so our family went to church three or four times a week. Basically, when my dad was at work, we were all at work. My mom was a school teacher but then got ill early in her career, so she shifted and focused more on her community work, community organizing, and related efforts. Being Haitian American meant that people my age at church were all first-generation, born in the States. All of our parents, the aunties, the uncles: they were from Haiti proper.

Those shared realities motivated everyone to be in service of each other. I think that's part of the reason why, with my previous commercial career in advertising, I couldn't take it seriously. It was just making stuff to make stuff. I made money, that's it. It wasn't sufficient, it wasn't substantial. I work to be of service. I want to be of service to Haiti, to the struggle, to Africans, to humanity.

THINKING AND READING THEORY

I've been approaching theory as a framework or as assumptions for ideas to flourish underneath. Frameworks are like guardrails. It's just like, *Hey, whatever you're exploring, whatever you're looking to like, discover, or on the path to discovery, use these parameters to help you reach that destination more precisely*. Right? Whether it's a historical framework or a conceptual framework, or sometimes a geographical framework, it allows me a kind of specificity in guidance. It's also a starting point. It's like, *Okay, this framework has these three core elements. This is where we begin.* And again, I think destination is the key statement for me. This is not the end-all. This is the road you're going to be moving toward.

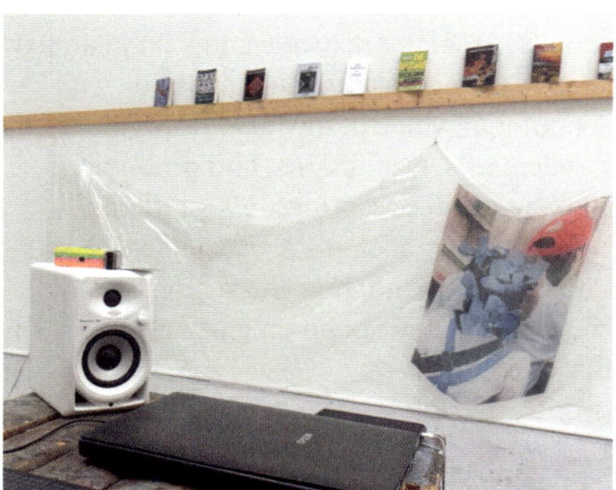

Jelsen's studio space, including his collection of books. Image courtesy of the artist.

I'm constantly engaging with political theory and how it actually manifests today. It is really grounding that I get to engage with people and organizations doing activism and community work in different ways. It's not only a scholarly engagement. I sometimes collaborate with my parents, community members, and friends in Haiti, Mexico, and stateside. That's really the stuff that gets me fired up. It also provides a clarity that would otherwise be impossible while I'm situated in Norway. It's not only this scholarly engagement.

For theory, I've been going into books for sure. I also find ways to use digital tools like YouTube or AI to explore ways into research that may add unpredictable layers to my process. Things can unravel, giving me more things to inquire about. I'm often at the point of, *I don't know aaanything! This is amazing!!*

YouTube Premium is the best subscription I have. It's the only app worth paying for every month. Period. If a writer whose work I'm reading has a lecture or talk on there, I really get to dig into their language, which further contextualizes their work in ways the singular text couldn't provide. So I'm actually reading the book with them because I got their voice in my head now. And then also watching reflections, discussions, and groundings around that book by reviewers, professors, students, anyone who uploads their take—it's always different and revealing. Because of the pandemic, there are so many classes and courses that have been online, you know? I'm now a perpetual student.

AI has also been a helpful research tool for sure, it's been useful in how I discover voices across academic disciplines and my own expanding interests. An example prompt I'd ask would be something like: I drop in a draft of my bio, my CV, or an essay that I wrote—I'd spent forever getting those two paragraphs together. Then I'd ask something like, "Provide three scholars or theorists that would complement and contrast the key themes in this text." Cool, then I'd be good for a month, because I'd be introduced to three thinkers I didn't know before. I'd go into their methodologies, their theories, their schools of thought. And then I'd get even more specific and ask, "Name three women thinkers from the Caribbean who work with opacity in a social context and colonialism between 1900 and 1965." You know, Sylvia Wynter pops up. It's fantastic. Then I'm gone for another two months.

I've been assigning "Papa Homework" to my son, and this month we're getting into 18th-century Haiti. Seeing, talking with, imagining the world from the point of view of a 15-year-old is fascinating. You know, he thinks of an '80s movie as a black-and-white film and doesn't know what a decade of something is. It's just so rich with all sorts of interpretations.

There are a whole bunch of people who have been integral to me shifting how I approach art who come to mind right off the bat. But it's been hard living in Norway and not really engaging or socializing the way I'm accustomed to in the States. Being home in New York, I have friends and colleagues from different stages of my life.

I've been exploring questions of statehood, nationhood, and the infrastructures of control that govern populations. So whether it's architectural, ecological, or psychological, the legacies of control are constant and interwoven throughout our societies.

Kerry James Marshall definitely changed my whole

thing. There was something about his intention in centering Black folks and their stories into the work within and beyond the craft. The way he went about his craft is how I used to think about design; *I'm gonna kern the hell out of this goddamn sentence.* There's something about the language he uses, too. It was just so beautiful and inviting to me.

Firelei Báez is an incredible Afro-Dominican artist, and it's interesting the way she positions—or I don't think "positions" is fair to say—how she says being of Dominican *and* Haitian descent. Dominicans tend to have an anti-Haitian identity complex.

Being tapped into Haiti, its diaspora, and Black American activist organizations is anchoring, especially while I'm living so far away from the tangible struggle. The Signal and WhatsApp group chats are always popping off with information, breaking news, and calls to action. These organizers are truly on top of it. They're not even "talking politics" but intimately engaging in the politics of people, and I'm seeing how they mobilize and have impact. A lot of injustices are magnified against the same issues, same people. That means that there's been resistance to it for just as long.

MAKING AND DOING IN PRACTICE

In 2001, it was the first time I had a studio, like a real artist's studio. I had this fantasy of what type of art I'd be making and what kind of artist I would be. It was based on scale in general. I wanted to make "big stuff." I wanted the space to do it. And I made nothing in that space. Literally, I made nothing... maybe one thing in 2 years.

Later, I had inherited a new space. I was reading more

and engaging with other artists more frequently, so I was in a space where making was finally necessary, not recreational. At the time, I had the time and space to be with myself and focus on intention, while incorporating material exploration simultaneously. It wasn't leading to a specific outcome. I was working through things by making. That led to a lot of experimentation at a smaller scale. I would play with different materials, use resources like workshops and technicians. I was literally experimenting every day. *Oh, what's that? How do you make it if I wanted to do this or that, minus that? What would it take? What are you doing Tuesday?* That was my conversation with people, constantly. I knew I'd be working toward a larger scale. I had access to a team of technicians who were very helpful, open, and enthusiastic. I developed tests and methods that I was able to execute at scale with three other people. As a creative director in my past life, knowing what and how to delegate work collaboratively was essential. It's, *Okay, maybe I have to help you help me*, and being able to facilitate that. They were absolute professionals, skilled and willing to explore ideas with me, too.

With previous work and shows, I had a residency in Slovenia in 2017 or 2018. That was my first residency. It was more or less the same idea. They flew me out and had the facilities for anything I was ready to make. I was there for about a week and a half, stayed up every night working up until the opening, then flew back the next day. Now, as I'm looking for a new studio, I have more defined intentions. I need a space where I can go and think, dabble with some small-scale material explorations, knowing I'll scale it up once I have the facility and the show to do that. I think this works in a practical sense, but also conceptually in terms of how I tend to approach my practice. I'm anchoring in thinking, reading, and sketching. It's a great reveal to then blow it up at scale in an exhibition space. Like, *I know exactly what this is—at a tenth of the scale.*

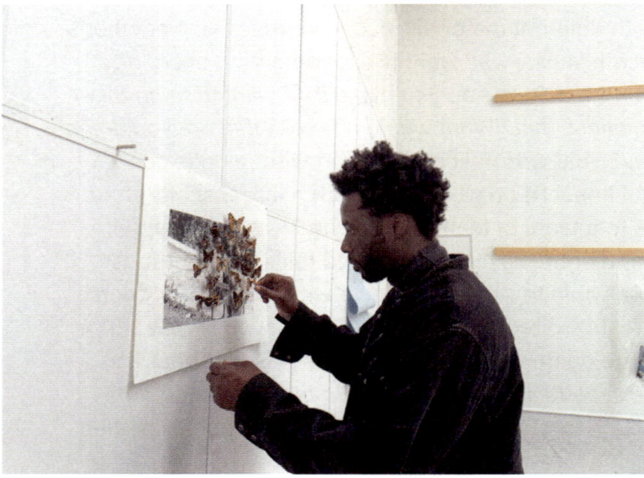

Jelsen in his studio. Image courtesy of the artist.

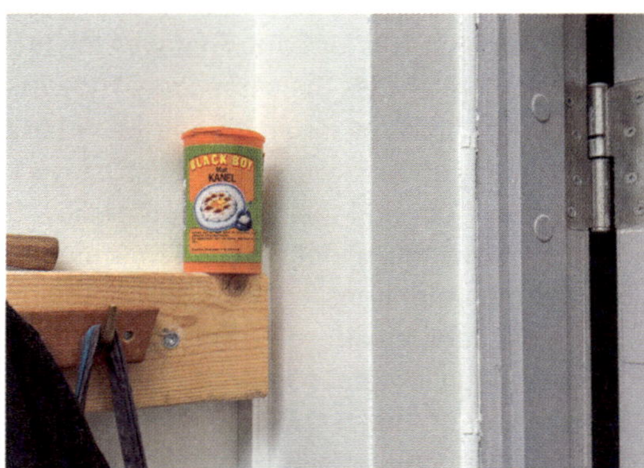

A Norwegian cinnamon package branded "Black Boy." Image courtesy of the artist.

I'm working with textiles more now than ever, denim and silk specifically. I work with polymer resins, video, and commercial building materials, from tiles to tile glue to different kinds of hangings and framing materials. I also used carpets for a piece. I work with printed matter too—printed media, publications, and archival materials. Me and eBay go way back. We have a good time. Writing is also part of my practice. Now, this is a terrifying process. I work with visual media because I am pulling from films and pop culture. I've been using meteorologist newscasts as an analogy for the omnipresence of the American Military Industrial Complex. I work with found objects too: a Norwegian cinnamon package branded "Black Boy," American-branded rice bags found in Haitian markets, and a 1968 Haitian stamp commemorating a Norwegian skier. Imagine what else we don't know about in terms of the relationship between the Nordic and the Caribbean. I intentionally have different degrees of abstraction throughout my works. So there are certain things that are just made plain. Now, sound is getting its way into the practice. I've used a WikiLeaked recording of an American military operation in Afghanistan that was eventually used to prosecute those involved in war crimes. Integrating social engagement and community impact is becoming more central to the projects I get involved in as well.

An initiative I started in August 2024 called *Peer Review*, which is for Black folks in Norway, was first done in conjunction with artist Cauleen Smith's show at a large institution here called the Astrup Fearnely Museum. About 25 Black folks participated in the two-day reflection, where we spent time walking through the exhibitions, and on the second day, we printed out local reviews of the show and collectively broke down the language and subtexts in Norwegian.

Peer Review is about establishing and normalizing our point of view first, moving any other "official" accounts secondary. We anchor what we think as a community, and that's how we move forward. I later extended Peer Review to another art institution, Kunstnerforbundet, also in Oslo. It continues to expand as a private space where we engage in critical dialogue around Black art and media. We meet twice a month for about three hours each time, and we go deep. Sometimes we review exhibition texts, asking, *How accurate is this compared to your experience? What do you think?* The goal is to develop a language, a vocabulary, and build confidence to attend shows and say, *This is like this because of that.* This raises the bar for what we consider quality.

It's rare for me to look at my practice as this constellation of things. I'm slowly recognizing that my practice isn't separate from, but extends across just about everything I do. They all feed into each other. They all leverage one another for the next thing. They even justify the next thing. *This practice is the effort.* Yeah, I like that. There's a commitment to putting in effort. Some of that practice gets to be witnessed in an exhibition, in a text, the material output that happens, but it's not the whole thing. The complete practice isn't confined to a material output.

BETWEEN THEORY AND PRACTICE

Practice Speaking Back to Theory

I appreciate being brought into an expanded universe that the art introduces me to. I want a journalist, a scientist, or the folks I'm reading to think, "Jelsen's touching on some things that we're also touching on."

Theory and Practice Are Inseparable

Every work anyone does has a level of autobiography in it because you're literally making the work. But there's just too much going on in the world and too much going specifically against my family and community for my work to be centering myself. That's not enough. My political values are going to directly inform the work that I do. I can't imagine a separation, and it still being my work.

Temporality Between Theory and Practice

I want the work to be transient. You can't pin down when it was made. I'm pulling from archives in order to complicate today's questions with something that was published in 1967. How exhibiting an issue of *The Liberator* magazine featuring Papa Doc [Haiti's late dictator, François ("Papa Doc") Duvalier], in my show titled *Truth Has No Friends In The West* (2025), can speak to both the past violences against his own people and those foreign alliances that continue to cripple Haiti today.

I'm constantly trying to find a way to be contextually relevant, and that context requires current affairs and also historical intervention. These things are cyclical, and if they are not cyclical, they are linear, but ultimately they are histories bound to each other. For instance, last year, Americans, Trump, and right-wing media were accusing Haitian migrants of eating their white neighbors' cats, and to most people, that sounds shocking. But I can pull out a 1925 *New York Times* article from the American military occupation of Haiti, producing identical dehumanizing lies about Haitians eating cats and why these savages needed U.S. presence and civilizing. This rhetoric can be traced back to publications from 1804 and even the 1700s. This long history of redundant Western propaganda against the same people sheds light on how little distance from white supremacist systems we're operating in today.

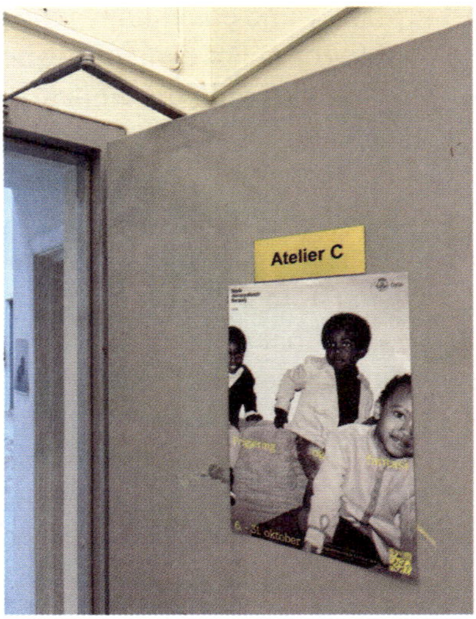

A door to Jelsen's studio space.
Image courtesy of the artist.

Zakiya Collier[4]

BETWEEN THEORY AND PRACTICE:
"I would be on the train reading, getting my life, getting mobilized. What I read was integrated into my mind and the way I work going forward."

•

In a certain aspect of the archival field, one aspect of my work is more of a pedagogical or educational approach to intervening in a lack of equity and access to education and training. I'm intervening through the creation of a training program specifically for Black memory workers, archivists, and folks that are interested in incorporating web archiving into their practice. That project centers mostly on folks who are on the ground in their communities. My work is around the creation of an actual container for this program, shaping the curriculum, and shaping the extracurricular pieces that will support their learning processes, and also the feelings of community and co-learning. I'm thinking about what will be taken away from the co-learning process—what the project and the field will learn and gain from, for the first time ever, having a cohort of 22 Black folks learning this skillset together. I'll be part of pulling that together and seeing what ways of knowing may be unique to this particular process, and the ways Black people use this technology and set of tools.

Another instance of my work is as a co-producer on a film, *Somebody's Gone* (2026), that looks at the specific home video collection of one man in particular, who has documented the life and career of his father, Brother Theotis Taylor, a spiritual gospel singer. In the process, he

4 zakiyacollier.com

has also documented his community in a small town in South Georgia, and he holds the most adequate documentation of the Black side of town in this mostly racially divided but integrated community. My role in that process is shaping the archival arc of the film and, of course, producer duties like sourcing funding and thinking about impact. But overall, I'm shaping the narrative as it relates to the archive he has kept and maintained for all these years, and how it speaks to the larger field of institutional archives versus home or community archives. I'm asking, *Where do they go, who is the steward, and how do they get taken care of outside institutional spaces?* I'm also thinking about, outside of the film, the long-term plan for this particular collection in this community.

I'm also Artist-in-Residence at The Laundromat Project and working with elders and organizers locally who have been part of a long history of preserving Bed-Stuy in central Brooklyn through a variety of programs. Many of these folks are no longer associated with the organization, but they have a long history that is largely under-documented in local archival institutions. There are a few oral histories, but I want to think with them about the stewardship of their materials long term. This stems from being in community spaces with elders who say things like, "There are no Black archivists," or "Nobody wants to help me—my family members don't want to dig into my archives," or "No one wants to buy or take my collection." They feel unsupported in this area, and while we know elders are under-supported in many aspects, this one connects to all of us—it is all of our history and responsibility to care for. My artist residency, which is meant to create change locally, aims to foster a network between local Black archivists and Black elders and community members so they know archivists are here to support them, to provide training through workshops on what they can do with their archival materials, and to guide them toward routes and processes to preserve them or find an institution that will if they don't want to steward them themselves.

Outside of that, my work is in advisory board capacities for community-based archives, or in project-based capacities to help think through how a community-based archive can be sustainable. This includes considering what kinds of programs are needed to engage the community and support them in their own stewardship, or in working with an institution to do it. I also work with elder artists and artists' foundations, thinking about storytelling and long-term preservation there. A lot of it centers on collective stewardship, communities, equity, and sustainability.

Archiving has colonial roots, so it was never intended, never meant to contain Black people. So it is still antagonistic toward Black people. Even as Black people are included in collections, there are always issues. We can't resolve anti-Blackness just by documenting more Black people or having more Black people in institutional archives. That only gives us more representation, but it doesn't solve who has access to archives or the structure of archival practice. Archives are still only open during business hours. So, only researchers or people with flexible schedules and a purpose can access them. Not just anyone can benefit from archives. Those realities have informed my skepticism and vigilance. It's like, *Okay, this is nice, but we still have to contend with anti-Black-*

ness. Where are our practices that are liberatory, not just inclusive?

THINKING AND READING THEORY

I was working at the Schomburg Center in 2019 when I was reading Saidiya Hartman's *Wayward Lives*. I would be reading it on the train to and from work. Yeah, I feel like I would be on the train, getting my life. Like, *Oh my gosh, yes, yes, this. Yes, that!* It's such a wild experience to feel so affirmed, fired up, and mobilized by something while you're on the train with everybody else in their own world. And you're just like, *What? Nobody else is getting this fire right now. You're probably dreading going to work.* Maybe I was, too. But at least in this moment, I'm getting this fire. To remember the connection that I made while reading, because they can be happening in such chaotic moments, like on a plane, on a train, sometimes at home, sometimes in a waiting room, so I need to come back to this. I want to remember the connection that I made.

I come back to my notes from things that I'm reading just to check in with myself—being my own primary source. It's a process of revisiting inspirational texts or ideas that have informed me. Sometimes I realize I said something related to this, or I just want to get to know myself again. Like when I was applying for The Laundromat Project residency, or preparing a presentation for the board a few weeks ago, I flipped through different places in my notebook asking, *How have I articulated this before?* I sometimes don't get a chance to get back into a book again until some time has passed, but when I read my notes, I'm just like, *Yes*, I remembered the fiery excitement that I felt when the connection was made.

In between the actual reading, I keep sticky notes in the back of the book. There's not enough room for me to really get everything out on the page, like in the margins, and so I need somewhere else to write that can stay with the book and the specific text. That way, I don't have to, in my notes app, be like *Page 132, top of the page, this is what this is in reference to*. So I have these transparent sticky notes. They're colorful but transparent, where I can put it directly on top of what I was reading when I threaded the needle to something in my work.

I definitely tend to travel with a notebook. Not constantly, like if I'm going to physical therapy, I'm not taking one with me, but I have multiple notebooks. There are notes between you and me in here, notes from different professional development offerings, and it has also become kind of my learning space notebook, mostly because it's my largest notebook. I am thoroughly fascinated by how we use notebooks differently. I've been like that my entire life. Like in elementary school, I couldn't figure out what kind of notebook structure I wanted, and I would switch halfway through the year, where I'm like, this isn't working anymore. Or my mom's like, "I'm not buying you any more notebooks. So like, figure it out." It's still in my life: I have my learning notebook here, NEW INC incubator, The Laundromat Project, creative practitioner dreaming, planning, resourcing notebook, therapy journal, and then I have, like, the work notes notebook. I'm still figuring out which notebook, but also thinking like an archivist, this would be chaotic to process as an archival collection.

I use Zotero, a citation tool, which I really get deep into if I'm working on a specific project, when I transcribe a quote and have notes next to it.

My phone is pretty much always with me. So if I need to take notes on something, I go to my Notes app. I have a couple of different folders there, so I can file things away. For example, I have a Research and Future Ideas notes section, where I map out notes from books I'm reading if I don't have something to write with, like a sticky note or notebook. I just take notes there. A lot of different things fall into this folder. I could be at an event, something comes up for me, and I just add it to the list. Or I'm out in the world, see something random on the train, bus, or car, and I think, *Oh, that makes me think of something connected to that.* So I put it in this note, even if I don't have any specific intention of investigating these things tomorrow. Sometimes I just make up words that feel right. If you look at the bookshelf behind me, the top shelf is

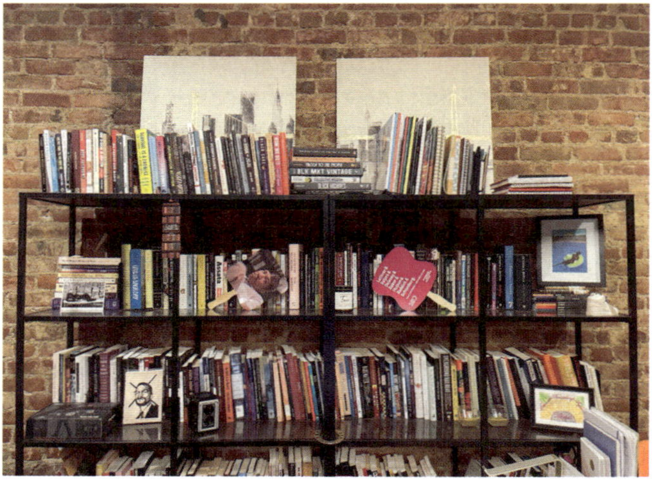

Zakiya's bookshelf in her home office. Image courtesy of the artist.

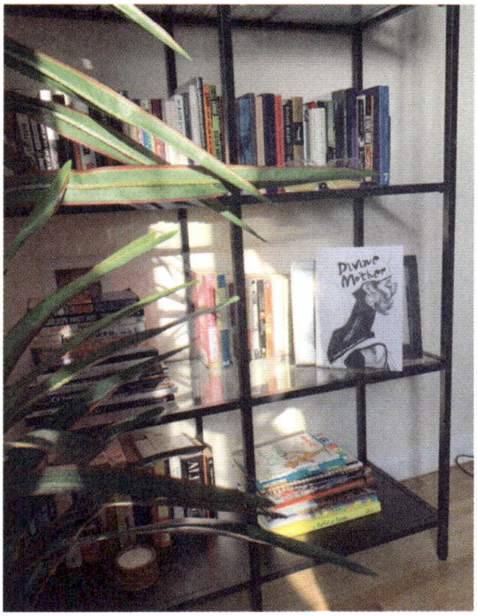

Zakiya's bookshelf in her former apartment. Image courtesy of the artist.

really Black women writers: Octavia Butler, Alice Walker, Toni Morrison, Assata Shakur, Zora Neale Hurston, Toni Cade Bambara. The writers are here on the top shelf, strategically placed. I've since had to add things on top of the top shelf, but that's the space. Right now, that shelf holds my more recent purchases or things I've been thinking through lately, including spiritual practices and Black feminism, Black feminist books on archival practice, some fiction, and information activism. I'm teaching a course on that this fall. So there are texts on surveillance, sousveillance, and digital Blackness.

The shelf below is more Black Studies and theoretical work: Saidiya Hartman, Alexis Pauline Gumbs, Black historical texts thinking through slavery and archival issues we run into. These texts deal with documenting Black folks who usually enter archives through encounters with law enforcement or being labeled as "bad." They aren't documented intentionally for the fullness of their personhood or contributions to society as creatives or just as people.

I'd say that the work of Christina Sharpe, Saidiya Hartman's *Wayward Lives, Beautiful Experiments*, Marisa Fuentes, Irma McClaurin's *Black Feminist Anthropology,* and Katherine McKittrick form where I entered the profession. I really started thinking about archives from an anthropological perspective. I studied anthropology in undergrad and came into archiving knowing about the issues around documenting Black and Indigenous life. That's not the case for a lot of people. They enter the field and are like, "Whoa, this is wild. I just wanted to be a librarian and archivist. I didn't know it was this bad in here." Archival practices have colonial roots, and anything developed in colonialism continues to do what it was intended to do.

MAKING AND DOING IN PRACTICE

When we are in community spaces and doing things, I see archival practice as one of the weapons in terms of fighting dispossession, or even documenting the dispossessions that are taking place, that have already happened. It can be used as a tool for liberation, and memory work should be a tool for liberation. When we are doing, say, an archival workshop, the memory work is more than just about the documents; people should be feeling supported, be fed. I care more about the people than the documents. Yes, we want documents and the VHS tapes, and everything else to be preserved. But if you're just not okay, I don't care about what's in your basement. There is a kind of urgency: *This person is aging, they're going to be gone soon. We need to figure out what's going on with their stuff.* But we can figure out what's going on with them, and that can be part of the conversation: "My basement has actually been leaking for years. That's what needs to be fixed first." I see that as part of the process of stabilizing and having sustainability and improving material conditions for Black people's lives, and then people can actually think about preserving materials. But if they're trying to preserve their lives, preserving materials is not a concern and shouldn't be. I'm not going to tell an unhoused person, "Well, what did you do with your documents before you were evicted?"

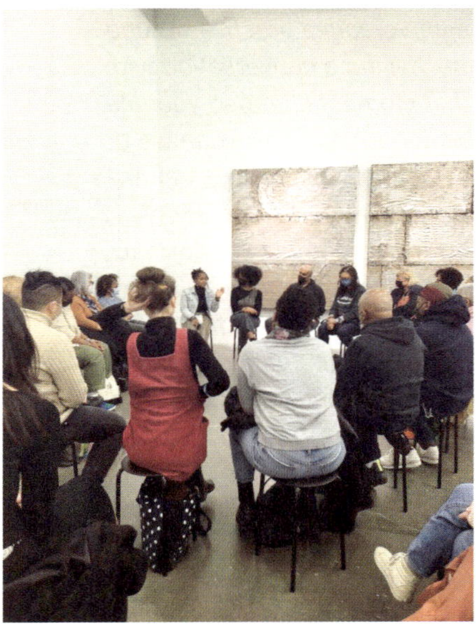

Zakiya facilitating a discussion at the New Museum, January 2023. Image courtesy of the artist.

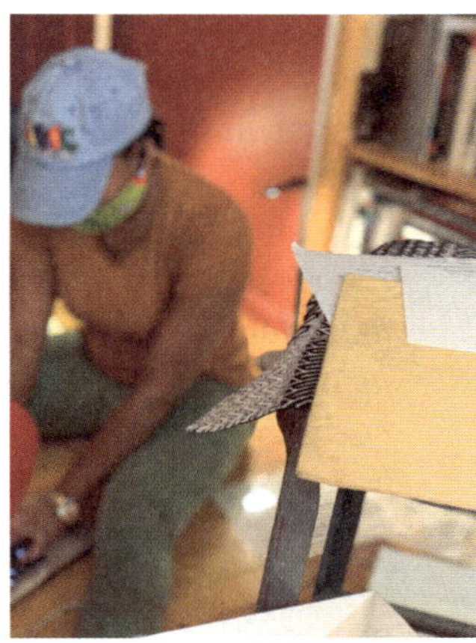

Zakiya processing papers in a client's studio. Image courtesy of the artist.

Whether I'm in a community space, a board meeting, or in someone's basement, I am thinking about what we are centering. Not just how we can sell this collection and get it into the closest institution, as in, "It would be great to go to 'X' institution, so students and faculty can come look at them." I carry things I've read into the work. Archival documents are not always safe; sometimes, there are things we don't want because they're too traumatic or violent. Maybe we need to redact things or add a note—not just in the sense of a trigger warning on a library website, but for a community. *Why is this too painful to interact with? What else can we do? Do we just completely forget that moment in time?* Which is fine, or *is there something we could do, engaging in some creative practice around that moment—writing poetry, having a conversation with someone else about how that moment changed your life, drawing something, dancing it out? What else can we do to remember or forget, or remember differently?* I think about how Black and Indigenous material conditions inform what documentation gets created, what formats, and where it ends up.

Instead of thinking, *I have this collection. I feel burdened by it. What do I do? I want to get rid of it. It's too much for me to handle,* or *I want to offload this; I wish my family wanted it.* Whatever the details may be, I encourage people to activate those who have shown interest in their history, to bring these things up at regular family gatherings, or moments when everyone is together. *I want you all to know what's in these boxes you think is junk—* explain things, be vulnerable, lean on others to sustain the collection, and don't see ourselves as sole individual stewards. That burden often leads to collections going to institutions far from their communities of origin.

I encourage people to bring others into the conversation about how we are going to take care of this. *How often can we do regular calls just to talk about what's here, to talk about a plan?* Or when we're hanging out, at least look at a few things every now and then to stay active in the process.

There are so many people who have been displaced—from natural disasters, forced displacement, eviction, or being refugees—so they will never have access to their archives. How do we need to, or how do I need to think about memory work for those people? There may be more people who have been displaced and don't have archives than those who do. I don't know if there are statistics on that, but we're all one step from being displaced. The archives I hold dear could be gone tomorrow. So yes, it's important to press the issue of archival practice, whether that means physically preserving things or being in conversation with elders, storytelling, oral practices, remembering, journaling, and so on. But we can lose these things at any time.

In my future work, where can I support people rebuilding their lives who just don't have documents and won't ever have documents or photos? Those things are actually gone—then what? That's something I'm thinking about in terms of my political commitments to the reality we live in and the reality for the communities I work with most—Black and Indigenous communities who are fighting for their lives in places impacted by climate change and violent displacement.

BETWEEN THEORY AND PRACTICE

A Separation Between Theory and Practice

I've read theory and have been informed by it. So they're with me in my practice, whether in someone's basement or in someone's digital files. But they aren't necessarily front of mind. I'm not, you know, looking at someone's photos from their racially segregated prom in the 1950s and thinking, "There's no way to memorialize something that is still ongoing!" You know? [Laughs] That's a Christina Sharpe reference. I might notice the applicability of the theory of what's been said in the moment. If I'm looking at slavery records, then yes, I can recognize what someone has written about the dynamics of how slavery records were created. I'm not the biggest fan of large cultural institutions for a lot of reasons, but I can be visiting or working remotely with colleagues who work with these institutions and think, *Yeah, I can totally see the applicability of theoretical texts that I've read to what we see here.* I have learned these things from these scholars and reading their texts, but I think it doesn't come up because it's not directly informing what I'm doing in that moment. Those are things that are figured out between me and the other people I'm with, based on my experience, expertise, and the things I'm informed by.

Theory and Practice Are Inseparable

It's really hard to separate my practices from what they're informed by because it's informed by so many people—how they talk about their work, how they experience it, and how they discuss it. That's informed how I understand my existence, like, *It makes sense now that my orientation is to have Black people experience and benefit from their own archival practices.*

Carrying Theory in Practice

The theoretical texts that I have read have put into focus some larger dynamics that I've been able to thread the needle between what they said and what I'm seeing in my work. Theory is something that I carry with me, not physically, but in my approaches to the work. I would say that in that instance of taking the A train to 135th Street, it was separate from the work I was doing day to day. It's more like a specter. It's there, but it's not. It was definitely integrated into my mind and into how I was thinking about my thoughts and the way I want to be involved in the work going forward. But it wasn't necessarily implemented immediately into the work, because I was working at an institution that, in some ways, participates in and enforces some of the things that are critiqued in that text. In other ways, we're talking about who gets documented and how, and about wayward women being documented. I'm working in an institution that was founded, which makes sense for the time period, on celebrating Black people's contributions and achievements. But 100 years later, that is still the mission: to highlight important people, people who've made positive contributions to society, people doing innovative, avant-garde things, but are Black. And that's not what that text is about. So yeah, it was a kind of double consciousness thing going on there, a separation.

Dissing and Disregarding to Bridge Theory and Practice

I bridge theory and practice by being very okay with dissing and disregarding the profession I'm a part of, and doing so publicly while decentering them in conversations. In the sense of what the best practices are according to the profession, according to "X" institution, it is easier to share those out to people. When people ask for resources, I can say, "Here are the best practices that this institution shared." But I encourage people to think about what works for them and their family, community, and capacity. I encourage people to build on their existing networks to sustain their archival practices.

Becoming a Different Person After Reading Theory
I think it's hard to pin down exactly how I do the work, because it's kind of an amalgamation of everything that has informed my life—my personal experiences, reading Black women writers for a long part of my life, and being informed by them. It's hard to separate my own experiences from the things I've read that have informed the next day and the next day. You don't walk away from reading Toni Morrison and still be the same—the same person after that. You stay there forever, even if you didn't finish the book or had to come back to it or reread it again because it still didn't sit in properly. Toni Morrison, just how she says, *This is not for white people. This is about Black people seeing themselves and experiencing themselves*, pulling from historical instances and building this beautiful life for Black people to read and experience something new or old, or to have remembering experiences.

Baseera Khan[5]

BETWEEN THEORY AND PRACTICE:
"I never could figure out how to make a visual from reading, thinking, and annotating. It can take 10 years to arrive where I can make something from that."

•

The most recent work was a set of oil paintings, rather large oil paintings. I just had an exhibition, *Pocket Diary* (2025), at Niru Ratnam Gallery in London, which closed a couple of days ago. So there were two sets of paintings, two series. In one series, I'm using a lot of red pigment. So overall, when you approach the painting, it's very much hues of red, and images emerge from that. The second series has intricate wood carvings with floral kind of carvings. And I was thinking about that as I was painting these different floral arrangements on panels, and then I would overlay rays of light on top of them. So those are the two sets of paintings I was working on.

On some level, I was trying to think about the way we see—a kind of complication of what we witness with our eyes versus the photograph. And it led me to this place where I was thinking about a diary that my father used to carry with him, and he would write down all the different things that would happen to him, or happened to his family, or his loved ones. And it was this little red book with a kind of wood-carving interlay look to it, and it said "Pocket Diary." So, I was all of a sudden in this place where I'm imagining paintings that come from that little pocket book. The other memory I had was my father used

5 baseerakhan.com

to teach me how to expose photographs, and we would go into the clothing closet. We had this one closet where we'd stick all the suitcases and all the clothes, and it was a magical place because there were so many different jewels and fabrics and materials and things I was so curious about. I spent a lot of time in that closet. We would tie a red scarf to the bulb, and we would expose photographs.

I was thinking about the document—the way we see the document as the photograph. And I started inscribing the dates of birth and death, and gold standards, and whatever was in the pocketbook. I would inscribe those onto the panels to create a kind of activity. The white square is just so intimidating to me, so I was just trying to do something. I was rewriting the journal onto the canvas. Then, I would squeegee it and sand it and do that over and over and over again. There's this thickness of the journal as you approach it, but then you don't really see anything—you're just in front of a red field, and images emerge from that.

Back in 2017, I had a show called *iamuslima*. I just knew that it would become something we would be teasing out. There was a Nike shoe situation in 2016 that became the thesis of my whole agenda of being an artist. I think artists are more poetic—they don't really think in terms of academia, but for me, the Nike shoe became the thesis of my whole project in life, which is: they wouldn't let me inscribe the word "Muslim" or "Islam" on the shoe. I was able to make a shoe before they shut down the embroidery process they offered on their online shop, and that shoe became the thesis of the show *iamuslima*.

At the time, there was this huge lawsuit that cost

them billions of dollars. They have been adjusting as a company since then. You know, hijabi gear, Colin Kaepernick as the cover for their campaign, all this stuff happened because of the lawsuit, because they lost their bottom line. Apparently, Muslims have a lot of money, and they support Nike, so they were like, *Oh shit, we're losing our customers, we better adjust.* Also, Muslims were not allowed back into the country, and there were protests, and people were bringing prayer rugs out into airports. And I was just like, you cannot make this shit up. I'm one hairline ahead of the activity that happens. I fell into this whole world of lawsuits and boycotts because in the bylaws or the corporate text, it says that Islam can inherently cause violence, which is why they couldn't put the word on the shoe.

I have become so disassociated and heartbroken from all the things. I'm in this place right now where I don't want to think about content at all. Institutions are terrible places, but I have to understand their language. The art world is a terrible place. It's where rich people come to clean their money. But I have to understand it, and it has made me a very social, but also insular, person. I just want to think about form—what happens when I'm connected to the surface and I'm painting, and what the material, the color, and the form are doing to me and for me. I think that's why I use the word selfish. Maybe what I'm experiencing is content overload. The content is in me, and maybe there's a block between the content and me, and instead of trying to take the block away to access the content, I'm just staying here.

THINKING AND READING THEORY

I don't want to be insincere in terms of my exterior motifs or influence from literature, music, or poems. I have gotten myself into a situation where I haven't been reading a lot since grad school. I graduated in 2012. It has become something of a problem since 2020. I think I got to a place where I didn't want to read the news anymore, I didn't want to engage, and then I couldn't concentrate when I was reading a book. Though I read almost every day. I read a lot: emails that come to me, I'm writing a lot, I'm processing a lot. I have to read a synopsis of an artist's work or a press release. I'm always reading, but I'm not really reading a collected artwork like a novel or a collection of essays. I can't really say that anything in my immediate year or the last two years has influenced me. I don't have a great book collection here at my house, but I'm in a stage right now where I'm thirsty again. I feel empty, and I feel like that foundation of knowledge I had obtained—I can't remember the shape of the nose or the face anymore. I'm feeling very vulnerable and wanting to learn again. And because I feel vulnerable, I'm really retreating and wanting not to be around too many people. Painting again is giving me the grace I need right now.

There are books I read deeply in grad school that have carried me, one of which is a collection of essays by Jean Genet, the French writer. He wrote a book called *Prisoner of Love*. I have five copies. I have my first original "holy grail" copy with all the little text, and I have a copy I left at the Brooklyn Museum for a year, tethered to the wall so other people could write in it. I have several extras in case my heart tells me to hand one to someone. It's almost like a Bible. You have a bunch, so you can pass

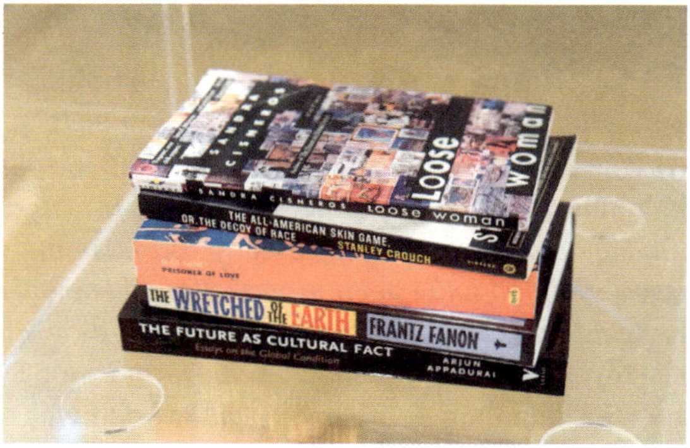

Stack of books selected by the artist. Image: Lynné Cravens. Image courtesy of the artist.

them out. A brief synopsis: *Prisoner of Love* is very much about memory. It's not a memoir, but it follows a political figure known for writing novels about his queerness and daintiness. He was also a war journalist in France, sent by the government to do interviews and research on political groups. He was sent to the Palestinian Liberation Organization (PLO) and spent time in Jordan. He was also sent to America to be with the Black Panthers. He stayed silent and didn't report back to the French government because he became so dedicated to those political groups. He decided the best way to keep everyone safe was to say nothing. In the 1980s, he bore witness to another kind of political warfare in Lebanon. Much later, from when he had been with the PLO and the Black Panthers, he realized he had to write something because tomorrow wasn't promised. The book is pictorial, jumping from timeline to timeline, geography to geography, because it follows his memory pattern. There are unreliable facts, but he's trying to remember the past and understand the present, and all of it is unreliable.

I was very lucky in grad school. I had a Sudanese professor, Salah Hasan, who started the Africana Studies Department at Cornell. There's an interesting history. The money was promised, but the school withheld it, so the Black Panthers arrived at gunpoint and held up the union. I was in New York City working at a nonprofit, hating my life, wondering, *Should I get married? Should I have kids? What should I do?* I was building my life, but I didn't know my past, my present, or my place in the world. I look South Asian, and I am South Asian, but my dad was also East African and Afghani. I'm not really treated like I'm on the inside of Islam, of India, of Iran, of Somalia—wherever it is I'm from. I don't have access. I worked with Salah Hasan, Distinguished Professor, and Professor Iftikhar Dadi, who was the Chair of my art department. Yes, they were men. Dismissive, all the things. But there were semblances of care I still haven't received from anyone else who wanted to teach me something.

The syllabus from a course I took was called Global Aesthetics. Within that, I learned about the Suez Canal, the French Revolution, and the Haitian Revolution—tactics to teach me about the future. We learned about the Bandung Conference, the Third World Order, the Washington Consensus, the UN, and how these so-called organizations of "care" were actually banks to keep decolonized countries indebted to their former colonies. There's no such thing as decolonization.

The Jean Genet book I read came from that syllabus, alongside learning the politics of Aimé Césaire, who had written a resignation letter to French Marxism. I wanted to be agile in theory. I read Lukács, Freud, Derrida, Deleuze and Guattari, Frantz Fanon, Aimé Césaire, Levinas, Judith Butler. I tried to keep up, but I would often set the book aside and imagine the world they lived in when they wrote it. I spent more time trying to picture their conditions than finishing the text. I ended up reading summaries—bless those who make difficult texts digestible. I was fascinated by Lukács and Freud because they were trying to understand the "modern man" during a Holocaust that hadn't happened yet, and a Third World Order that hadn't happened yet. They were writing before World War II, which changed humanity's course, rippling into genocides in the Congo, in India, and in Palestine. They were bridging society, and some of them even wrote these works in Israel in its early stages. I'm interested in how theory emerges from daily life. I tried to be an annotative, cold-pressed, panini kind of person about theory, but I have too many emotions. I miss that world, and I feel a little empty now. I think about a future where I can go back to it a little.

I am an artist, so I want to learn about artists. There's an Indian artist named Arpita Singh I'm discovering—she's an elder, and she was at the Serpentine Gallery when I was in London. I knew Noah Davis was an important artist before he had his Barbican show. I studied him closely—his complexity reminded me of Césaire or Fanon. He died young, like many of these men. He was a painter who started a gallery in LA to counter the modern museum archive, creating a Black history archive when the Getty had none before 2020. Ariella Azoulay calls herself a "perpetrator." She says any Israeli is a perpetrator. She's a theorist who has built a school of knowledge around the photograph. One of her ideas is that a photograph exists even without the click. She frames it as a pyramid: the subject, the photographer, and the event. The image exists even if it doesn't physically exist. She constantly rethinks occupation. Her book *Civil Imagination* is dear to me. After reading her, I asked myself, *What would it be like to make public art?* I got to do that a little.

MAKING AND DOING IN PRACTICE

The last eight or nine months, I've tried to wake up and do all my admin, thinking, and planning here at home, and then I purposefully leave my computer behind. When I walk to the studio, I can get there in five or six minutes. From my place, you pass a really yummy Mexican restaurant with the freshest food. I know the owners, and they're very sweet. I'm only saying it because it's a distraction—you know, like, I want to see what Maria's up to, maybe get a coffee real quick. But I look at the place, and I'm like, *Nope, not today, keep walking.* Then there's all this construction, because my neighborhood has turned into a haven for young Asian professionals or white kids from Ohio who can't afford Williamsburg. And then there's this mosque that on Fridays has all the men spilling out onto the street praying. I feel like these are my people, but I'm wearing shorts, so I scurry along.

I get to my studio. It's a keyless entry with an app on my phone. I walk up to the top floor because I decided I have to have a view to feel safe. My studio's a single-door space, which at first made me sad, but it's fine now. There's a lot of daylight, and I built a platform above me. I used to sleep there, but I don't anymore. It's about 750 square feet of open space. To the left is a janky little woodshop I built in case I need to cut or spray something. Floor-to-ceiling windows, two or three of them, and my big wall is where I usually paint. It's not the perfect setup, but I'm getting more specific about my decisions. You know how sometimes that hoarder mentality is like, *I might need this one day*. I'm starting to let that go because I want a bunch of space for the things that bring me prosperity.

I do have a computer at the studio, but it's almost ten years old. I can't use Safari anymore because it can't update enough, so I jump between search engines. I keep it mainly for safety—if something bad happens, I have internet. Or if I need to send something time-sensitive and can't walk home. The battery doesn't work, but I also use it with my projector when I need to draft something on the wall. I'm really trying to make the studio a place without internet, even though my phone is there. Sometimes I find myself doomscrolling Instagram, but

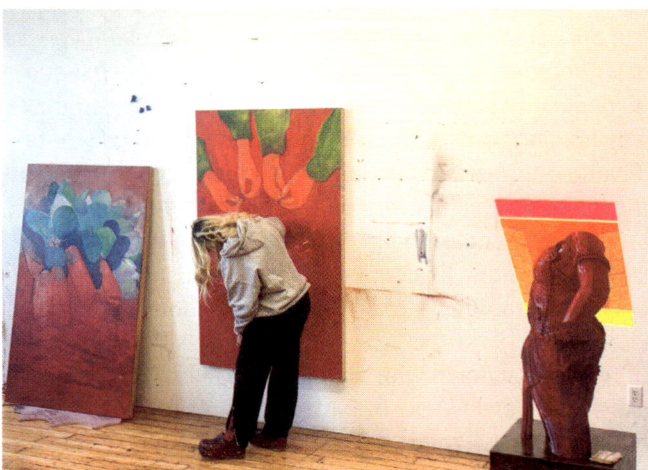

Baseera working in her studio. Image courtesy of the artist.

I'm trying to behave. I want the studio to be outside of technology. Everyone's talking about AI and Gemini, and I'm like, *Great, I'm just going back to the fundamentals—pigment, image, hands.*

I'm in my studio, being quiet, painting, and being really selfish and insular and emotional, because I think painting is a very selfish act. It's all about the self, and it's all about recording your movements and everything that's going on inside, you know? I moved in mid-to-late 2022 on a five-year lease, so I've got about three years left. They might price me out after that, but I've had rent stabilization so far.

BETWEEN THEORY AND PRACTICE

A Separation Between Theory and Practice
I arrived at the color red. I arrived at the idea of *Let me just put content away and just work with the repetitiveness of writing the text from the documents and erasing it and writing it and erasing it.* Eventually, a hand emerged that was holding something, and I just let my mind go where it wanted to. I decided to leave the block between me and the content, which is very unacademic. The pigment of red is the first color that a child experiences after seeing shapes and light, like dark spots and light spots. The first color that emerges is red. I didn't really know that until later.

When I sit down with people or do talks, I'm just like—*I don't even know who made that work.* I can't even remember how I made it. I'm trying to let a lot of things go, because I think what it ended up doing was building a lot of walls around me. It also made me become attracted to people who were argumentative, because I didn't feel comfortable just being at ease and having peace. There was so much bad in the world that I learned about. How could I be at peace? I literally had to stop reading so I could make.

Practice and Something in the Air

When I'm in the studio now, making the cuts or painting, I just feel full. I feel settled. I feel abundant. I have to believe I'm on the right path. There's a lot of magical thinking. I know that's not a theoretical or practical answer, but in hindsight, because I'm 45, I can look back. Since my 20s, I've been moving in this direction of wanting to be a creator. Now, I have the studio. I have the time, my work's in museums, so I can have shows. It's not a perfect life. I don't have the big galleries behind me, but I can see that the intuition that led me here has always been on my side. It never distracted me or wasted my time. It was all worth it because there's just something in the air.

Temporality Between Theory and Practice

When you see a show of mine with titles like *iamuslima* (2017), *I Am an Archive* (2021), *Weight on History* (2022), or *Pocket Diary* (2025), I'm always referencing the indexical self. I'm always referencing the archive, but it's not an official archive; it's an emotional archive. I liked the way of writing in *Prisoner of Love*, where the experience happened, the witnessing happened, the document was there—but then ten or 15 years later is when the work actually happened, because it took that long to digest the information. I think I could do that, and then I arrive somewhere where I can make something from it.

Theory as Practice

I would steal away what I was really reading back then. I was taking notes, writing, and I realized I was making art. That the book with the scribbles and the text was my artwork. I had fulfilled the creativity. In hindsight, I never could figure out how to make a visual from reading something heavily and annotating and thinking and bookmarking. I could never read a text and then derive a visual world from it, because there are people whose jobs are to illustrate text, and that's not my job.

I got so frustrated that I started taking my hands and scanning the book, then printing the photograph from that. If you look at my collages, you'll see I'm holding documents or objects, and I scan myself. I started thinking about how scanning, FaceTuning, 3D printing, and Roomba vacuum cleaners and drones are all surveillance tools. But they're also tools for desire.

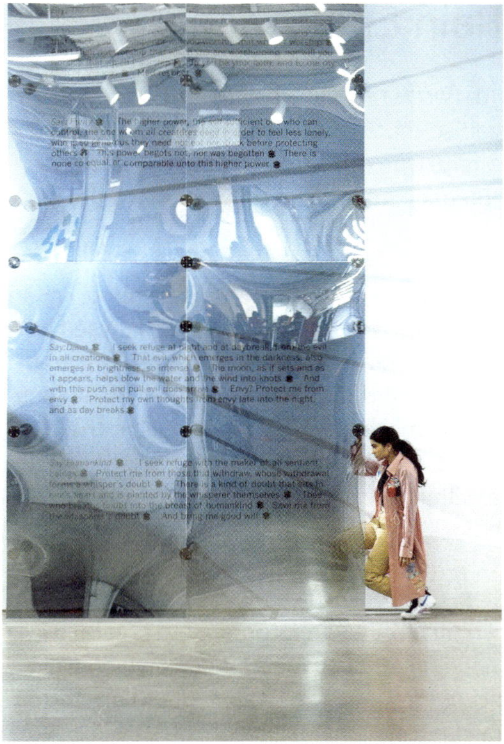

Privacy Control (2019). Installation at BRIC Arts Media, Brooklyn, NY. Photo: Benny Krown. Image courtesy of the artist.

Rain Embuscado[6]

BETWEEN THEORY AND PRACTICE:
"I've internalized so much of those readings. I spend 90% of the time there. One out of ten times, I will separate theory and practice and reflect on what that's doing."

•

I have a ceramic practice, and then I have painting. I'm an installation artist, and what I've learned about myself is that I like treating spaces as my canvas or my work area. I like creating assemblages, and I like making installations that respond to and make full use of the space rather than just existing as a painting. If I create a painting, it has to make sense within the larger ecosystem of the entire installation I'm designing.

For my MFA thesis exhibition, I've been using 11 Labs, GPT Builder, and two other software programs to create my virtual clone, my *Rain Embuscado AI* model, which will be featured as part of the show I've designed and organized. It's not the crown jewel of the exhibition, but it will be there. I'm thinking about sculpting what a personality looks like. In the process of trying to be the architect of this model's personality, I'm also reflecting on who I am, who I have been, and who I aspire to be, not in a singular sense but in a prismatic one. I don't see it as a linear relationship.

This project also incorporates the graphical interface of how news is expected to look—what you might call journalism aesthetics: headline, subhead, byline, image, image credit, article text, another image, or maybe a

6 rainembuscado.space

video embed from Instagram. These are signals for how information is supposed to be represented within a format. I'm playing with that format because I'm interested in format as function. The medium as the message. Not a new idea, but I want to see how it either perpetuates or interrupts people's expectations of reality. That's what I'm trying to do with this piece.

The exhibition as a whole is approached from an Audre Lordian perspective: we cannot trust these tools because they are intrinsically embedded in a system that perpetuates a certain vision of power distribution. I can already anticipate the backlash: "How could you even use Audre Lorde's name next to AI? That's crazy." Fine—everyone to their own. But I approached this project the same way I approach most of my work: from an embodied perspective on epistemic authority.

From a philosophical standpoint, I'm intrigued by Deleuze and Guattari's rhizome—different clusters of networks existing in tandem, never static, constantly shifting and changing like a neural network. One of my professors once told me, "The problem with you, Rain, is that you're slippery—it's hard to pin you down because you're constantly changing your mind." And I think that's the only way I've survived.

THINKING AND READING THEORY

I'm usually alone when I think about theory. I'm not distracted by anyone, so it doesn't matter what I'm doing—it doesn't really impact when that reflection happens. I do it whenever I have the chance to be alone, which is pretty often. So I'm honestly thinking about and reflecting on theory and my practice all the time.

One of the scholars who has had an enormous impact on my practice is both a scholar and an artist. That's what I want to be remembered as, too: a scholar and an artist producing work that responds directly to my own scholarship. The scholar-artist I'm referring to is Johanna Drucker, a professor at the Education and Information School at UCLA. She wrote a book called *Graphesis: Visual Forms of Knowledge Production*. It's a small book, about 200 pages, with an iconic red cover and white text, published by Harvard University Press in 2014. Deceptively small, because each page is dense with exquisite information on the histories of how humans have visualized knowledge, dating back to Babylonian tablets.

It's been exciting to think about how I organize information for myself through her theoretical framework. While I'm not limiting myself from generating new forms of knowledge visualization, it's convenient to be able to draw on models from this book. They're models that I think we can inherit as a species today, if we choose to. I'm also aware of the political and economic paradigms that shaped how these visualizations were forged, so I understand the utility of each model I use.

Rain Embuscado AI pushes this further. I'm curious to see how people reflect on their own reality when interacting with a model that sounds like me, talks like me, and occupies part of my exhibition, critiquing the mass production and circulation of information. I've been thinking about Nicolas Bourriaud's book *Relational Aesthetics*, in which he argues that a generation of 1990s artists took human relationships—and the spaces between people—as their medium. If the medium is the message, relational aesthetics assumes that art lives in the phenomena perceived in the interactions between people.

I wouldn't say I fully agree or disagree. The theory I'm actually testing in my thesis is what I call *reality aesthetics*: the idea that reality is the one thing we all share, even if our versions of it differ. There's already research on consensus realities, which are shared sets of fact-based information that form a collective reality, which may be completely inconsistent with another group's reality. People in Tehran today likely live in a reality vastly different from someone in Columbia, Missouri.

I went to Hunter College, where Audre Lorde taught, and it was almost impossible to take a humanities course without her being on the syllabus. She was larger than life there. Whether I mean to, I subconsciously think about everything from her perspective. I'm always asking how Audre Lorde might view my work, and I critique it as I make it, because she was deeply resistant to epistemic authority. I've internalized her work so much that when I revisit her texts—on eros, the erotic exchange, or systems of power—I read them with an understanding that she was using the formats available to her as a scholar and public intellectual of her time. The product she gave us, decades ago, was forged within those academic expectations. I take her writing for what it is, at face value.

My approach to the relationship with theory is shaped most by my sister, M, who passed away. She was a scientist, artist, poet, and pilot—she was of her own mind.

She never simply internalized what she read; she rejected everything at first, and through that rejection, she could stand alongside anyone in their reality. She never discriminated about who she shared space with. She could walk alongside someone so deeply that she would sometimes lose herself in their perspective.

To this day, I've never met anyone more empathetic. While I'm proud to have internalized Audre Lorde's way of life and thinking, I still struggle to be entirely fixed in that position because of what I learned from my sister: you cannot be fixed in your perspective, because that limits your ability to expand your horizons of consciousness for any living being. I spend 90% of my time in what I've internalized; one out of ten times, I separate theory from practice and reflect on what that's doing.

A big reason I could accept Audre Lorde so fully was because of my sister. She raised me without ever labeling it feminism—it was just the way life was. I remember going to high school and hearing classmates talk about Judith Butler or Jacques Derrida and asking, "Who's that?" They'd say, "Feminist scholars," and I'd think, *Why is this even a thing? Women are superior.* I understand now that's also toxic, but my sister raised me on action figures like Lara Croft and Lady Death, on Jewel and Lauryn Hill, Toni Braxton. You know? Like, I was the girl.

MAKING AND DOING IN PRACTICE

I think it's important to emphasize that I am critiquing myself and the work as I'm making it, which is a difficult place to be. Some of my artist friends, classmates, or professors will say, "Oh yeah, I go into subspace, I totally

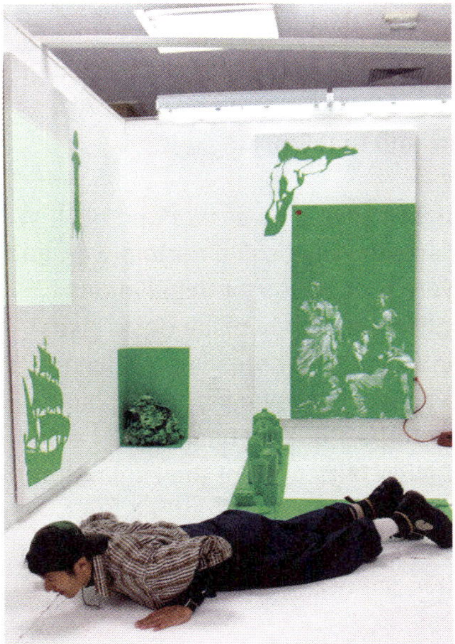

Rain's studio at the University of Missouri's School of Visual Studies. Image above: Bianca Turner and Igor Arume. Images courtesy of the artist.

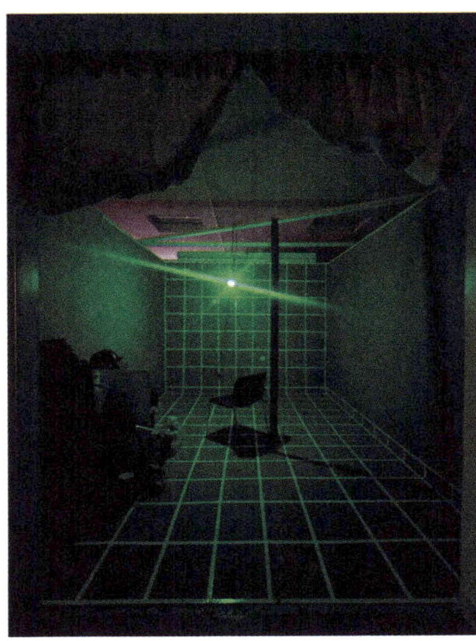

check out, I just enjoy." I wish I could. Even when I'm making, I'm asking, "What is the purpose of this? What is it signaling? Am I perpetuating something?" Still, it's interesting to move through that tension.

I didn't realize it at first, but even if I was working at NEW INC or Artnet, I would arrange my desk a certain way, and those arrangements were prototypes for installations I was thinking about, right there on my office desk. I was prototyping installations I would eventually produce at half scale in my studio space. For reviews, I would stage my installations in that studio. Looking back, I see I was doing this at Artnet, at NEW INC, even at the Huffington Post, even back in college. I put things together, but I didn't have space, I didn't have people who saw me as an artist and would invest in me or my vision.

When it comes to the traditional pillars of art—painting, ceramics, sculpture—the *how* isn't a problem for me. I'm classically trained in painting, I'm improving in ceramics, and I understand the basic chemistry of silicone production, resin, and related materials. The *how* is secondary to the *why* for me.

BETWEEN THEORY AND PRACTICE

Theory Lives in My Heart

When I reach for theory, I reach in myself. Whenever I re-encounter Audre Lorde's work, for example, it's more of a confirmation that, *Oh yeah, I did interpret this symbolic cluster of words at the right time*, or at least in the way I think was right, whether the first or second time many years ago. It's so embedded in the way I think about life that, as I'm making, I can now tell you in retrospect, and in the spirit of earnest transparency, that when I do make, it's built in. I don't necessarily carry the ethos so much as embody it. It lives in my heart.

A Separation Between Theory and Practice

I'm a little more critical of my own preferences and my stubborn refusal to de-internalize Audre Lorde. I understand she's there. I just don't want to give her up. But I also have to understand she doesn't represent me, and I don't represent her. Still, I don't want to let go. It's hard, and that's where I start to see the separation.

The "why" is when I start to separate theory and practice. When I have to think about why I'm doing this, why the work is important, why it's advancing our collective knowledge in the way I think makes sense. Why am I justifying the production of whatever I'm working on from what I perceive to be my own perspective on what matters?

Signals Between Theory and Practice

I've been experimenting with voice recordings recently, but ultimately it's all in my mind and in my heart, too. I try not to create a distinction between the two. Sometimes I do, when I'm under extraordinary stress and pressure, and I'll sever any interconnectivity between them. But for the most part, what happens here, in my mind, directly informs what happens here, in my heart. Usually, the reason it's happening in my mind is because my heart is sending a signal that I need to start doing some work there.

Theory as Omnipresent in Practice
I do this everywhere, all the time—when I'm walking between points on campus, when I'm sitting in my apartment with my sister's ashes and reflecting, when I'm making a sculpture unrelated to my thesis. I think about theory when I'm coding, too. I've been working in Python, and I just got a Raspberry Pi Model B with a motion sensor that I'm programming.

Promises Between Theory and Practice
It's more of a performative gesture. My whole life, I've been performing: *I promise I'm worthy, I promise I'm smart, I promise I'm good enough, I promise I'm capable, I promise I can deliver, I promise I deserve even minimum wage.* Now we're getting really personal, but ultimately that's where it's coming from—I feel like I have to justify my existence that way. The optics of identity are still real for me, from a certain era of my life. I'm still trying to outrun that and accept that I am valuable, that I have value, and that I can come forward with valuable things to say. I'm like, *Am I just supposed to not relate to other theorists in general? Like, I might, but am I not allowed?* You know, that raises a lot of questions for me. Do I need a theorist exactly like me in order to say I can relate? That's when the moves between theory and practice stop, and I start to see the differences between us, but again, it only returns me back. It's a centrifugal effect. It pulls me back into the oscillation.

AK Wane[7]

BETWEEN THEORY AND PRACTICE:
"It's like riding a bus. You're looking out the window and experiencing this passage of time and society. Of course, you can make your own theory. But it does feel like theory exists outside for me."

•

I studied documentary filmmaking. At a certain point, I wanted to question everything because of this notion of truth and the way that I was taught documentary filmmaking. That's how I ended up in the arts, because I realized I could make experimental films and call them documentaries. Someone told me not too long ago, "You're afraid of the camera," and I think that's true. I was like, *Yeah, I am. So what?* All of these social and political readings, all of these theories, are ever-present. I am so aware of the power of the camera to the point where I film something once a year. It's my practice technically, but it takes a lot for me to get to that point. That's why I predominantly film myself: I can have this discussion with the camera as opposed to filming someone else, where I am then exerting power over them.

At the moment, I work mainly with archives. And probably for a few years now, I've been focusing on the myth of objectivity in the archive, which I believe to be a colonial myth, and basically bringing into question what the notion of truth is and questioning the narratives that are in the archive, thinking specifically through a feminist lens, an intersectional feminist lens. The archive that I'm

7 annakwane.com

speaking about specifically is the institutional archive. For example, I went to France to the *Archives nationales d'outre-mer* [National Archive for Overseas Territories], which is this kind of colonial archive where they have everything that shouldn't be there. It's about these things that have been considered worthy of being kept, specifically by institutions, specifically by people in power, by power structures.

I'm also preparing a lecture on social practice in the arts, interested in widening the definition of art practice. I literally taught a course last semester about journaling as an artistic practice—we wrote love letters. If I'm on the bus, I write on my phone, but I like actually writing, feeling it. I have so many journals.

Being from Senegal, growing up there, leaving and then coming back, I feel like an important part of it is that I went back home, and then I was like, *Oh*. All I could see was colonialism.

I went to South Africa for boarding school. That was rough. I always think about how I wasn't even out there like that—but still, you could feel violence. The same thing with the US. I've spent a lot more time in the US. I make this joke that living in the US leads you to believe in conspiracy theories because everything is so messed up, and there's always something going on. There's always some hidden agenda, some lobby group, something that's making it that way. It really woke me up.

Going back to Senegal, suddenly I could see colonialism everywhere. It hit me so hard that I felt so powerless, like we're just being dragged along in the march of history, like we don't have any power, like every decision is being made completely outside of us. That's how I feel a lot of the time when I'm walking in Dakar. Of course, we have the power of making our everyday, but even that is very limited sometimes. I just saw so much violence. It's not just over there where it's obvious, and people are talking loud and being completely unhinged, but it's also here—quiet—and we don't talk about it often.

My mom already has some consciousness that she definitely tried to instill in me when I was growing up, and my grandfather was a politician, a socialist. My grandfather's older brother was one of the people who wrote union regulations in West Africa. This is my context. Every day, the news was about how many bodies were being fished out of the water—young people trying to migrate in very dangerous ways. You can't hear that and then just continue living normally, whatever that is. A lot of the specters are everywhere around us, but you don't have the time to actually reflect on that because you have to survive, you have to keep moving. I don't want to speak in general terms about my home and the way that we interact with history, but I think it's difficult. I've always said we never healed from all of the stuff that happened. I think it's very important to say, *Okay, this is what I read in the history book, this is what has been taught to me, and what if I just refuse that?*

THINKING AND READING THEORY

Theory is taught in a presentation, and you're like, *Well, this isn't the reality for a lot of us.* And also, coming to Finland for me, I was like, I am curious about Finnish exhibition history. I would love to know more about what art looks like in Finland. But instead, it's all aspirational.

Lola Olufemi wrote this book called *Experiments in Imagining Otherwise*. She's coming to Helsinki this week, so I've been reading, trying to understand a bit more about what she's writing about. For example, yesterday I was reading it on the bus, and I had so many moments where I had to close the book and let it marinate. Because I also write a lot. That's part of my practice. I pick up things she's writing and think about them. I think it's a really interesting book because it's about things that are not static, that the otherwise is not this goal that we have but something that is ever-changing and elusive. I'm there on the bus, well, on my phone actually, I don't know why I said to myself, *Close the book*. And then I need a moment of, *Okay, in what ways am I working through this?* I think about my own projects, like the one I'm working on called *Subverse*, which is a kind of discussion platform about what we can do. I don't use the word otherwise, but that's what it is: how do we survive in ways other than the status quo?

I found *Venus in Two Acts* in a text about the work by Tourmaline, an American video artist who made a piece in 2020 that you could watch for a limited time online. A curator had written about the work and quoted *Venus in Two Acts*. The work imagined the life of a trans woman in 1800s New York, something that was already very much speaking to my practice. *Venus in Two Acts* by Saidiya Hartman has completely shaped the way I think. She talks about history and the theory of critical fabulation, but it's also a practice. To present that theory, you have to actually do it. I find the dialogue between theory and practice particularly interesting because she's a historian and is expected to traffic in the truth, but instead she says,

No, I'm going to do my thing, write, and fabulate—which I find beautiful.

MAKING AND DOING IN PRACTICE

People ask me now, *Do you have a studio?* And I'm like, no, I pay rent, so I use my house. Also, because a lot of my work happens here, it's mostly overthinking things.

In the US, when I was studying at Yale, we got a studio quite late in my studies. At that point, I was filming mostly outside and using the editing rooms, so I didn't really use the studio much. It was literally just an empty room. There were two of us in one room; my studio mate was making this huge installation, and I was in the corner. It was all BFA students mixed together—mostly painters, a few sculpture students, and I may have been the only film person because it was a new program.
At Uniarts Helsinki, I was in the Time and Space Arts department for lens-based media and other work. I had two studio mates who worked with photography and analog film. We were all working with media and discussing, while painting, sculpture, and printmaking felt more hands-on. The rest of us were mostly talking to each other in a room, then shutting ourselves in the editing room until further notice.

In the first year, the studios were on the second floor: cubicles we called "stables." Very separated, everyone had their own nook, some with curtains—very compartmentalized. In the second semester, because you're preparing for the thesis show, they moved us to the bigger, nicer studios. Two windows. A corner office. It was like, we have an amazing space, we should share it with others, we can't just keep that for ourselves. It really became a very funny situation that even people from sculpture would come in. It was just everybody, because we also always had snacks. A friend once told me that whenever they see me, they get a sugar craving because I was always baking. I stress bake. So in the lead-up to the show, I was baking every day.

I can show you a few mind maps—there's always something. I have notes, timelines, project notes, and to-do lists. That's my biggest archive.

BETWEEN THEORY AND PRACTICE

Separation of Theory and Practice

The thinking part is really important for me—it's where most of the stuff happens. That was a critique I got a lot during my thesis show: "Stop thinking and make the work." I got that advice a lot. "Okay, we get it, there are a lot of ideas, just do something." Maybe it's a block for me. Or maybe it's just that it takes time, because I enjoy thinking and questioning everything. It's hard to get to something because I'm always asking, *What if this? Why that? Why not this?*

For me, it's like riding a bus: You're in your brain, looking out the window, experiencing the passage of time and scenery—the theory. And you're in your body, a person in the world, interacting with others, not in Finland, maybe [laughs], but you would be interacting with people if you were in another country. There's a lot of input. Of course, you can make your own theory. But it does feel like theory exists outside for me.

Theory and A Changing Practice

Working at Raw Material Company in Dakar shaped my thinking a lot. I went in thinking, *Oh, I'm an artist, this is what I do*—and I left a curator somehow. I learned so much from the people I was around, from conversations I was part of. I could see the in-between: it's not black and white, it's not theory or practice. You can do both, and you can participate in different ways.

Fei Liu[8]

BETWEEN THEORY AND PRACTICE:
"Once I start to name the theory, I start to create this distance from my work. It starts to create this rubric. This rubric and the practical, material things that I'm trying to do don't go naturally together."

•

During COVID-19, I just didn't find any interest or, I'm going to be very blunt, any value in traditionally considered art, and especially in the fields that I was making things in, which is creative technology. I could not spend time on the computer creating a speculative emergency when there was a real emergency happening.

I just stopped really making anything. I did a lot of volunteering, basically moving money and goods from one place to another, and a lot of Instagram-based fundraising for different things. I was kind of surprised. I was like, *Wow, people just give me money if there's a good cause and I ask.* I was shocked by that, and it made me think there are so many ways to do financial redistribution. Obviously, this is all under the condition of the state not providing these things, so we have to ask our peers to do that. Kind of like a GoFundMe. The trap of GoFundMe and medical fundraising is a whole separate thing.

That turned into a lot of trying to alleviate food insecurity in New York City, and in Bushwick in particular. I would cook food at home and walk around asking, "Hey, do you want food?" I got to know my neighbors better that way and met some really interesting people at the hot food kitchen, where I did a lot of shifts. I feel like my

8 trytobegood.com

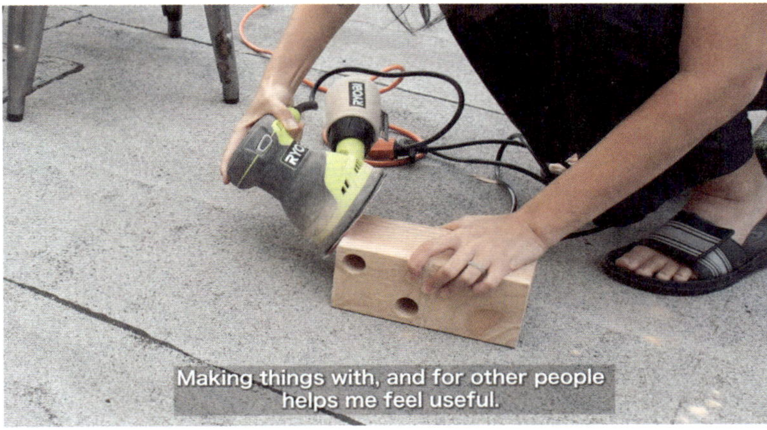

Fei sanding down one of the 28 domino pieces for the project, *Our Good Bones*, on her rooftop. Image courtesy of the artist.

involvement was pretty much: I'm going to show up, I'm going to advertise for you, and I'm going to try to help.

In 2022, I started *Our Good Bones*, a game of dominoes reimagined as a collective effort to create a community bank. That was a lot of woodworking at home for a year, and it was really therapeutic. I deployed the game at the park across the street in Bushwick, and people came and played. It was interesting because we didn't know where anyone was from, so there was dialogue: "Oh, you play like this. Oh, we play it like that."

You have to collect coins to fill up the domino pieces in order to play. I collected a lot of the coins for the dominoes. That came about because I wanted to make something that leveraged trash. We don't really think about coins as having value anymore. The US might stop making pennies soon, and maybe nickels as well.

Thinking back, it's like a rare artistic medium, pennies. I was trying to make value out of something that could be assembled and become more valuable as it was assembled.

I've done this publicly two or three times. Each time it's very ephemeral. It happens, and then it's over. The two times I did it for the general public, I had a game facilitator and a translator. My friend, who mostly does sound art, came and did the one in Maria Hernandez Park. He spoke Spanish and, even before the project began, was obsessed with dominoes as a child, so he got to live out some version of that. The second time, I brought it to the soup kitchen, where there were a lot of asylum seeker families who would spend hours there. One of the founders is Iranian, and the asylum seekers spoke Dari, which is close to Farsi, even though Dari is spoken by people in Afghanistan. The third time was for the canners association in October of 2024. I'm a big fan of the canners in my area, the recycling workers. They honestly have a lot of fans. It's a very collaborative, creative space. Bands come and play for their fundraisers. It's very Bushwick.

One small thing I made was a sculpture using the penny as a starting point. They become little zinc blobs, and I wanted to make a sculpture with them. The idea that the metal is worth more than the penny itself is interesting to me. The penny costs more to produce than its face value. I forget the exact number, but the process is interesting. I wondered if I could sell this art for much more than the worth of what I got it for, which is true of any art practice. If I sold it, the money would go back into some mutual aid sphere that I have.
The actions I do—like cooking at home and giving the food

to people—aren't remarkable in themselves. Anyone can do that. But the fact that I feel a certain way and express those feelings is what makes it art. I've always had this conflict: why is it that mutual aid work can be considered art? It is a lot like charity, because I'm in a different financial position and a different position of privilege than the people I'm helping. There are interesting dynamics there. I really want to give money away in amounts that are not insignificant, and I want more people to do that—especially for people outside their own sphere. Artists will sometimes redistribute their grants to other artists, but what about non-artists who need money? How will you access them, or interface with them? One of my other ethics is that if you get funding, you should try to distribute it as far away from the source—in terms of social connections—as possible. Like the Six Degrees of Kevin Bacon, except it's an ethics degree.

I had another thought about how my identity as a designer and artist influences each other. It's something like performing or simulation. In UX and design thinking, you're supposed to imagine platonic users and empathize with them by coming up with motivations and needs. Some brainstorming exercises call for roleplay or simulation of how the user would behave. The more I think about this, the less I identify as a UX designer. A fellow artist described my latest blood plasma project as a combination of journalism, performance art, and direct mutual aid support. But I wouldn't call it journalism; I think of it as "performing journalism."

THINKING AND READING THEORY

I have a really hard time remembering the specifics of theories—why is this novel, or why is this different? It all lives in this murky cloud for me. I do put the tabbies in books, I watch YouTube, and then I have been actually typing out the quotes that I like into a Google Doc. I'll write stuff in my art-making notebook with little sketches and things.

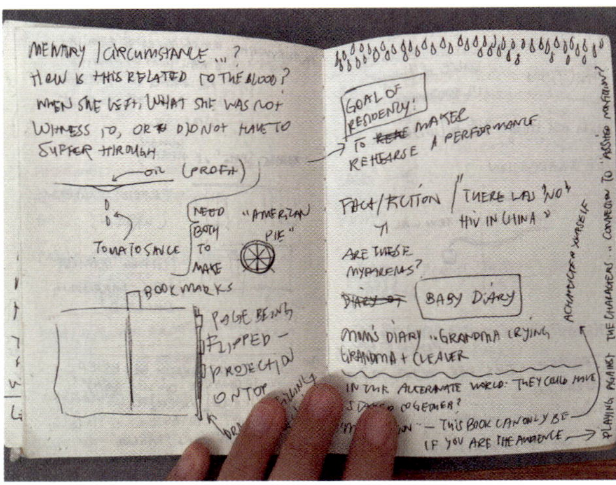

Notes from Fei's notebook pertaining to her project researching the blood plasma industry in the US. Image courtesy of the artist.

What I've been researching is about blood plasma donation. I did get connected to the journalist who published the first book I read on the blood plasma industry, *Blood Money* by Kathleen McLaughlin, who I'll be chatting with soon. The project is about commodification, body politics, and economic ethics. And I think there is some sort of ineffective altruism here. Ineffective altruism. Okay,

I just came up with this term, and I kind of like it. It's something about mutual aid, maybe doing it while illuminating some darker aspect of it.

I have the book *Solidarity: The Past, Present, and Future of a World-Changing Idea*, by two people who have done work on the Jubilee Debt Campaign. They talk a lot about philanthropy and how, in philanthropy, there's this quote from *Solidarity*, "The arbitrariness of philanthropy is adjacent to domination," and how it's opposite to freedom, in a sense, because "freedom requires the absence of domination—where domination is defined as the arbitrary interference in the lives of others." So the things I do are the random interference in other people's lives.

I have this one book I've been slowly making progress on, but I think there is theory here, right? Yeah, *Planetary Mind: Territories of Extraction Under Late Capitalism*. There's stuff about labor theory and geopolitical issues. It's a really well-cited book. Particularly what interests me is the soft colonial powers of China and how much of that is labor- and resources-driven. The penny project was why I bought the book.

There's a university lecture or something on Marxism, but the professor, Dr. Taimur Rahman, breaks it down super well so far. But we're only in chapter one, and there are so many chapters.

Another book I really liked is *Artificial Hells: Participatory Art and the Politics of Spectatorship*. It's by Claire Bishop, and it's super readable. She does a critique or commentary on a lot of community-oriented art. It's an interesting survey of those types of projects through time. What were the political situations? How were different artists or groups responding to other things happening? Where were the pitfalls? And how, when you present work through a more official channel like a biennial, a lot of the essence gets diluted.

MAKING AND DOING IN PRACTICE

When I had the idea for a pregnancy suit that would distribute soup out of the stomach, I was walking around on my phone outside. A lot of these ideas came from walking around my neighborhood or sitting at the park. Or I would watch *The Rehearsal* and *Nathan for You*. Nathan is a comedian, but the way he approaches his projects is, for me, the zenith of what art making is. He's an artist. I'll have an instinct, and when the image is strong in my mind, I can't let it go. It's good to be a little bit weird, you know? And I feel, for the most part, anecdotally, people I do the volunteering stuff with seem so normal, and I feel there is this sense that you have to be pure about volunteering. Purity policing. But it's so human to have perverse thoughts.

In the blood plasma project, I want to donate plasma in order to collect money. I don't really know what I'm going to do with it yet, but a lot of these projects are making it extremely complicated for yourself to squeeze little bits of money from the capital cloud. The artistic, conceptual research part of it is me watching videos about Marxism and value, and researching how the plasma industry is exploitative. It has marketing gimmicks to reward you for coming in often or agreeing to sell your plasma for months. I don't think this should be how it's run. I'm going to try to go donate this weekend, but I'm scared of the needle.

The materials of the project are like the plasma, the red blood cells, and they also inject saline solution. There's a plush reclining chair. I forget the gauge of the needle—maybe 16 gauge. The collection sites are often in areas with more income disparity. One is in Weeksville or Brownsville, that triangle, and another in downtown Brooklyn. There's one in the Bronx, one in Harlem.

I feel weird doing this because this is what people do to pay off a credit card or gas bill. But I'm trying to work with it as a person of privilege. That aside, it's conceptually interesting. You get a debit card to spend the payment, but there may be a fee. That fascinates me, because when there's a fee, everything gets devalued. After I do this, who or what am I giving the money to? How many times will I go? People call it "plassing." On Reddit, there's a big plassing community. A lot of people do it, but I'm still scared. Even though I'm doing it for mutual aid, I don't want to do it. It's becoming more like 70s actionist artwork, which I've never done before. I might try to go on Saturday. I've been pushing it off because I'm into sports, and after I do this, I probably can't work out for a day.

I want to challenge myself to overcome this. Why is my body more precious than those who have to do this more often, usually in predominantly Black neighborhoods? There's a racist historical precedent—much of the plasma industry grew out of using prisoners' blood during wartime. The people selling the plasma made a lot of money compared to the pennies prisoners were paid. It was either you do this kind of labor, or you sell your blood. Selling blood was the easier option. That makes me want to do it more, even though I'm scared.

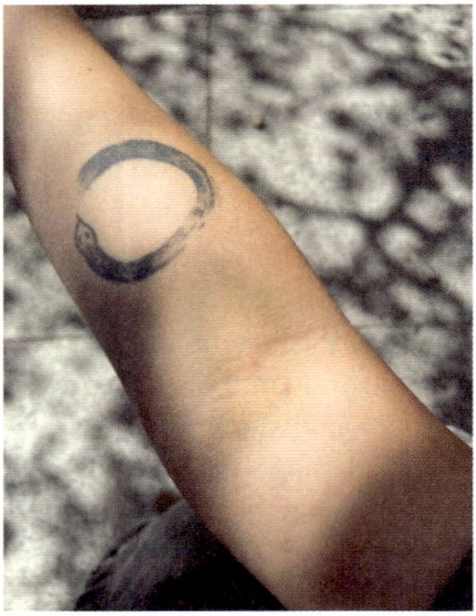

Not long after this interview, Fei donated her plasma. A bruise was left on the inner elbow of Fei's left arm after she received a "bad stick," causing a mild hematoma. Image courtesy of the artist.

BETWEEN THEORY AND PRACTICE

From Practice to Theory

I have the instinct about an idea first, and then I'm like, *Oh, is there theory about this?* One example was that I wanted to make this pregnancy suit that would distribute soup out of the stomach, like a spigot that comes out of the stomach. Then I was reading a bit of Julia Kristeva. A feminist, Freudian thing. She asks, Why do we reject the taste of milk? One of her first memories was the skin that grew on top of milk, which disgusted her. Then she went into why milk turns us off. Something about the mother, the milk, infants, and poop. So that somehow fits well with my stomach soup idea.

Between Official and Unofficial

Once you get into that space of providing services for itinerant peoples, there are official channels that work through institutional frameworks. Those make it so some acts individuals take on their own are not as good as a systematized approach. Walking around and giving out food is on the cusp of legality—you're not supposed to give people food you made at home. You need a license, health and safety inspection, and all that. So I was already on the fringe.

Separation of Theory and Practice

Once I start to name the theory, I start to create this distance from my work. There's the academic research about poverty, let's just say, which I think is not exactly theory, but that kind of thing starts to create this rubric. The practical, material things that I'm trying to do don't go naturally together. I don't want to be assessed according to a theory rubric. I want the freedom to do something weird, like my fiction about someone poisoning others. I think because of cancel culture, I want space to do something off, raw.

Practice Speaking Back to Theory

When I brought the dominoes to the canners association, the executive director, coming from a theater background, gave feedback: "Can you make this more community-oriented?" Before, if you won the game, you got the money. After talking to them, we decided the money should stay within the collective, and players vote on what the collective should do with it. It became less about individual gain and more about decision-making and communication. That was a shift for me.

Linda Dounia[9]

BETWEEN THEORY AND PRACTICE:
"Sometimes you see something, and that becomes a corpus of theory. Sometimes theory has a direct translation that can be made with hands. Sometimes it's indirect and percolates."

•

Everything I do has to do with technocapitalism—the merging of technology and capitalism into a new feudal world order where access to tech determines your geopolitical power. There's a bit of economics in how inequality is exacerbated by this new world order, and a bit of cultural studies in looking at how cultures are impacted by it—how humans and how we interact with each other are essentially shaped by algorithms.

What design did for me is that it cracked open the veil of how technology is built and who builds it, who's in the room, and how it's built. In a design studio, unless you're working on hardware, you rarely have to see or touch hardware, or even worry about it as a user experience designer or in interaction design in general. You don't have to be materially conscious. You don't have to think about human labor in any way. You're the last translation from raw software and meaningless algorithms to something someone could use. It's the glossy, well-paid part of the job.

The pandemic happened, and I couldn't go anywhere while I was in Ghana with my partner. I had saved up all

9 lindarebeiz.com

this money, was between four walls, and thought, *What am I going to do with my life?* I opened my laptop, made random posters for nobody but myself, researched things, watched documentaries, and stumbled on AI. This was before any generative AI tools—pre-ChatGPT, pre-downloading anything.

I'd been experimenting with blockchain. Nobody has to know who you are, so I went in with a pseudonym, sharing my work. Some people were really interested. I found a lot of people from Latin America, especially Afrodescendants from Brazil, building this beautiful internet culture that used their heritage and translated it into interfaces, experiences, and digitally native visuals. I had never seen that in my life. I didn't know what being a child of Senegal who uses only digital language to express themselves could look like. Seeing examples of Afrodescendants from Latin America expressing themselves through digital material was eye-opening.

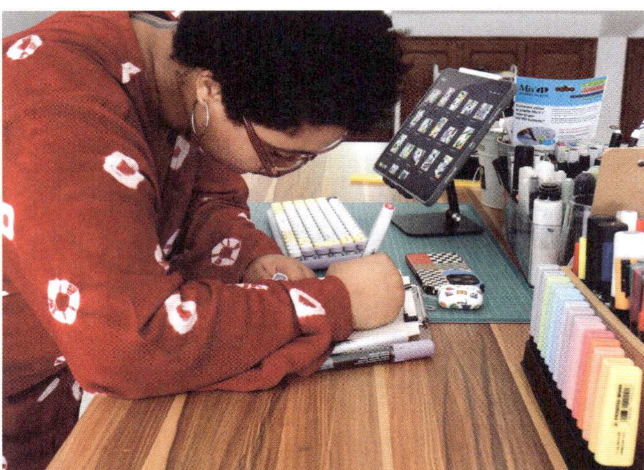

One of my main projects is the physical infrastructure of AI and tech in general. If you ask most people for a mental model of AI or the cloud, it's always abstract—numbers, a floating brain—completely disembodied from the concrete infrastructure and human labor needed to run it. I find that fascinating. Who decided we needed to disembody technology? What's hiding there? Kate Crawford's work, *Atlas of AI,* comes to mind. Mapping the physical infrastructure that makes any given model run. If you map the supply chain of AI today, it starts in the African continent and ends there. You mine raw materials and rare minerals, leaving devastating water damage in their wake. You use cheap human labor for content moderation, data cleaning, and other menial tasks. Then, you publish models that know nothing about Africa or are full of stereotypes. And finally, you dump server parts, computer parts, and cable infrastructure back to the continent, especially West Africa, in the name of recycling. The largest e-waste dumps in the world are there. It's a cycle of plundering and disposing, without even producing a decent model in return.

Of institutions that shaped my work for better or worse, in design, there's Stanford's d.school as a big authority, at least for beginners, and IDEO, with its distilled philosophy from Stanford and Apple. That shaped my work, along with local institutions in Senegal. Cheikh Anta Diop University's language center focuses on local language archives. There's a library with incredible books long out of print. The Archdiocese of Dakar has rich archives. I stay where I am and pull from these places. They only affect my practice if I let them, and I enjoy that independence.

Through my own studying, I've learned from Indigenous interaction not mediated by apps—how we talk to each other, how we relate, how we arrange space for mourning, joy, or celebration, how we place furniture, angle objects. These are teachers, things you grow up with and internalize without realizing how much they shape your worldview. I didn't grow up thinking these cultures were "Indigenous." It feels contemporary to me. Calling them Indigenous makes them sound like they belong in the past. My grandma is Diola, and there's Serer from where I grew up, and Lebou, from my grandpa's work in the fish industry. I speak Wolof, a derivative of the native language. Then there's Lebanese, specifically Maronite, from the mountains, where my grandpa is from.

THINKING AND READING THEORY

We have very sophisticated theories. Take a Serer theory—take a proverb from that, right? What is a proverb? It is something we use in speech, in everyday life. It's a very succinct understanding of something about the human condition. A theory about how humans behave or how they should behave. Sometimes a proverb is a theory, sometimes a judgment, sometimes a divination, sometimes a riddle, and sometimes a joke. Someone who speaks the language is able to determine, *Oh, that is a deep, fundamental theory about my culture that is channeled through a proverb*. It's so tangible. I always start with lived experiences, because I appraise them as the strongest theories.

Life and lived experience, to me, are as important as fiction and imagination, and just as important as an actual researched paper. You know how, when you write a paper, your literature review is stronger if you reference other papers? I've always thought—wait, but isn't that an echo chamber? Shouldn't your lit review include things that are not from the same circle of people who think the same? So my relationship to theory is that it has to come from different disciplines.

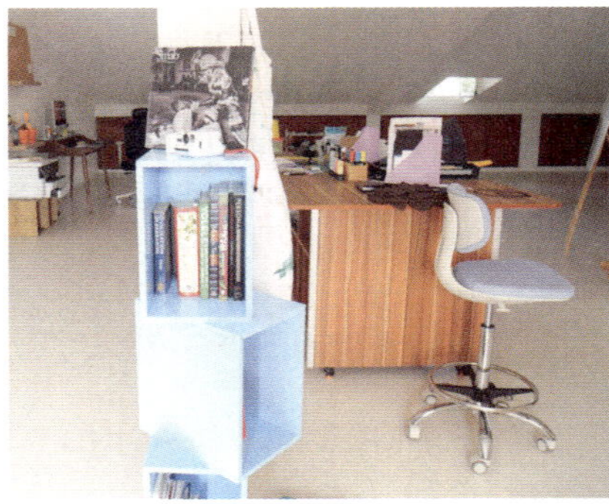

One of Linda's bookshelves in her studio. Image courtesy of the artist.

The state of theory, I think, is a vulnerable state. It has to remain open for scrutiny in order to remain theory. The strongest theories have the most scrutiny, and you can read a lot about different ways of thinking about the same thing or ways it applies to different things. But sometimes you have certain theories formulated to study or explain a phenomenon completely foreign to the person who theorized it. They become inscrutable because the person formulating the theory is doing so from a position of extreme power relative to what they're theorizing. The person, entity, or culture on the receiving end of the theory, which then translates into actions, often isn't in a position to question it. Like, what is a gang? A group with a common interest, willing to tear things up in the process of getting it. Sometimes they actively fight. I think academia sounds like that. I had no confidence with theory then, but I worked in a university that was kind of experimental. We worked with PhDs from different fields, and there was vitriol between departments: "We have to come at it from anthropology, ... No, from sociology, ... No, statistics."

When I approach papers and theories, even as an artist today, sometimes I have to read things completely beyond my comprehension, especially math-heavy things about computer vision. I just have to remind myself that *I'm not an idiot; I just don't get it yet.* I keep moving forward. Maybe in two months I'll come back to it and understand more. That's okay.

Since I was very little, when I asked my grandpa a question, "Grandpa, what's this?"—he would bring me this massive dictionary. Gigantic, with pictures of all kinds of things. He'd say, "Open the dictionary. What's the first letter? Read about it." Every single time. So, from about 4 or 5 years old, I learned that when you have a question or a doubt, open a book. In high school, I had seminal readings. In hindsight, I went to a really crunchy granola Pan-African high school in South Africa. Every semester, we'd be given a stack of papers to read. Not typical high school material. One of them was an excerpt from the book that coined the term *Orientalism*. That experience made me feel like papers were accessible. Then in college, a friend told me, "You don't have to understand every single sentence." I thought, *You're kidding!* That was liberating.

Theories I work with: *Critical Race Theory for Human-Computer Interaction*, a small paper from 2020, and it's more of a kind of survey of other papers. *Speculative Everything: Design, Fiction, and Social Dreaming* by

Anthony Dunne and Fiona Raby. *African Alphabets* by Saki Mudíqua.

Also, what's that book? Something about introverts and extroverts. *The American History of Graphic Arts.* Some things I know I'm gonna disagree with, and I'm just gonna read them anyway, just to disagree even harder: *The 48 Laws of Power* by Robert Greene.

There's this zine that I love, *Disconnection Practices*, and it's literally a practice about a little bit about low tech, how to approach phone addiction, but also just does a very good job at questioning your relationship to devices. *A Brief History of Curating. Philosophie de la Relation* by Édouard Glissant. Anything by Lev Manovich, like *Software Takes Command.*

I don't know if sci-fi counts as academic reading, but I read so much sci-fi. Top two: Ursula K. Le Guin, *The Ones Who Walk Away from Omelas*, which is a short story, and Frank Herbert's *Dune* series—but not just the first two, the entire series, which is six books. I feel like no one should just read the first two books. He was trying to do something, and we owe it to read the whole thing.

On geopolitical power and technocapitalism, from the enemy as well—Marc Andreessen and Ben Horowitz. He's the founder of A16Z, a big investor in tech. He has a text called *The Enemy of the State*, basically defending techno-optimism, which is anything but that. It isn't intuitive, but I think everyone should read it. *Invisible Women: Exposing Data Bias in a World Designed for Men* by Caroline Criado Pérez. I think the window is gender here, but it applies to everything. *Debt: The First 5,000 Years* by David Graeber. *Pedagogy of the Oppressed* by Paulo Freire. *Capital* by Karl Marx. *Goodbye, World! Looking at Art in the Digital Age* by Omar Kholeif.

I didn't mention any poets! I read a lot of poetry. It's because I do it secretly.

I have a folder of theories, with the dates I found them. I also have about 16 notebooks. I use one notebook for things that stick with me when I'm reading, and I have a little classification system—like CCEI03, for example, which stands for computer culture, BCC critical studies, BCCS.

One entry reads: "Software is a cultural practice made up of algorithms, human interaction, and speculative imagination." This comes from critical code studies—Wendy Chun. I think it's from her paper *Software's Ideology*. It's not something Wendy said directly, but something I gathered from reading. I circled it as an area for further investigation.

MAKING AND DOING IN PRACTICE

Most recently, I've been working with GANs: generative adversarial networks. I collage. I write a lot while I make. I've even won an award for my short fiction, a short story I wrote. I use the Notes app for rambles-type stuff. Every time I finish a piece of work, I usually have pages and pages of things I've written about it that I can use to make the description. Most of it is very intimate.

I use quite a bit of Adobe Suite stuff, like Premiere if I want to make animated videos, After Effects when I'm making large-scale artworks, Illustrator, things like that. I've also used quite a bit of generative AI, diffusion models, and video-generating models. I use code, both functional code like Python or JavaScript, and creative code like p5.js. Oh, and I paint. I love to paint with acrylics. My paintings are my secret garden. I don't sell them.

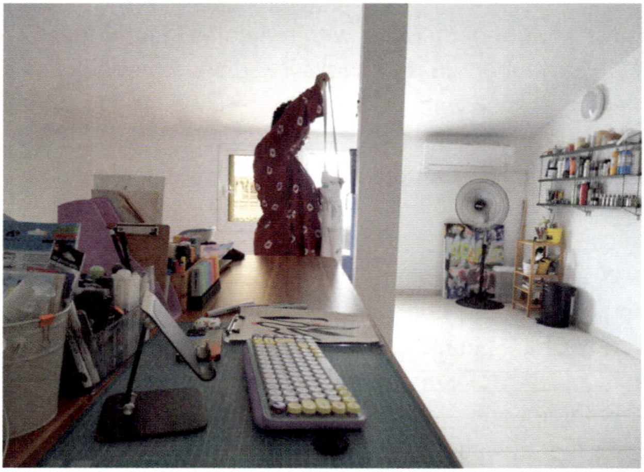

Snapshot from Linda's studio at 10 a.m. Images courtesy of the artist.

My studio is in the same office I share with my dad. He works for a charity that rebuilds hospitals and schools, so his side has the most random assortment of things—fridges, medical equipment, clothes, toys. There's a wall between our two doors. I have periods where I'm in there from morning to evening for the whole week, sometimes multiple weeks in a row. Now, I have to move my entire studio into my house because the building is getting renovated. Knowing I'll have to move makes me less likely to go in. I'm mourning it already. I love having a space to create in. I'm wary about mixing my everyday home life with my making in the same space. I like them separate, which I'm learning now. I do like to invite people over, but when I do, I'm usually not making. The space of creation is a fragile ecosystem for me.

This is my making corner in my house. The living room opens onto an enclosed balcony, and that's where it is. I like it because if I turn around, I can see all my books. There's a door with a patterned glass that sort of closes me in. Great sun too. This place is for soul-searching or just me time, like answering emails. I've never answered an email from my studio; it's too sacred for that. Right now, it's my birthday next week, so I'm in that weird "what am I doing with my life" phase, and I haven't gone to the studio in a minute. I've been writing instead.

I have a couple of friends who are artists. My plight is that not all my friends are in the same place, so a lot of them are remote. I'm collaborating on an installation with a friend. We do a lot of calls, use FigJam to make together, and of course, video. I have a friend here who's also an artist, and we have a monthly breakfast-slash-brunch where we just talk about life, careers, and projects.

There's my team too. I have an agency that represents some of my work. It's a non-exclusive contract—anything related to art I have to sell but don't want to sell myself. I can't code-switch well, and to get into the mindset of how to commercialize art in the art world, no matter how critical I like to be, I don't want to do that. I'm not an insider in those circles. I also can't negotiate to save my life, so I'd rather have someone else do it. They come into the studio virtually.

BETWEEN THEORY AND PRACTICE

A Curious Family Member Between Theory and Practice
My dad comes to my studio all the time. He's over my shoulder, asking, "What are you painting? What is that?"

He says, “Wow, that’s great. Why are you reading papers?” I had printed a bunch of papers for research on how the internet affects us as flesh-and-blood humans. I spread them on the table, stapling them, figuring out the order. “What are you doing?” he asked. “I’m reading papers for my next project.” He said, “Why?! I thought you were an artist.” I told him, “Yeah, but it also involves reading.” He was surprised, like it wasn’t just school that required that. Then he said, “Let me know what you find out.”

Temporality Between Theory and Practice
The things I read crystallize in my brain at different points in time, then are reinforced by experiences I go through, further things I read, conversations I have, talks, whatever, and they come into my work in a non-linear way.

Direct Translation from Theory to Practice
Sometimes you start with theory, write something down exactly as you’ve read it, quotable, immediate. It’s like highlighting a sentence that sparks an image. That image can have a direct translation into something made with your hands.

From Practice to Theory
Sometimes you make something with your hands, intending to do something else, and it reminds you of some theory, right?

Carrying Theory in Practice
Sometimes it’s a more indirect relationship. You read something, and it percolates in the back of your mind. You see something that reminds you of it, then you see more things like it, and it becomes a corpus you can explore

with your hands. I don't set out to make a work that speaks about debt, for instance. I've never made anything about debt. Graeber's book, *Debt*, is hugely influential for me in understanding my condition to begin with. That's a lot of the initial draw of reading it—asking, who am I, and what's my place in the world?

PART TWO

CHAPTER THREE

This chapter illustrates hands-on methods for activating the framework. It outlines the many contexts in which they can be applied.

1
DEFINING MY PARALLEL PRACTICE

As defined in Chapter 2, a *parallel practice* involves the mediums of a creative practice, an explicit political direction, an approach for studying the relationships of what is abstract and what is concrete, and the practitioner themselves. Fig. 4 summarizes the components of my *parallel practice.*

Parallel Practice

doing theory, thinking form

Practitioner	Myriam D. Diatta
Mediums	paper models and writing
Framework	*doing theory, thinking practice*
Politicized Direction	double consciousness

Fig. 4. My *parallel practice* between 2019 and 2021 and its characteristics.

The Practitioner

Between 2019 and 2021, my design practice involved facilitating workshops with a variety of clients. They included public health workers and university librarians to fellow designers and academics. To stay up to date, I also read literature about design and socio-political issues, attended seminars and conferences, conducted interviews, and wrote both independently and collaboratively for academic journals and personal newsletters. The facilitation work I did ranged from teaching a team of colleagues to use reflection in their cross-disciplinary project to collaborating with regional managers to put their organization's new values and strategies into practice in their local programs. Since then, my design practice has changed significantly, but I will contain what I describe in this chapter to this time period for the purposes of modeling a specific *parallel practice* and the methods I used at the time. In this book, when I use the phrase "my parallel practice," I refer to my *parallel practice* in this three-year period.

The Mediums

For my *parallel practice*, I draw on my proficiency in writing and making prototypes using sheets of paper. These basic mediums are adapted for the framework, becoming methods.

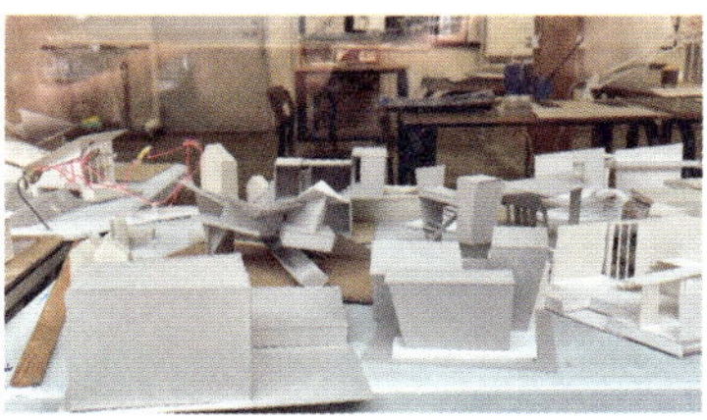

Fig. 5. Image of a typical spatial design student's studio desk, full of paper models.

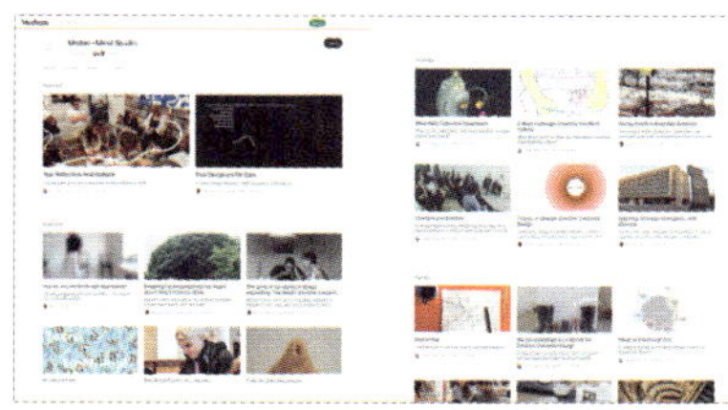

Fig. 6. Snapshot of the company blog of New York City-based design consultancy, Matter-Mind Studio. Co-authored by Myriam D. Diatta, Lillian Tong, and Colleen Doyle.

One medium used in my *parallel practice* is based on paper model-making exercises, shown in Fig. 5. This exercise is commonplace and fundamental in undergraduate industrial design, architecture, and interior design programs. As young students, we are taught to take abstract concepts like "solid and void" or "rhythm," for instance, and materialize them in Bristol paper models. Beyond representation and learning to make things look professional, this teaches early design students about spatial thinking, technical execution, conceptual clarity, iterative thinking, and learning through making.

I take this model-making exercise out of its original aims of training new design students,[1] and instead, reconfigure the making-knowledge we develop from the exercise toward answering, "How can making material forms make visible relationships between theory and practice?"

Another medium I used in my *parallel practice* is based on the writing I do as part of my design practice, shown in Fig. 6. Since 2016, I have been writing about my professional design practice in the form of blog articles. I wrote about the relationships with clients that my colleagues and I developed, the design tools we used to facilitate workshops, the concepts and themes we cared about, and how we started and operated a design studio in New York City. Years later, during my doctoral studies, I was introduced to critical autoethnography and self-reflective ways of writing in which I could manipulate the columns, text, citation styles, and the voices of the author or co-authors.

The Politicized Direction

In this period of my life, I was exploring many critical and theoretical concepts, but the main theory with which I was engaging for the purpose of my *parallel practice* was double consciousness. I wasn't attempting to work on a professional design project about double consciousness or teach the concept in a design classroom. It was first and foremost a personal endeavor to attend to some inner turmoil I was dealing with. I am trained as a practice-led researcher, so naturally, the questions I was asking—my inquiry—were led by practice, by making and being.[2] I did not override practice by

1 First or second year architecture, interior, or industrial design students may first come into contact with this exercise in introductory courses titled "3D Design," "Visualization/ Representation/Concept," or "Space/Materiality." The course titles listed here are names of actual courses from design education programs in the US and Europe.

2 See the Preface for more on practice-led research.

conducting a survey of literature—seminal or niche—about the concept. Depending on the day or season, I checked in with myself and what I needed—affirmations, dissection, validation, or redefinition of the way I move in the world.

From there, I sought literature and other references to meet those needs. I push the notion of "theory" out of its textual, disciplinary, and institutional confines. I use double consciousness as an apparatus, positioned between what is public and oppressive and what is private and interior—a deflective tool to manipulate the boundaries of what is cared for in private and what is exposed to the risk of the public. It became the primary theory on which I concentrated my *parallel practice* because of the institutional context in which I was working at the time.

W. E. B. Du Bois's 1903 conception of Black American double consciousness is a state of being that is derived from living in Blackness. This doubling is due to the particular kind of chronic, heightened self-awareness necessary to survive whiteness. In *The Souls of Black Folk: Essays and Sketches*,[3] Du Bois puts forth,

> It is a peculiar sensation, this double consciousness, this sense of always looking at one's self through the eyes of others, of measuring one's soul by the tape of a world that looks on in amused contempt and pity. One ever feels his twoness,–an American, a Negro; two souls, two thoughts, two unreconciled strivings; two warring ideals in one dark body, whose dogged strength alone keeps it from being torn asunder ... The history of the American Negro is the history of this strife,–this longing to attain self-conscious manhood, to merge his double self into a better and truer self. In this merging he wishes neither of the older selves to be lost. He would not Africanize America, for America has too much to teach the world and Africa. ... Such a double life, with

3 W. E. B. Du Bois, *The Souls of Black Folk: Essays and Sketches*. Project Gutenberg (A. C. McClurg, 1903), 76.

> double thoughts, double duties, and double social classes, must give rise to double words and double ideals, and tempt the mind to pretense or revolt, to hypocrisy or radicalism.

In his statements, Du Bois does not over-explain how double consciousness works or detail how it is done to others who do not live it. This gives the impression he intentionally writes for the Black reader who lives with double consciousness; he simultaneously performs his own doubleness. He makes a tenacious call for doubleness and for using it strategically to navigate whiteness. Alice Walker, with a Black Womanist take, clarifies that consciousness entails double vision, calling attention to the outside gaze and one's own self-awareness. She underscores the "remarkably silent accuracy" with which the Black southern writer, in this case, "is capable of knowing ... the people who make up the larger world that surrounds and suppresses his own."[4] I bring attention to the capability "to know" that Walker notes, which suggests there is a way of knowing the world that comes with double consciousness.

Du Bois' concept is also interpreted and appropriated to celebrate multiple identities, topics, or cultures.[5] However, I stick to understanding that double consciousness is a matter precisely of consciousness. Our self-awareness and plural "eyes"[6] in opposition to whiteness are worthy of study. Kevin Quashie remarks that Du Bois' concept has become "the preeminent trope of black cultural studies."[7] Through a literary inquiry, he calls out that the concept has been shaped by the white gaze, over-determined by how well Black folk are able to challenge anti-Blackness in the white public

4 Alice Walker, *In Search of Our Mothers' Gardens: Womanist Prose*, Harcourt Brace Jovanovich, 1983.

5 Anzaldúa, *Borderlands*.

6 Legacy Russell, *Glitch Feminism*, Verso, 2020.

7 Quashie, *The Sovereign of Quiet*, 4.

eye. However, we can decenter the white and public gaze and use our double consciousness to stay committed to the interior and the personal, shared, and political aspects within it. In a first-person inquiry of living with double consciousness, Robin M. Boylorn builds on Walker's notion of double vision and describes her own doubleness as operating through a "two-way mirror"[8]—partly transparent, partly opaque and reflective. Boylorn looks to her own lived experience and her practice to define double consciousness. When looking at accounts of firsthand experience of living double consciousness, the doubling is not textual academic discourse nor a trope that is overly consumed by public forms of resistance but a form of self-preservation and safety.

The Approach

The specific approach I used in my *parallel practice* was *doing theory, thinking* form. Through form—making pieces of writing with arranged bodies of text on the page[9] and paper models shaped with curves, edges, and shadows—I made visible what went on in past moments in my practice. I studied the interior structure of the writing and models to locate whether, where, and how double consciousness—both as a conceptual theory and a state of being—was present in each past moment. Critical explorations, personal story, anecdote, history, theory, and the ethos of theory are treated as the bases that make form something that is not fixed but continuing, open-ended, and living. I move first from recollections of my past experiences to present materializations and back, again, before, and again. The methods of reflexive writing and reflexive model making involve temporalities and betweenness that are necessary for triangulating personal history, theory, and the

8 Boylorn, *Sweetwater*.

9 Later, I also refer to arranging bodies of text on the page as "formatting" and the made thing that results from it as a "layout" or "composition."

everyday. The made things allowed me to trace the theory in the form. They offered ways of finding theory in the form's composition. It is the lived-in criticality of theory in this process that makes theory matter in practice.

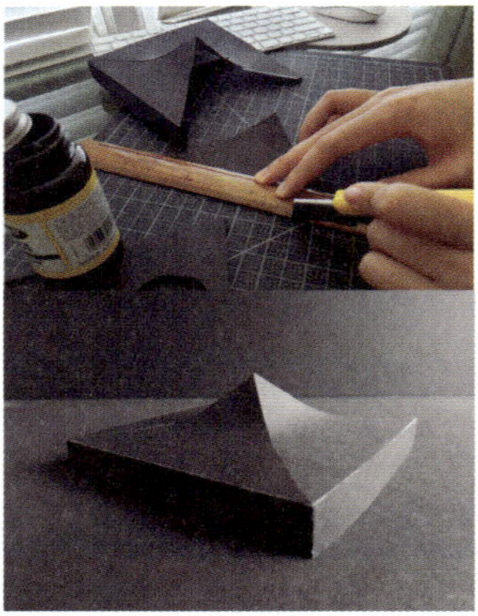

Fig. 7. Images of the reflexive model-making process I used and the material outcome. The top image shows a moment in the making process. The bottom image shows the final model made from black paper.

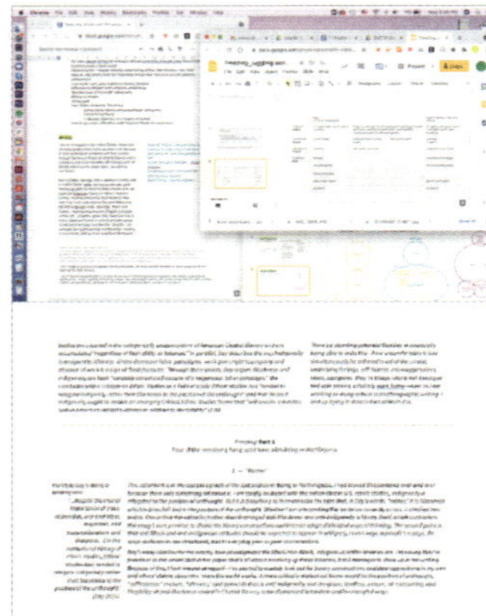

Fig. 8. Images of the reflexive writing process I used and the material outcome. The top image shows a collection of in-progress documents on my computer's desktop. The bottom image shows an excerpt of the final piece of writing and formatting.

Whenever I sat down to make a model like the one in Fig. 7, I began by recalling a challenging experience I wanted to unpack. I studied how my body felt out of alignment at the time. I sat with the sensations. I gave shape to that feeling—the aches and heaviness on my shoulders or the distorting and splitting on my back, for instance. Making visible the splits, masses, or empty spaces in the model itself was how I externalized my double consciousness in each past experience. I did this with an understanding and trust that, because of my positionality in the world, there in that confronting situation lies double consciousness. The models were not replicas of physical rooms or objects, nor were they an interpretation of previously written theory. I did not make any of them with the outside viewer in mind or try to incorporate visual cues or formal references so their meaning could be interpreted by others. Reflexive model making lets me tangibly trace critical theories about double consciousness and the ways I live double consciousness in the everyday.

Whenever I sat down to do reflexive writing, as shown in Fig. 8, I started by writing in the first person about a misalignment that I felt. I attended to a past experience by writing and formatting the text. At times, I restructured the columns, or shifted my writing voice, or altered the relationships between the body of the text and the footnotes. I used the first-person stories I wrote and the formatting of the page to open up space for theory about double consciousness to be folded in. Writing in the first person offered the situatedness necessary to write about my personal relationship with a set of ideas about Blackness. I incorporated references to theory, which is how my own experience with double consciousness and theory about double consciousness are made visible on the page at once. The reflexive writing and formatting was done within one select paragraph in a larger academic paper I was working on, or an essay in its entirety was a piece of reflexive writing and formatting. The process of writing prose and formatting it on the page served to make visible previous experiences. It allowed me to find critical theory between the lines and fold in my understanding of my double consciousness. Theory and accounts of everyday past experiences were brought together through reflexive writing.

2
METHODS FOR MY PARALLEL PRACTICE

A few things come into play when studying my double consciousness and strengthening how I enact it. In this section, I explain the methods in more detail by outlining how they build on notions of reflexivity and knowing through making. Fig. 9 contextualizes these elements within the broader framework.

The skills and knowing I use to format text and shape pieces of paper stem from my education and background in interior, industrial, and transdisciplinary design.[10] What I carry over to this process is less about the physical tools like rubber cement, an Exacto knife, or Adobe Illustrator used in these professional disciplines. What I used to give form to my embodied knowing involves a multitude of tacit sensibilities that I picked up in my design training. The processes of reflexive writing allowed me to negotiate both abstract concepts and everyday experiences related to double consciousness. The methods call for me to attend to a specific past experience and written critical theory at once. I could think with the making and the visual form. I used the methods to think, reflect-in-action,[11] and later to reflect back on what had taken place. I approach making with an iterative, prototyping spirit, assuming my recollection of the past experience with which I am working and my interpretations of theories are not fixed or stable. The design practitioner can be said to have a particular multi-modal way of knowing and, as

10 See Grocott, "Design Research & Reflective Practice" and Latva-Somppi, Mäkelä, and Gündeşlioğlu, "Traces from the Anthropocene."

11 Donald A. Schön, *The Reflective Practitioner: How Professionals Think in Action*. Basic Books, 1983.

design-led researcher Lisa Grocott argues, "iteratively negotiates the understandings that emerge from the practice."[12] As opposed to more involved processes—like manufacturing a product in a technical workshop or processing rare materials in a lab—the malleable, low-stakes nature of working with sheets of paper and text on a screen allowed me to reflect-in-action[13] and make multiple adjustments to the form as I went. Without attempting to finalize or fix anything in place, I revisit a specific bodily sensation or an impression of a particular past experience. I then illustrate it through prose and formatting or through pieces of paper. I give material form to the impression of heaviness with which I am left or the inundation I sense.

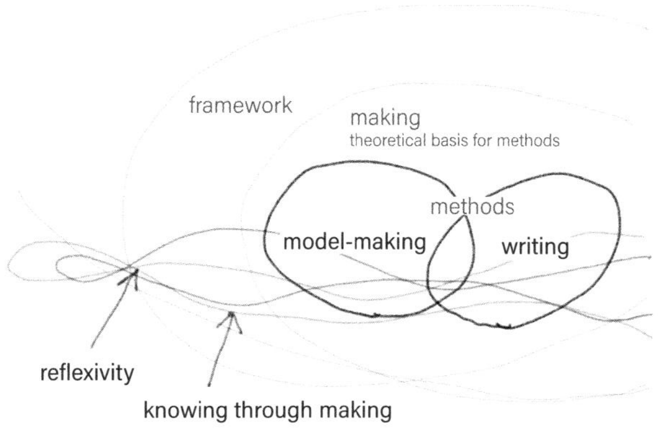

Fig. 9. The methods are shown in the context of the wider theoretical frame introduced in this book. The winding thin gray lines suggest the influences that contribute to the process of using the methods.

12 Grocott, "Design Research & Reflective Practice," 51.

13 Schön, *The Reflective Practitioner.*

Knowing Through Making

Once I made a piece of writing or made a paper model, I accessed the material record[14] of the made thing in different ways. With reflexive model making, I studied the abstract forms I was creating and interpreted the shapes in the model in front of me. The space, mass, shadows, edges, and gestures of the model suggested different understandings of the initial past experience from which I had materialized the model. The shapes I recut or the creases I pressed presented different understandings and framings. With reflexive writing, it was not only the visual composition of the text that indicated different framings as I worked on them. In the middle of putting a piece of reflexive writing together, I went back and read the ideas, references, and shared meanings of words in the writing I had externalized. The content and elements of the format told me about the situation I was writing about, and I made adjustments as I continued writing.

In the process of making, the models and pieces of writing "suggested," "indicated," "presented," and "told me" things. The act of reflecting and negotiating in-the-making becomes new framings and reframings of the situation. Grocott describes this kind of conversation as "not just reflecting upon material, technical and physical decisions but also a broad range of social, environmental, cultural and conceptual concerns."[15]

Reflexivity

I intensified my double consciousness while I was materializing and exploring the material record of what I made. I deepened my understanding of what my lived-in knowing entails—the many forms it takes, when I need it, how I tend to it, and how I value doing it. The methods call for me to deepen my awareness of myself through my

14 See Chapter 2, Doing Theory, Thinking Form, On Making and Unmaking

15 Grocott, "Design Research & Reflective Practice," 18.

lived experience and written theories. This is done from an intersubjective position. My firsthand accounts are in conversation with situations and places where social life happens, not only contained in my own self. The methods are inspired by critical autoethnographic practice, though the methods are not aimed at studying culture or used for ethnographic ends. Autoethnography centers the self as a site of inquiry,[16] setting out to "analyse (graphy) personal experience (auto) in order to understand cultural experience (ethno)."[17] Autoethnographic inquiry may begin from the self, but the process, purpose, storying, and analysis in autoethnographic practice are intersubjective.[18] It is concerned with "self-and/with-other" or "self-in-relation-to-others,"[19] a matter of ethics that subverts the fragilely invented crutches of "objectivity, control, and predictability."[20]

As subjective, vulnerable, and strongly reflexive as we can be,[21] without a commitment to the contexts in which it rests, reflexive research reinforces and holds up dominating ideologies. Where reflection leads to an insight into a past or ongoing experience,

16 Sherry Marx, Julie L. Pennington, and Heewon Chang, "Critical Autoethnography in Pursuit of Educational Equity: Introduction to the IJME Special Issue," *International Journal of Multicultural Education* 19, no. 1 (2017): 1. https://doi.org/10.18251/ijme.v19i1.1393.

17 Carolyn Ellis, Tony E. Adams, and Arthur P. Bochner, "Autoethnography: An Overview," *Historical Social Research* 36, no. 4 (2011): 273-90.

18 Robert C. Prus, *Symbolic Interaction and Ethnographic Research: Intersubjectivity and the Study of Human Lived Experience*, State University of New York Press, 1996.

19 K. C. Hernandez and Faith W. Ngunjiri, "Relationships and Communities in Autoethnography," In *Handbook of Autoethnography*, ed. Stacy Holman Jones, Tony E. Adams, and Carolyn Ellis (Left Coast Press, 2013), 264.

20 Stacy Holman Jones, Tony E. Adams, and Carolyn Ellis, eds., *Handbook of Autoethnography* (Left Coast Press, 2013), 35.

21 Leon Anderson and Bonnie Glass-Coffin, "Learn by Going," In *Handbook of Autoethnography*, ed. Stacy Holman Jones, Tony E. Adams, and Carolyn Ellis (Left Coast Press, 2013), 73.

reflexivity mirrors back and asks us to question our own ethics and values.[22] No matter how well a practitioner or researcher recalls details of an experience or how sensitively they express their relationships with others, reflexivity alone is not built to confront the practitioner with critical perspectives on social life. By looking through a universalized perspective on the subjective researcher, matters of reflexivity can be critiqued as doing "nothing more than mirror mirroring."[23] More candidly, as Jared Sexton argues, it keeps the researcher in a self-serving echo chamber of their own experience.[24] Another liberal danger of adopting reflexivity is that it assumes the practitioner's agency to pull themselves up by their bootstraps and shape the norms around them.

If more common approaches to reflexivity are described as mirroring, I change the metaphor and use the kind of reflexive device that Du Bois, Alice Walker, Kevin Quashie, and Robin M. Boylorn articulate. The notions of double vision, two-way mirroring, and seeing yourself twice that I detailed above offer a framing relevant to the methods here. If, traditionally, reflexivity is used to see oneself situated in culture, I use reflexivity for the more specific task of seeing myself situated in the white gaze. My take on reflexivity has drawn from Black scholarship that understands mirroring as an instrumental part of matters that are "self-and-other." Because the methods in this approach are embedded in theoretical grounds dedicated to lived-in knowing, like twirling, loitering, and grinning,

22 Nancy N. Chen, "'Speaking Nearby': A Conversation with Trinh T. Minh-Ha," *Visual Anthropology Review* 8, no. 1 (1992): 82-91. https://doi.org/10.1525/var.1992.8.1.82; Jones, Adams, and Ellis, *Handbook of Autoethnography*, 30; Anderson and Glass-Coffin, "Learning by Going," 73.

23 Barad, *Posthumanist Performativity*.

24 Minelle Mahtani, Ann Morning, and Jared Sexton, "What's Radical About 'Mixed Race?'" APAInstitute, May 18, 2015, https://www.youtube.com/watch?v=jSMQpRzcGpA=.

they do not ask me to transcend qualities of Black subjectivity[25] but to better know my own doubleness. Critical reflexivity reflects back to me the socio-political realities surrounding my professional practice. It is what enables me to recognize what is between theory and practice.

The Making Process

My day-to-day work on reflexive writing and reflexive model making was not a step-by-step procedure but was a flexible process. However, each method had a starting point, and both began the same way: I first recalled a specific experience I had in my practice. When I sat down to make, it was because I was confronted with external expectations to reject my double consciousness or because I did something that felt out of alignment with it in ways that left me wanting to attend to it more carefully. Taking time to write or setting aside part of my day to make a model offered me a slow pace and criticality to care for how I am (not) aligned with my politicized commitments in everyday life.

While there is an impetus to the process, the process of making is not linear. For example, I may sit down to use the methods immediately after an unsettling situation arises, or I may use the methods days later while referring back to personal notes. A memory may suddenly well up one evening, leading me to revisit the event from years earlier. Sometimes in the process of making a model, I dug up a book or article to find a line in a theoretical text, a video essay on YouTube, or a poem that would keep me company as I explored the misalignment. At times, while revisiting a piece of reflexive writing I had made a few weeks back, I took to making a new model, riffing off the writing to further understand my double consciousness.

I put written theory and creative practice in conversation. The limitations of strictly text- and discourse-based modes of theorizing

25 Hartman, *Scenes of Subjection*.

and their privileged status in creative academic fields traditionally marginalize the actual knowing through making of creative practitioners.[26] As a creative practitioner exploring lived-in ways of knowing, my practice is based in my firsthand experiences and relationships with a diversity of contexts. Adopting a practice-led approach encourages me to prioritize material knowing and self-reflexivity while also developing an approach that is in constant conversation with theory.

The qualities and affordances of the two methods I developed for this framework are summarized in Fig. 10.

26 Grocott, "Design Research & Reflective Practice"; Mäkelä, "Knowing Through Making."

doing theory, thinking form

	REFLEXIVE WRITING	REFLEXIVE MODEL MAKING
Creative medium	Works with written language and written theory.	Works with conceptual thinking and material inquiry, forgoing written and spoken language.
Materializing	Past experiences are embodied through writing. Theories are engaged through citations and quotes. Both past experiences and theories mutually influence each other in one piece of writing.	Both past experiences and theories are remembered in the mind's eye or in the body and expressed at once in three-dimensional form.
Locating theory in the material record	Located through the content of the writing and by studying the formatting of one's own piece of writing. Located through bodily sensations.	Located by studying the finished model; identifying the physical features of the made model and thinking through metaphor. Located through bodily sensations.
Strength of reflexivity	With the possibility of composing, reading, moving around, layering, and laying out written accounts of past experiences and textual theory, they are both more readily accessible to engage with.	As the final artifact is not easily legible to others, the process and its output feel private, offering opportunities to attend to delicate issues and with less at stake in "going there."

Fig. 10. Outline of the qualities of each method.

REFLEXIVE MODEL MAKING

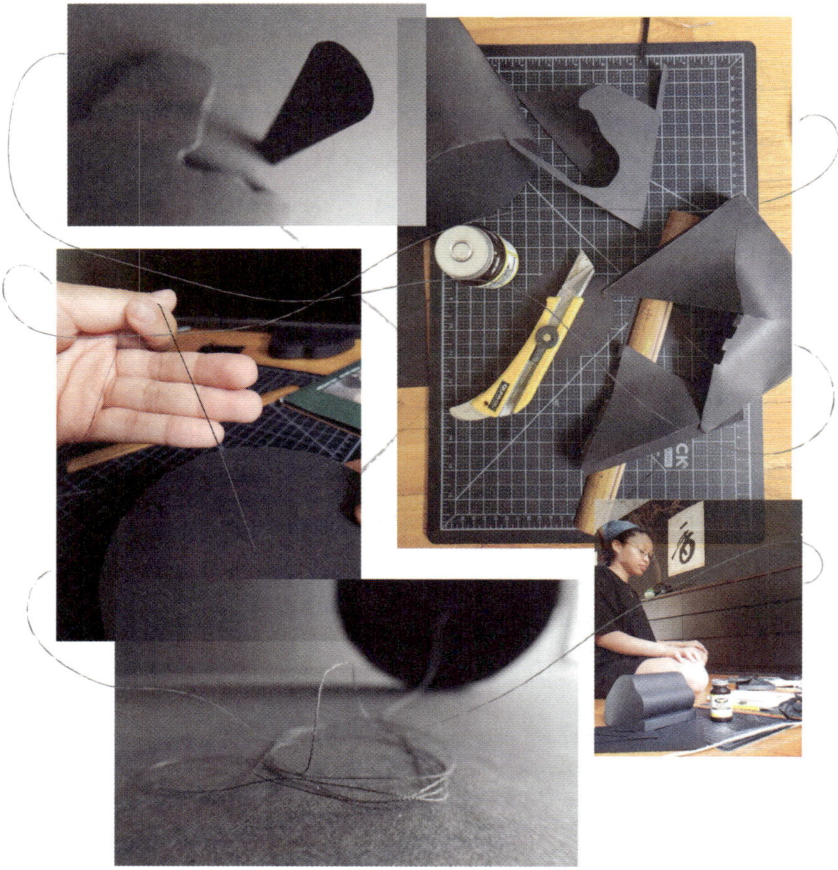

A cluster of snapshots from making and documenting the models. Includes photographs pertaining to four of the models and the processes involved. The gray lines suggest the reflexivity and knowing through making that contribute to reflexive model making.

REFLEXIVE WRITING

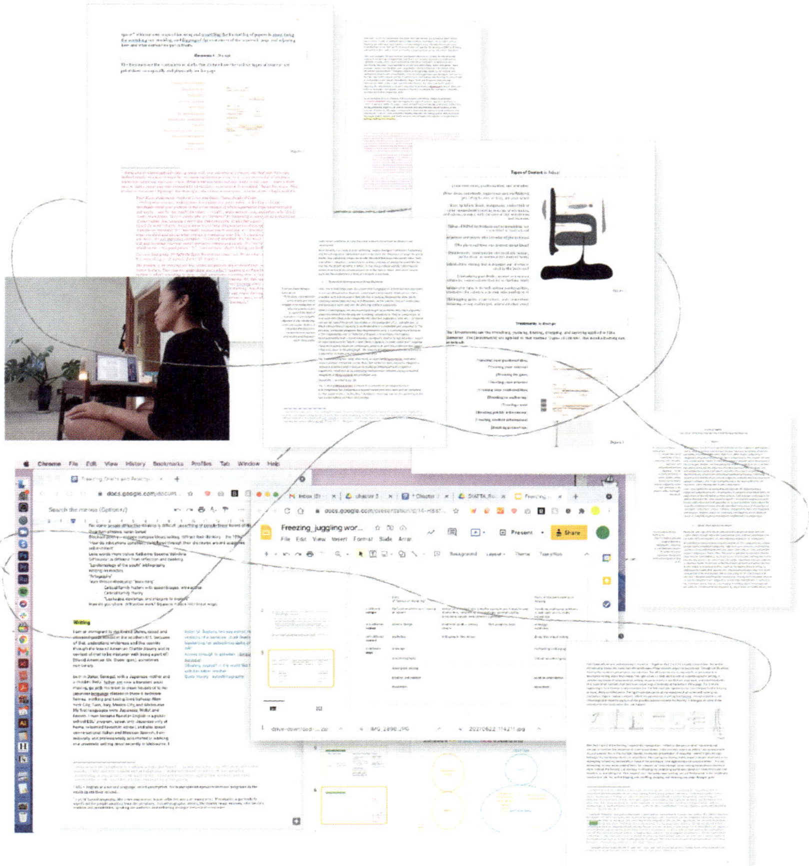

Images and screenshots taken from a mixture of reflexive writing pieces and their process. Includes images pertaining to two pieces of writing. The gray lines suggest the reflexivity and knowing through making that contribute to reflexive writing.

Given that reflexivity serves to mirror back lived-in knowing in order to study it, the methods create both privacy for and access to one's own inner experience. In the table above, I do not aim to compare the two methods against one another. Reflexive model making and reflexive writing are both explorations of form. Together, they offer a multitude of ways of *doing theory, thinking* form.

3
AREAS OF MY PRACTICE

In professional practice, one's interiorities are not quite part of the usual concerns. Bringing private matters into the formal work at hand may be emotionally and practically destabilizing. Furthermore, involving personal, inner investigations of oneself into the realm of professional contexts risks exposing what is personal and private and having it consumed by others. These complexities are present in *doing theory, thinking practice*. This process allows room for the stance that a political practitioner's embodied knowing is relevant to and inseparable from professional practice—while also encouraging us to be illegible and opaque when necessary. The kinds of situations that require being accountable to oneself are much more permeable and ever-present than the formal boundaries created around one's own professional practice.

Accordingly, the areas of my professional practice include

1. how I listen to my physical body,
2. how I facilitate in structured settings,
3. how I engage with others' ideas, and
4. how I engage across my communities.

These four widened areas of practice can cover as intimate a scale as one's own body to a larger scale of community. The areas involve places, bodies, and ideas. And they engage with professional, structured, informal, and casual contexts. This is what a "practice" entails in this framework. See Fig. 12 for details. In line with the authorized and unauthorized knowing I noted in Part 1, the framework does not aim to formalize the contexts to more closely resemble traditional or commercial professional practice. It presents the everyday, personal, professional, and formal settings as contexts for inquiry.

Each summary in this section serves as background information, originally written between 2020 and 2021. This section is not where I show how I used the methods of reflexive writing and reflexive model making. The purpose here is to set up context for the following chapter, Chapter 4, which is the heart of what I am modeling with my *parallel practice*.

Fig. 11 presents an outline of how the contexts will be covered in this chapter. The descriptions will have the following structure:

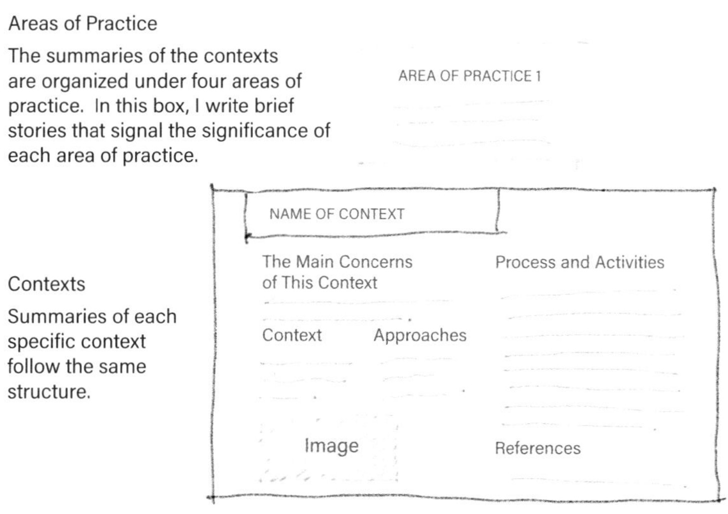

Fig. 11. Outline of each context description.

AREAS OF PRACTICE	CONTEXTS	PERIOD
How I listen to my physical body	My body	Jun. 2019 - Jan. 2021
How I facilitate in structured settings	Interviews in living rooms, bedrooms, and a prayer room	Mar. 2019 - Mar. 2020
	Workshop with designers	Aug. 2020
How I engage with others' ideas	Reading literature and writing about my worldviews	Mar. 2020 - Jul. 2020
	Reading literature and writing about the politics of writing	Jan. 2020 - Mar. 2020
How I engage across my communities	My father's home village in Senegal	Jun. 2019, Aug. 2019, Mar. 2020
	Collaborative space to write an academic paper	May 2019 - Apr. 2021

DURATION	PLACE(S)	PARTICI-PANTS	**METHODS**
Intermittent, 13 months	Helsinki, Mexico City, Atlanta	1	**REFLEXIVE WRITING** **REFLEXIVE MODEL MAKING**
Intermittent, 11 months	Atlanta, Brooklyn, New York City	4	**REFLEXIVE WRITING**
One time, 1 day	Online	9	**REFLEXIVE MODEL MAKING**
Continuous, 5 months	Online	1	**REFLEXIVE WRITING**
Continuous, 3 months	Online	1	**REFLEXIVE WRITING** **REFLEXIVE MODEL MAKING**
Intermittent, 3 months	Dakar, Thionck Essyl, Online	1	**REFLEXIVE WRITING**
Intermittent, 2 years	Melbourne, Online	1 (+2)	**REFLEXIVE WRITING**

Fig. 12. A summarized overview of the everyday contexts of my design practice. This figure should be used as a reference to navigate this chapter and the many contexts and methods detailed herein.

AREA OF PRACTICE 1

HOW I LISTEN TO MY PHYSICAL BODY

We were in a spacious, light-filled room in a former monastery along the Hudson River in New York. There were 25 of us, and we were asked by a facilitator to find a partner for a listening exercise about the first time we "felt seen." I had noticed the stress building in me due to what the facilitator was asking of us. I sat down with a friend, looked around at all the other pairings of people, focused on feeling my feet on the ground, scooched up nervously to sit knee-to-knee with my friend, and straightened out my back. My friend seemed to be doing the same kind of fidgeting and grounding, and breathing. He spoke about the first time he "felt seen," and I listened. I then did the same, and he listened. That experience, in 2017, left a deep impression on me about how big a feat it was to go there in front of others, even a friend, and in a room full of people. I had managed to listen to my body closely enough to know I desperately needed to make adjustments and scooch and fidget before I could have the capacity to hold space for my friend. I had listened closely enough to know how much we needed it.

SITTING WITH THE SHAPES MY BODY MAKES

The Main Concerns of this Context

This context became concerned with proper, respectable movement and refusing it. It was an exercise in bringing awareness to the tacit and constantly active changes in my body. It resulted in experiments where I physically leaned into everyday physical pain in white-dominated spaces or the sensation of wanting to scream or get up and leave the room when restricted from doing so with ease.

Context

Every day for two weeks in June of 2019, I spent an hour sitting with my eyes closed in my living space at the time and in a public silent space. Because I had access to personal time in this period of my life, I was intentional about using my personal alone time for experimenting with meditative sitting.

Six months later, when I had a similar pace of life and available personal time, I revisited the experiment. It was during that winter that I built on and mixed mediums for attending to my body and the surrounding social implications.

Approach(es)

Neither of the experiments is over-orchestrated or used instrumentally in pursuit of a specific outcome or to demonstrate a particular method. It was a personal exploration of attending to my physical body.

As I sat in the summer of 2019, I used the body scanning and awareness techniques I learned as a former student of Vipassanā meditation.*

In the later winter experiment, I built on the approach I exercised that past summer by turning to doing an hour of stream-of-consciousness writing, inspired by the dream-like writing structure in Lynda Barry's graphic novel, *What It Is.*

Process and Activities

For most of the two weeks in June, I stuck with the traditional awareness techniques I had come to learn. During three of those days, I experimented with my meditative sitting. I deviated from traditional techniques and adapted them so that I could express the sensations in my body. Traditionally, the technique I learned has the sitter sitting still and focusing on the present. In this personal experiment, I stayed with the present but allowed my body to respond to the intense pulsing in my shoulders or to the peculiar sensation that my torso, neck, and head were elsewhere. Responding to these sensations meant physically leaning into them or moving my body with the sensation, rather than resisting them in stillness. I made this adaptation to how I sit because it was a way to show myself the inner responses I have in any given moment that I often numb or tend to pummel through. By doing this exercise, I opened myself up to listening to my physical body and what it was communicating about interpersonal conflicts and tensions in the moment. Neither of the experiments in June or December were about clearly or emotively communicating my inner experience to outside viewers or readers. The work of the experiments was in the act of meditative sitting and of giving words to experience. Later, these two experiments came to be a great influence on my development of the methods.

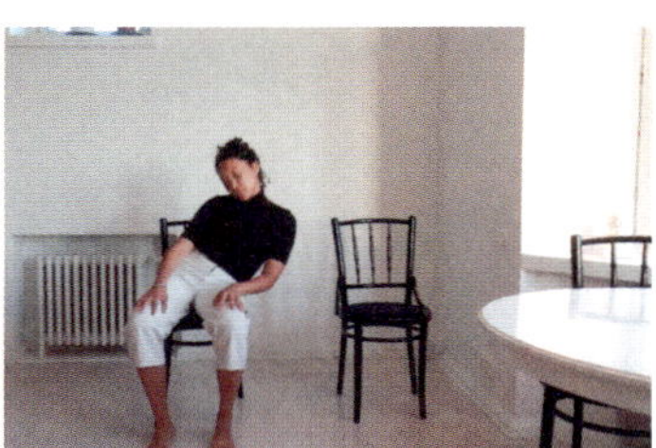

* As taught by S.N. Goenka in the form of ten-day and more extended silent, residential meditation courses.

Image: A video still from the awareness experiment in June 2019.

AREA OF PRACTICE 2

HOW I FACILITATE IN STRUCTURED SETTINGS

I facilitated one of my first design workshops as a 22-year-old. It is hard to remember the content or aims of the workshop, but what I do remember is standing on a chair above the group of 20 or so participants to give instructions. I hopped up and down from that higher position of standing on the chair throughout the workshop. From that position, I explained an exercise or two and gave time cues. Looking back, being higher up and above the participants may have partially been an implicit tactic I used to deal with the tested history my co-facilitator and I both had with the white participants. It may have also been what I thought facilitation was, and I may have had a skewed understanding of leadership, credibility, and authority.

IN-HOME INTERVIEWS: OUR EVERYDAY FORMS

The Main Concerns of this Context

The concerns in this context were about my complex role as a facilitator–interviewer–friend–cameraperson–guest–host. It was about my ethics of bringing the intimate, vulnerable stories shared during the interviews and exposing them to academic, formal analysis. The concerns of the context had to do with participants' private spaces and how the subjective experiences between us interrelate.

Context

In March 2019, a year after beginning my PhD, I conducted the first two in-person, in-home interviews. Before beginning this PhD process, I conceived of the in-home interviews and began planning them as part of the PhD. I was looking for a way to talk about and document the material things and private spaces that Black, Indigenous, and folk of color use to cope specifically with everyday racist, homophobic, xenophobic, transphobic, elitist, carceral, and ableist incidents. A series of semi-structured interviews about the coping tools became a publication on an open online platform and a project entitled *Our Everyday Forms.* I described these specific coping tools as *objects of resistance.*

Approach(es)

Our Everyday Forms is a mixture of interviewing, facilitating brief grounding exercises, casual conversation, and video filming.

Process and Activities

When I enter a participant's home, we start casually, sometimes with tea. We spend two to four hours discussing why they want to share their tools for resisting harm. I check again, in person, if they're comfortable being recorded. With consent, they choose an area to start, and I ask them to silently walk through their space to note objects or spots used as tools for resistance. We then walk through together, and they pick one object or spot to discuss in-depth, answering questions like where they got it, how they use it, and what prompts its use. . I ask questions such as, "Where did you acquire this object? Where did you learn to use it this way? What incident or part of your life prompts you to use this as a tool for resistance?" We repeat this for two or three more tools. The interview ends with a silent walk-through of their space to acknowledge themselves, their belongings, and their relationships to them.

After leaving, I note immediate reflections on the session, including tensions, deviations, or personal reactions. Later, I watch and transcribe parts of the interviews, incorporating notes into an academic paper about my role. These transcriptions and notes became a draft essay exploring the complexities of my roles, my relationship with participants, and the ethics of the project.

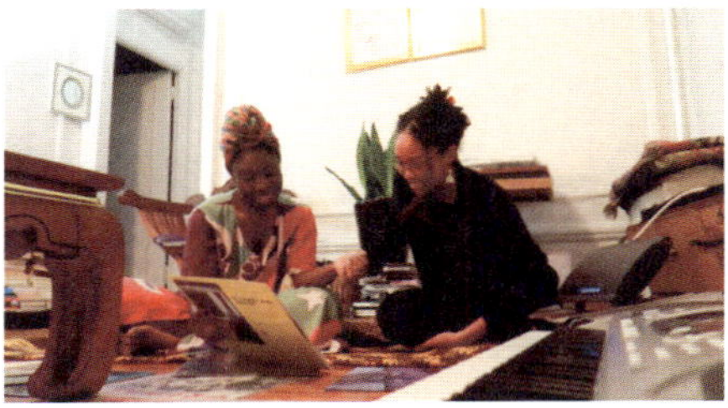

Image: A participant and I discussing a record they used as an *object of resistance.*

FACILITATING A SESSION WITH DESIGNERS

The Main Concerns of this Context

This context—online at an international design conference—was concerned with creating situations in which the aims I create are not aligned with my values. Despite how prepared or observant a facilitator I may be, this context was concerned with putting myself in situations where the professional culture is in the way of my and others' relating with one another in ways I care to.

Context

For an hour, I facilitated an online workshop with (mostly) strangers. My proposal for an in-person, four-hour workshop was accepted by an established design research conference, but because of the COVID-19 pandemic, the workshops during the conference were required to be cut to one hour and held online. In the online workshop in August 2020, I aimed to discuss "Design research that is by, for, and with Black, Indigenous, and folk of color" and be a "way to talk about what we're working to resist and undo as Designers."

Approach(es)

Workshop facilitation involved giving a presentation of concepts and a matrix framework. For the second half of the workshop, participants engaged in individual work and shared their explorations as a group.

Process and Activities

For the first 15 minutes of the workshop, I gave a presentation that centered on how—in the formal design fields of which I was a part (consisting of conferences, community projects, and papers)—the complexity of a designer's positionalities in relation to participants and colleagues is "neutralized," tucked away, collapsed, and conflated. I presented a visual framework, a matrix, that, if used, brought together the analysis of the systems and ideologies in which we live with our politicized positionalities among participants and collaborators. In the presentation, I gave everyday examples of how these two concepts intersect and how the matrix may facilitate those kinds of reflections. The remaining half of the workshop was for participants to pick a past situation in which they had been a part and use the matrix to reflect on their own positionalities and the structures they were navigating. In the last few minutes of the workshop, they reflected on the difficulties and how it felt to do the exercise.

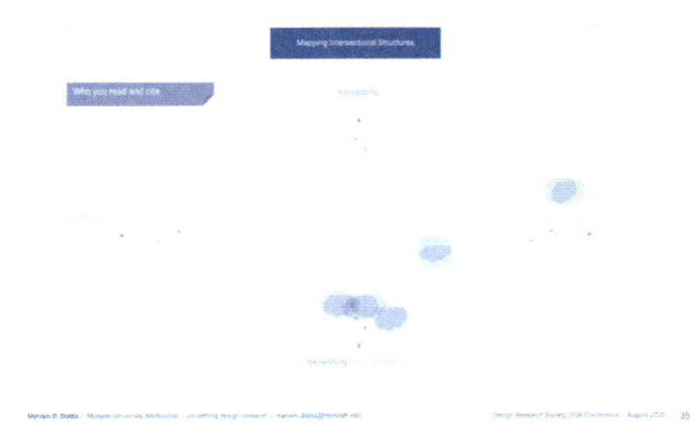

Image: One of the frameworks presented in the workshop. A matrix to consider one's positionality in social design projects.

AREA OF PRACTICE 3

HOW I ENGAGE WITH OTHERS' IDEAS

I have two novellas in my hands as I walk up to the checkout register. I am at an independent bookstore on Prince Street, down the street from where I worked in 2018. I dropped in to find a new book to read. It was the person working behind the register who had me considering why I had dropped in that day. It was a brief exchange in a quiet hour at the bookstore. At the register, I told them I was not sure which of the two books I put down on the counter to purchase and take home. By the end of our brief exchange, I had chosen the one I needed at the time, rather than the seminal or best-selling one. The person working the register was pointed and kind, suggesting our experience with literature is about what ideas you may need to keep you company that day. I walked away from this encounter appreciating deliberate, intentional relationships with others' ideas—more specifically, others' writing.

ACADEMIC WRITING WITH OTHERS' IDEAS

The Main Concerns of this Context

The aim of this context was to challenge a convention in doctoral research—specifically, the claiming of ontologies. I used the luxury and space of the academic setting to begin undoing the dominating, Western, white-centered ways of seeing, thinking, and doing in my work.

Context

In Spring and Summer 2020, I worked on a project to name the ontological foundations of my research. I called the project "Freezing Ontologies."* Though it has changed, the initial intent for the project was to write a draft of a chapter for my doctoral research. In the earliest attempts at writing this chapter, I struggled with the blank page and the expectation to demonstrate a stable, fixed worldview. Rather than conform to the expectation, I attended to this struggle and considered why the stipulation felt discordant to the degree that it did.

Approach(es)

The conceptual approach for the paper was built on what Shana Agid and Yoko Akama offer as an approach that makes room for "mess," "incompleteness," and "situatedness." Writing from the field of service design, they offer an approach that resists "functionalist" and deceptively "complete" *fixing* of ideas and systems. Instead, they offer a *freezing* of things that allows for emergent nuances to temporarily be traced and oriented. I adopted their approach, taking it out of its original context; what I held onto is how they problematize the conventional ways of negotiating and documenting complexity, and I apply it to this theory-based project of naming worldviews.

Process and Activities

I put "Freezing Ontologies" together in two parts. Part 1 contextualized Day's *Being or Nothingness* in the research project and in my experience with it. Part 2 is a selection of four leftover hang-ups I have after reading *Being or Nothingness*, which I kept returning to and replaying in my mind. This jam-packed, extremely challenging, prickly essay is written by Iyko Day, a Canadian scholar based at Mount Holyoke College in the northwestern United States. I found this piece of writing in a search for theory that would help me think about Indigeneity and Blackness. Through its citations and the concepts it notes, it would later lead me to other influential theories and scholars. In "Freezing Ontologies," I worked toward finding a stance (whether elation, disappointment, agreement, or critique) among the ideas claimed in the reading. Combining the aim of challenging normative ways of "owning" worldviews and the aim of making visible my relationship with Day's paper, the project resulted in a paper whose form is visually fragmented, sometimes illegible, intersubjective, multiple, and fluid.

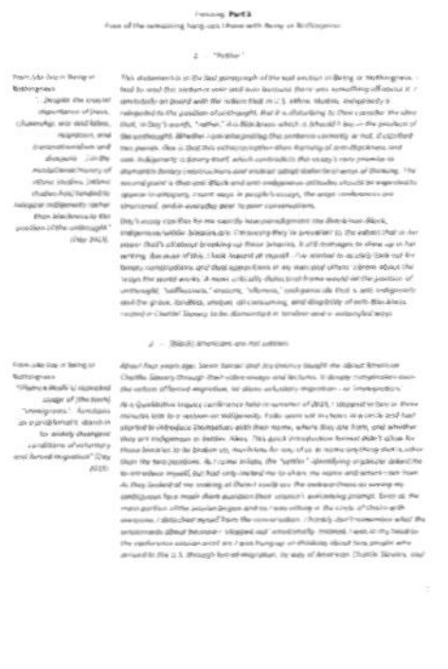

* Myriam D. Diatta, "Freezing Ontologies: Making Visible the Messiness of Working with Theory," *Text and Performance Quarterly* 42, no. 2 (2022): 97–110. https://doi.org/10.1080/10462937. 2022.2058076.

Image: One page from a longer essay, "Freezing Ontologies"

REMAKING TO WHOM AND HOW I WRITE

The Main Concerns of this Context

This context—an academic paper—analyzed the codes of conduct set by citation manuals and journal templates. It saw these codes as being further enforced through our compliance with them from early on in our secondary and university academic experiences. This context was concerned with how to take care of multiple aligned and discordant theories and author backgrounds. It was concerned with resisting showing up with an authoritative, static objectivity toward producing knowledge.

Context

In early 2020, I worked on an academic writing project to politicize the way we write and engage others in writing. I called the project, "I Paid Attention to the Footnotes." It was a context that served as a small training ground for remaking the worlds in which we live. I started the project based on a statement made by Indigenous scholar Eve Tuck in a lecture about reading Linda Tuhiwai Smith's work: "I paid attention to the footnotes because I believe that Indigenous Women and Women of Color are always writing to each other in our footnotes."

Approach(es)

This context, the academic page, was an interactive, discursive writing project. I approached the paper as a proposal for approaching academic writing.

Process and Activities

The main proposal of this writing project centered on the three components of any academic paper: the elements of a paper, like the paper title, body text, and in-text citations; the types of content, like your own voice, others' ideas, or underlying past drafts of the paper; and treatments of your positionality, co-authoring, or omitted prickly information. I listed the parts of these three components in detail and put together three visual illustrations to accompany them. The elements, types of content, and treatments were not the structure to abide by, but I analyzed and listed them to undo the academic page. Working to name and visualize these components exposed the anatomy of an academic paper and called for disruption within it. I concluded the project by reflecting on the scholars and practitioners across fields and disciplines whose work I kept in my mind's eye as I wrote "I Paid Attention to the Footnotes."* I asked readers, "What may it look like to unsettle the formatting of papers as a symbolic, metaphoric case study for taking up space?"

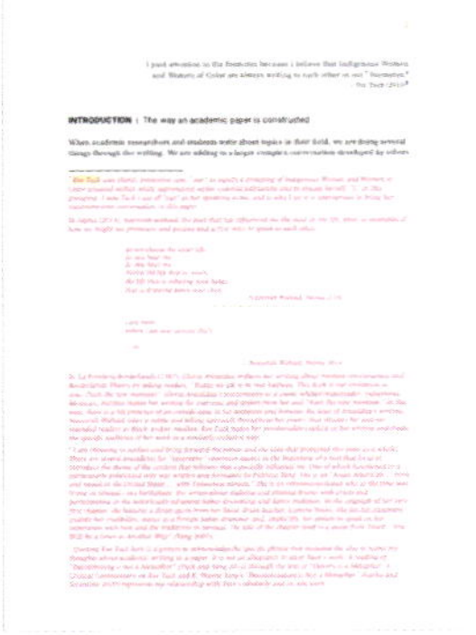
INTRODUCTION | The way an academic paper is constructed

Linda Tuhiwai Smith and Eve Tuck. "INQ13: Decolonizing Methodologies," The Graduate Center, CUNY, April 29, 2013, 88:09, https://www.youtube.com/watch?v=rIZXQC27tvg.

Image: First page in a longer essay, "I Paid Attention to the Footnotes."

AREA OF PRACTICE 4

HOW I ENGAGE ACROSS MY COMMUNITIES

We got a message from a friend sharing that she had made the difficult decision to formally leave the politicized community that she had organized with for years in college. In that message, she expressed gratitude for this other one we had more recently built together. She called our online space her political home. We share music playlists, garden-harvesting tips, and relationship advice. Our more explicitly politicized activities range from study groups, listening parties, and documentary film nights. The planning for building this online community was collaborative, with a group of friends whom I had met on the internet. We set up routes and channels to exchange ideas and everyday concerns. We also built designated spaces for our politicized commitments to shift, become undone, or be fortified. To do this, we spent months planning how to maintain safety and criticality in such an open, public, growing community of people.

REVISITING A TRIP BACK TO THIONCK ESSYL

The Main Concerns of this Context

This context—in Thionck Essyl, Sénégal—prompted a conversation with a friend, a poem, and a video. The concerns were to do with how I understand my positionality with my family and my father's home village. The concerns were about how I negotiate my personal, private experience and share it in a formal, academic setting.

Context

In Summer 2019, for the first time in over ten years, I flew with my family back to Thionck Essyl. This is where my father was raised and where he was born. Thionck Essyl is an area full of mangroves in Casamance, the southern region of Sénégal. It is a place where the Diola language and people make up the largest social group. Since 1982, the region has been home to a radical self-determination struggle with the post-colonial French and Wolof regions in the north, where the capital, Dakar, is located.

Approach(es)

My trip to Sénégal largely stays out of reach of this academic research project, but I used a recorded conversation between a friend in the US as a way to revisit the trip. Many lessons I learned from family members continue to affect the research. My trip to Sénégal was not an anthropological, ethnographic endeavor; so, as a context, it does not expose details or understandings about my family or the region.

Process and Activities

For this research, I recorded a conversation with a friend in Atlanta (US) in August 2019 in which I casually recounted my time with family in Thionck Essyl. It was part of a longer conversation where we generally caught up as friends. I carefully listened back and generated a short piece of poetic writing about what had stuck with me. I picked up on recurring matters: being there, arriving, the situational greeting in Diola, how my name, Myriam, is shared across generations ("homonyme"), and boundaries within family and the village and forest. The 500-word piece took the form of poetry with stanzas of short phrases. This articulated how that time with family continues to affect the research, referencing my trip without divulging specifics to the academic gaze.

Four months later, I edited video footage from Thionck Essyl, layered in the poems, revisited footage, collaged family photos, juxtaposed landscape and words, underlaid music in a 5-minute film, sent it to family, posted online, and shared it in a PhD presentation.

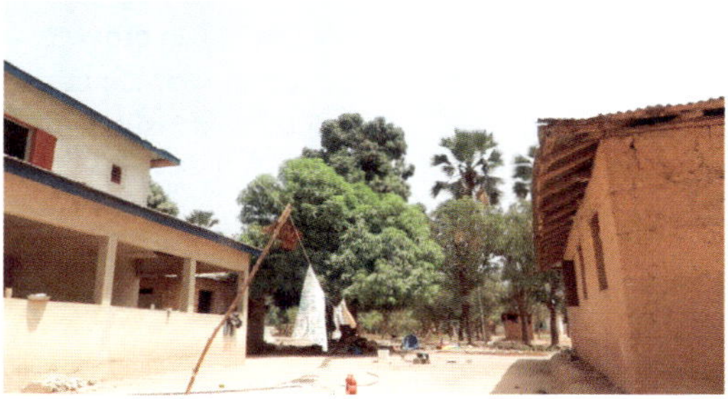

Image: Photograph of my family's home in Thionck Essyl and the surrounding area.

A CO-AUTHORED PAPER

The Main Concerns of this Context

This context—a long-term, two-year writing collaboration—was concerned with expressing through a series of case studies the intangible qualities and sensibilities practitioners bring to their work. From my position, it was concerned with how I show up as a co-author. While the content of the paper we co-authored had to do with themes of materiality and embodiment, this context is set in the collaborative process that led us to write the content in the way that we did. It was concerned with creating balance and upholding ethical integrity while co-authoring. This context was concerned with setting up a slow, quiet pace of my participation, our conversations, our writing, and our ideas.

Context

In May 2019, friend and fellow PhD candidate Ricardo Dutra Gonçalves and I talked over lunch at a Japanese restaurant on campus in Melbourne, Australia. This conversation set off a long-term writing collaboration, and this context spanned two years, across continents, and was set in a paper that would eventually be called "A Family of Sensibilities: Toward a Relational Design Practice Grounded in Materiality and Embodiment,"* published in *Design and Culture: The Journal of Design Studies Forum.*

Approach(es)

I saw what we were doing as deliberately bypassing inclinations in the beginning of co-authoring processes to quickly and efficiently claim and produce knowledge to be published, in order to productively participate in the academic institution.

Process and Activities

At that lunch, we discussed how our past work and early PhD interests connected. Ricardo suggested audio recording the conversation; months later, he transcribed and shared it as a launching point. We then held multiple 1.5-hour calls, producing pages of notes with themes and ideas. By November 2019, we had five pages of first-person writing capturing our sensibilities, reflections on other practitioners, coded themes, theories of working with materials, and a poem-writing process Ricardo introduced to engage readers laterally and poetically. After a pause, we resumed in spring 2020, exchanging writing prompts. A new third author, Lisa, altered the collaboration's dynamics, testing my ability to maintain pace, dissent, and ethics.

Ricardo and I then wrote a meta-reflection, "Threading Notes,"* to articulate our collaborative approach. Inspired by discussions with friends, we outlined phases of our work together, including "stumbling upon each other," "trust," "entering," "constantly entering," "nudging," "making boundaries," and "stopping." It emerged from an hour-long writing exercise documenting the qualities we brought to our collaboration.

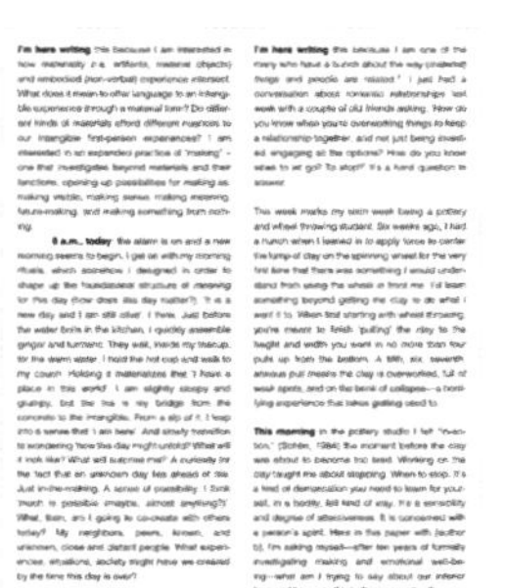

* Myriam D. Diatta, M. D., Ricardo D. Gonçalves, and Lisa H. Grocott. A Family of Sensibilities: Toward a Relational Design Practice Grounded in Materiality and Embodiment. *Design and Culture* 14, no. 2 (2022), 205–29. https://doi.org/10.1080/17547075.2021.2018539.

Image: A page from a longer paper, "A Family of Sensibilities: Toward a Relational Design Practice Grounded in Materiality and Embodiment."

ENTERING THE INTERIORITIES: USING THE FRAMEWORK IN CONTEXT

CHAPTER FOUR

Embodied and inwards, this chapter sinks into nine cases in which the framework and methods are put into action.

There are nine instances where I have looked back at a past experience and used reflexive making to investigate my double consciousness. In this chapter, I describe each instance one by one. In each section, I make visible much of the slow, inner wrestling with, recognizing, negotiating, and teasing out that I did. I recount how hand-making the models and shaping the writing on the page allowed for that slow inner work.

Chapter 4 dives into what I did to intensify my double consciousness. I unpack how I aligned theory and practice, brought them closer and closer together, and messed with their binary separation. In Fig. 13, I illustrate the relationship between Chapter 3 and Chapter 4, showing that here, I enter into granular accounts of how I used the methods.

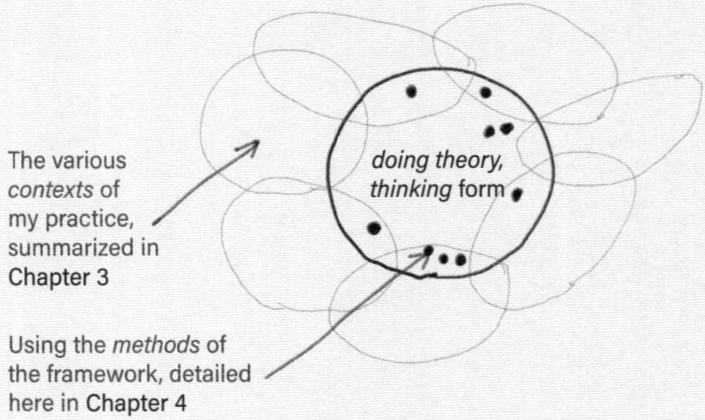

Fig. 13. The image shows the relationships between aspects of my *parallel practice*. It includes the framework I use, *doing theory, thinking* form; the contexts of my creative practice I reflected on; and the methods. The nine black points symbolize nine instances where I used the methods.

The nine sections in this chapter each vignette a piece of reflexive writing or an image of a paper model generated from reflexive model making. The vignettes are a window into the things that resulted from using the methods. Following this illustration, I look back and expand on what went on as I made the piece of writing or paper model. Within each of the nine sections, you will find the following structure:

A cover page including

a title that describes what was aligned: "Aligning double consciousness and [an everyday context]."

a repeated statement of "The Main Concerns of This Context" and a thumbnail image from the context, which was originally presented at the end of Chapter 3. They are repeated so they may be used as a reminder to link the context summarized in the previous chapter with the granular description that will follow.

A vignette of reflexive writing and/or paper model. Vignettes of reflexive writing are presented in areas of white text with a black background. Vignettes of reflexive model making are presented in black and white photographs of a finished paper model.

A description of my process. I story the past experience relevant to what was vignetted, recognize how I made aspects of my double consciousness visible, and name how the method allowed me to investigate and intensify my double consciousness.

Footnotes: Some descriptions include footnotes that lead to quotes and references to critical theory. The footnotes are integral to the descriptions. In line with the practice-led approach of this framework, some of these theories were referenced in Part 1 of this book, signaling how they were first engaged with in practice and later presented in Part 1 to describe what I did in practice.

Importantly, the task of writing the "description of my process," noted above, is not where I did the work. It is not where I attended to my double consciousness or aligned my values and actions. I did so through the actual hands-on process of reflexive writing and reflexive model making. What I documented for the purposes of this book and what I did in practice are distinct. What the "description of my process" does is document the tangible and ineffable activities behind what I did in practice. The descriptions serve as documentation of the theories that are not accessible by looking at an image of a model or reading a story about a past event. The descriptions are there for you, the reader, to access the abstract negotiations and thinking with form that went into what I made.

This chapter showcases a breadth of uses for the methods but does not aim to comprehensively unpack all the ways I used the methods. The following pages follow this outline:

A. Using Reflexive Writing

1. Aligning Double Consciousness and [How I Interview]
2. Aligning Double Consciousness and [How I Write with Theory]
3. Aligning Double Consciousness and [Talking About Family]
4. Aligning Double Consciousness and [How I Co-author]

B. Using Reflexive Model Making

5. Aligning Double Consciousness and [Who My Work Is For]
6. Aligning Double Consciousness and [The Company I Keep]
7. Aligning Double Consciousness and [How I Decide to Do a PhD]

C. Using Both Reflexive Writing and Model-Making

8. Aligning Double Consciousness and [How My Body Moves]
9. Aligning Double Consciousness and [Whom I Write To]

A. USING REFLEXIVE WRITING

1. ALIGNING DOUBLE CONSCIOUSNESS AND [HOW I INTERVIEW]

IN-HOME INTERVIEWS:
OUR EVERYDAY FORMS

The Main Concerns of this Context

The concerns of this context were about my complex role as facilitator-interviewer-friend-cameraperson-guest-host. It was about my ethics of bringing the intimate, vulnerable stories shared during the interview and exposing them to academic, formal analysis. The concerns of the context had to do with participants' private spaces and how the subjective experiences between us interrelate.

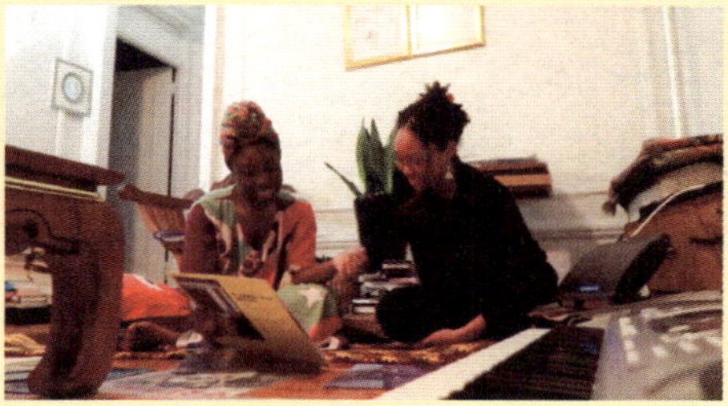

Back in Brooklyn toward the end of the interview, I asked Ace to name who their story is for. I gave them time to think about it, and they began. They addressed their "peers," their "diasporic Asian community," and their "queer community." Hearing their message to them, I watched them bring back up the subject of the collection of objects in their bookshelf that they previously passed up. In this address, they explained they did not want to talk about it because they felt their mom watching. With that period of self-awareness, they passed on advice to their peers and queer community that it is ok to have objects that are not from your culture. I sat behind the camera they were looking into as they spoke and took in that healing advice for myself. From this, I personally gained awareness of the effect of my own family's traditions and judgments on other cultural and spiritual traditions. Ace gave me permission to feel ok about my own tools for resistance.

Fig. 14. An excerpt from an essay, "Our Everyday Forms."[1]

Before I began any in-home interviews, I found myself feeling disturbed about filming and sharing the interviews with others. I struggled with my role as a facilitator, interviewer, and cameraperson. I was asking Ace and other participants to divulge things about their politicized lives as Black, Indigenous, and/or folk of color while

1 Myriam D. Diatta, "Our Everyday Forms," Medium, n.d., https://medium.com/our-everyday-forms.

exposing images of their private spaces or things they may never have said out loud prior to the interview to an institutional audience.[2] As a critical part of "Our Everyday Forms," I invited participants to name specifically who their stories were for. See Fig. 14.

At the end of my visit with Ace, I asked them to speak into the camera and begin their sentence with "Dear..." so that they could direct the inner stories they had generously shared with me, on camera, to the folks with whom they cared to share them. I decided to make this part of my approach for these interviews, knowing that the objects around which our conversations centered were connections to one's spirit and inner life.[3] I understood there could be a rich, historied, deeply personal process[4] by which they came to be tucked in a drawer, on the floor, or on the wall.

2 When I made the decision to ask participants to name whom their stories were for, I carried with me this statement from a conversation between filmmaker Arthur Jafa and scholar bell hooks that I had watched years before. Jafa states, "If you point a camera at Black people, on a psychoanalytical level that camera is also functioning as the white gaze even if a Black person is behind the camera. So I said, 'I'm just not going to point a camera at people at all.' ... It's about surveillance ... and the whole idea that the way power is structured, it always drifts upwards ... presumably going to be a representative of white power ... We can't very much go forward with this whole idea of never pointing a camera at Black people ... I want to privilege the idea of Black people being able to speak freely." See bell hooks and Arthur Jafa, "bell hooks and Arthur Jafa Discuss Transgression in Public Spaces at The New School," The New School, October 15, 2014, 13:45, https://www.youtube.com/ watch?v=fe-7ILSKSog.

3 Originally published in *The New Yorker*, an essay by Teju Cole titled, "Black Body," recounts how James Baldwin had to "bring his records with him in the fifties, like a secret stash of medicine, and he had to haul his phonograph up to Leukerbad, so that the sound of the American blues could keep him connected to a Harlem of the spirit."

4 In "In Our Glory: Photography and Black Life," bell hooks reveals that "to enter black homes in my childhood was to enter a world that valued the visual, that asserted our collective will to participate in a noninstitutionalized curatorial process" (61).

It was after I began asking participants to name who their stories were for—and after my interview with Ace—that I decided to note my reflections about my time with her. I did so as part of a much larger essay about my role in the home tours early on in my PhD endeavor. I was not calling this "reflexive writing" at the time, but I had carved out time for writing and for revisiting specific moments during the interviews. A handful of instances came to mind. I first recalled how we both sat on the floor in front of their bookshelf and how I waited as they paused and considered whom they wanted their story to be for. Writing and reading and rewriting and rereading what is vignetted here allowed me to notice something in the writing—how much "watching," "self-awareness," "awareness," and the presence of a camera went on in that moment. Typing out the words about this moment let me link the judging gaze of a family member Ace was talking about with the belonging gaze of their queer and diasporic Asian communities and the gaze of many "others" that I was aware would be on the video footage one day. It was seeing the dynamic of each of us and the camera written out and placed on the page together that allowed me, at the time, to make this connection. I was intentional and explicit about participants looking into the camera to name whom their stories were for, but I came to appreciate the multiplicity of the gazes upon us by making these links in the writing.

While it was not until two years later that I would explicitly center double consciousness in my research, this short piece of writing made visible the gazes present in that moment on Ace's bedroom floor. My doubled self-awareness was heightened, making all the more significant what appears in public and what is private.[5]

At this early stage in the research, the reflexive writing itself did not make explicit my double consciousness or make a visual intervention in the layout. However, the process of writing let me recognize the double consciousness I was doing. It let me bring theory with me to reinforce how important it was to put an intervention in place to address the outside gaze and preserve our interiorities. Understanding this better mattered because I set out to grapple with my position as the person bringing the outside gaze into the room (with the camera), as an interviewer and a facilitator.

5 Jared Sexton offers a metaphor of Sonny Rollins' jazz ensemble performing in front of an audience: in the middle of their session, the microphone cuts off. The sound technician rushes on stage as they continue and attempts to troubleshoot. The drummer, while continuing to play, tells the technician to stop by saying, "If Sonny can hear himself, and we can hear him, we don't care if the audience can hear us or not." Sexton goes on to explain, "We're not here because of the microphone, we're here because of what is being produced on this stage." See Jared Sexton, "People-of-Color-Blindness: A Lecture by Jared Sexton," UC Berkeley Events, October 27, 2011, 61:58, https://www.youtube.com/watch?v=qNVMI3oiDaI.

2. ALIGNING DOUBLE CONSCIOUSNESS AND [HOW I WRITE WITH THEORY]

ACADEMIC WRITING WITH OTHERS' IDEAS

The Main Concerns of this Context

The aim of this context was to challenge a convention in doctoral research: the claiming of ontologies—worldviews. I used the luxury and space of the academic setting to begin undoing dominating, Western, white-centered ways of seeing, thinking, and doing in my work.

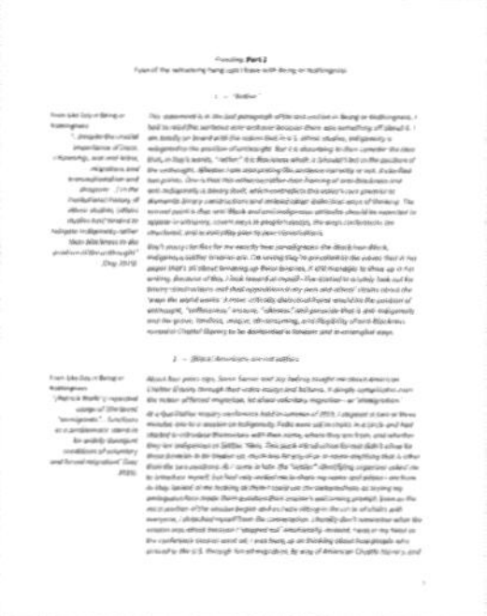

A reading of "Being or Nothingness"

Iyko Day's "Being or Nothingness: Indigeneity, Anti-Blackness, and Settler Colonial Critique" is an essay that works to break up two binary constructions: Indigenous/settler and Black/non-Black. She does so because, in her conception, the binaries are used by abolitionist Afropessimists to fall into victimhood and exceptionalism and by theorists who put Indigeneity into the "position of unthought" or nothingness. She breaks up these binaries and tendencies using the lens of dispossession: dispossession of land and dispossession of bodies and labor. Day cites the Afropessimist formulation that situates Black labor as a figure of "anti-labor." Black American bodies are situated in the categorically unique system of American chattel slavery and are accumulated "regardless of their utility as laborers." In parallel, Day describes the way Indigeneity is assigned to idleness. Under dominant labor paradigms, work gives right to property and absence of work is a sign of "bad character." Through these points, Day argues Blackness and Indigeneity are both "similarly constituted outside of a hegemonic labor paradigm." She concludes with a critique of ethnic studies as a field of study: ethnic studies has "tended to relegate Indigeneity rather than blackness to the position of the unthought" and that instead, Indigeneity ought to enable an emerging critical ethnic studies frame that "will enable a durable Native American critical existence in relation to the totality."

....

18. "i "if the ocean can calm itself so can you. we are both salt water mixed with air. — meditation."

Fig. 15. An excerpt from the beginning of an essay I wrote, "Freezing Ontologies."[6] Includes a footnote featuring a poem.[7]

6 Diatta, "Freezing Ontologies."

7 Poem formatting edited; Nayyirah Waheed, *Salt* (CreateSpace Independent Publishing Platform, 2013), 94.

When I started the essay in Fig. 15., "Freezing Ontologies," I wanted to work with the ideas in Iyko Day's paper.[8] Throughout the two months of putting this piece of writing together, I was constantly resisting the pressure that my position on Day's essay needed to be a figured-out, "cleaned up," and complete narrative.[9] The decision to write this with a two-column format took away the immense pressure of needing to forcefully conflate everything (i.e., the theories presented in Day's essay, my questions, things I had forgotten, all my personal experiences with it, and everything unsaid[10]) in obediently lined-up blocks of text. It invited me to deal with the sweaty airlessness that came with trying to begin writing the essay in the first place. I could speak to the fact there were things that were unsettling for me and leave them there, visible in the text and footnotes, rather than "getting over it," suppressing it, or pretending to myself that I had a hold of it. I sat in it.

Working with columns on the left and right—running up, down, and across the page—encouraged me to work iteratively and temporally. I attended to anxieties when I was ready to write about them; reserving empty openings and slowly filling it in as I went. Over time, this skipping and meandering around also let me find the homes and shapes of Day's work. Not only this, but the fragmented

8 Day Iyko, "Being or Nothingness: Indigeneity, Antiblackness, and Settler Colonial Critique," *Journal of the Critical Ethnic Studies* 1, no. 2 (2015): 118, https://doi.org/10.5749/ jcritethnstud.1.2.0102.

9 Dionne Brand argues, "Narrative contains our demise. ... Pressure of that shape on Black life. The bargain of narrative is an exchange of death for less death" ("Dionne Brand," 28:25).

10 "In this regard, signifying is extraordinary expressiveness, relying unreliably on interplay between said and unsaid, public and not; one cannot appreciate it by only paying attention to what is explicit. And yet the general discussion of signifying as verbal exchange tends to focus on its demonstrative quality rather than its capacity to reflect what is unsure and interior" (Quashie, *The Sovereignty of Quiet*, 12).

layout[11] also created space for the contours of the work of Jared Sexton, Frank B. Wilderson, Tiffany Lethabo King, and others to make their way into the essay, even in the midst of me grasping and processing them. The left-hand column is reserved for quotes and descriptive writing about Day's essay. The right column is dedicated to reflexive writing; it contains my stream-of-consciousness writing, recounts events in my life from years back, and is sprinkled with superscript numbers that lead to an outpouring of footnotes at the bottom of the page. This is where supporting critical theories and backstories live. The left-hand side is the basis for the *freezing*: an essay, "Being or Nothingness." The right-hand side carries all the messiness that comes with attempting to name worldviews.

In the first part is "Freezing Ontologies" I introduced Day's arguments and this introduction took up most of the space on the page. The sweatiness and discomfort that came with reading and writing about *Being or Nothingness* had so little space, narrowly constrained to the right-hand side of the page. In the second section of "Freezing Ontologies," a shift happens. The small right-hand column in the first part expands and widens in the second part of the essay. In the latter, rather than overriding traces of my initial impressions, embodied responses, and thoughts in progress, I leave resting as much as can fit on the page. The right column expands and narrows the left hand column.

It is in this multiple, layered, incomplete presentation of ideas that I intended to gain a stronger footing on my worldviews. I used the form of the writing to be doubled, creating a new approach for

11 Jared Sexton puts forth that getting a grip on a coherent, stable conception of the world is a matter of survival ("People-of-Color-Blindness"). In the same way, flexibility within that conception is an absolute necessity. Flexibility is necessary for persisting against fixed conceptual and physical borders. As Gloria Anzaldúa puts it, "rigidity means death" (*Borderlands,* 101) for la mestiza who fights to navigate her plurality and whose psychological borders are swamped by Western modes of logic (*Borderlands*, 101). To remain flexible and stretched, convergent and divergent is to move towards a more whole conception of the world (*Borderlands*).

myself to act on my double consciousness. The essay is a lightly pinned-down frame that momentarily allows one scene from the worldviews of this research project to be pictured. This meant the reader found themself in the middle of a construction site. As they read, they would be tripping over, shuffling, dodging, and retracing their steps. Navigating the messiness, illegibility, temporality, and lived-in qualities built into the *freezing* may be as unsettling for the reader as it was for me to put it together. I reserve space to process my inner thoughts in writing, resisting the expectation to be coherent and linear. My experience navigating theory was made visible through the process of composing writing. This reflexive process is what eventually led me to name the worldviews in Part 1 of this book.

3. ALIGNING DOUBLE CONSCIOUSNESS AND [TALKING ABOUT FAMILY]

REVISITING A TRIP BACK TO THIONCK ESSYL

The Main Concerns of this Context

This context, in Thionck Essyl, Sénégal, prompted a conversation with a friend, a poem, and a video. The concerns were to do with how I understand my positionality with my family and my father's home village. The concerns were about how I negotiate my personal, private experience and share it in a formal, academic setting.

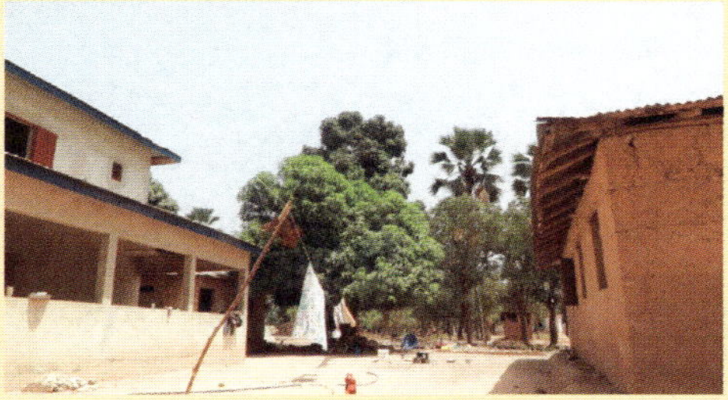

There's a way to say hello
to a group.
a person standing.
A group that's walking.
A couple sitting down and working.
When they're leaving.
When a person's come back.

When you greet an aunt
they respond to your greeting
with "Kusumuy"
along with their relationship to you—"aunt."

You repeat,
echoing back
that relationship.

We were walking from the houses,
through the mangroves,
to the river.

As we walked, he moved me
from his right-hand side to his left-hand side.
He told me that for a long time,
the forest has dedicated areas.
He was protecting the area
of the forest
and protecting me.

Fig. 16. Excerpt from a poem derived from a conversation with a friend.

This vignette shows part of what I learned from my cousin. There were too many memorable family moments to count on this trip, but when I came back to this PhD, I sat down to reflect on a couple of personal lessons that were profound for me. That is when I began to piece together a poem, excerpted in Fig. 16. I took all the days and cities and family members we visited, and let themes rise from them, stanza by stanza. One of those themes can be found in the last two stanzas in the vignette here. This process led me to describe my cousin moving me from one side of him to another as his "guiding" me. He taught me that the forests have been divided for ages and physically moved me to the side of the path on which I *should* be walking. I appreciated his gesture as a determined and generous move.

Meanwhile, at the same time as I was back working on the PhD and writing this poem, I was also struggling with my role as an interviewer. In "Our Everyday Forms," I was reflecting on how I was (not) managing to juggle my positions as an interviewer, a professional, a friend, a facilitator, a cameraperson, a guest, and a host, simultaneously, in someone else's home. While I was working with one participant of the home tour, I really struggled with stepping in and "correcting" their interpretation of a prompt I gave. Correcting what happened would have meant a risk of physically ignoring their experience—the objects they had vulnerably brought out for us to talk about. In that interview, I went with it and our time together lasted a rich four hours. We eventually said goodbye, and I took the train home. I missed chances to ask questions. Frankly, I was not always being present while internally juggling many roles at the same time.

I bring this issue into my reflections on my cousin's actions because one has come to inform the other. By describing what my cousin did as "guiding" me, I was able to make the connection that my role in the home tours should be that of a "guide," first and foremost. At the time, there were power dynamics (of being tied to a university) and logistics and planning to take care of, which made it difficult to find clarity in how I wanted to show up with Azar, Ace, and Akeema. I chose to lean on my cousin's offerings and his clarity, which changed how I planned to move forward with the project,

"Our Everyday Forms."

Choosing to center what my cousin taught me has some weight to it. I come from a design background, where facilitating groups of people is instrumentalized and serves the agenda of a company or institution, whether it is made explicit or softened and tacit. Although I had become wary of these approaches and detached myself from them, I inevitably needed to come to my own terms of facilitation if I were not prescribing to design facilitation. I looked to what I knew about the most prominent filmmaker from the same region of southern Sénégal. Ousmane Sembène, known as the "father of African film," was once asked in an interview if he thought his films would be understood by French audiences. Leaning forward, he stated, "Let me be clear. Europe is not my center; Europe is in the periphery. ... My future does not depend on Europe."[12] Centering the way my cousin guided me made the design facilitation toolkits on my bookshelf peripheral. It made all other authorized places I could have looked peripheral. Prompted by writing a few lines in a poem, I engaged with my cousin and Ousmane Sembène's ways of knowing as theory.

12 Translated from French to English language, Férid Boughedir, *Caméra d'Afrique: 20 ans de cinéma africain (Twenty Years of African Cinema)*, documentary film, 1983.

4. ALIGNING DOUBLE CONSCIOUSNESS AND [HOW I CO-AUTHOR]

A CO-AUTHORED PAPER

The Main Concerns of this Context

This context—a long-term, two-year collaboration—was concerned with expressing the intangible qualities and sensibilities that a set of practitioners bring to their work. From my position, it was concerned with how I show up as a co-author. This context was concerned with setting up a slow, quiet pace of my participation, our conversations, our writing, and our ideas.

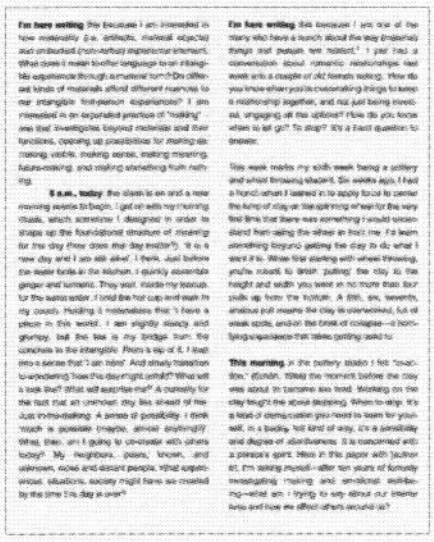

I am here writing this because I am interested in how materiality (i.e., artifacts, material objects) and embodied (non-verbal) experience intersect. What does it mean to offer language to an intangible experience through a material form? Do different kinds of materials afford different nuances to our intangible first-person experiences? I am interested in an expanded practice of "making"—one that investigates beyond materials and their functions, opening up possibilities for making as making visible, making sense, making meaning, future-making, and making something from nothing. ...

8 a.m. today, I am slightly sleepy and grumpy, but the tea is my bridge from the concrete to the intangible. From a sip of it, I leap into a sense that "I am here." And I slowly transition to wondering "how might this day unfold? What will it look like? What will surprise me?" A curiosity for the fact that an unknown day lies ahead of me. Just in-the-making. A sense of possibility. I think, "much is possible (maybe, almost anything?)." What, then, am I going to co-create with others today? My neighbors, peers, known, and unknown, close and distant people. What experiences, situations, society might have we created by the time this day is over?

I am here writing this because I am one of the many who have a hunch about the way (material) things and people are related.7 I just last week had a conversation with a couple of old friends about romantic relationships, asking, "How do you know when you're overworking things to keep a relationship together and not just being invested, engaging all the options? How do you know when to let go? To stop?" It's a hard question to answer...

This morning in the pottery studio, I felt "in action," the moment before the clay was about to become too tired. Working on the clay taught me about stopping. When to stop. It's a kind of demarcation you need to learn for yourself, in a bodily, felt kind of way. It's a sensibility and degree of attentiveness. It is concerned with a person's spirit. Here, in this paper with Ricardo, I am asking myself—after ten years of formally investigating making and emotional well-being—what am I trying to say about our interior lives and how we affect others around us?

Fig. 17. An excerpt from the introduction to a co-authored paper, "A Family of Sensibilities."

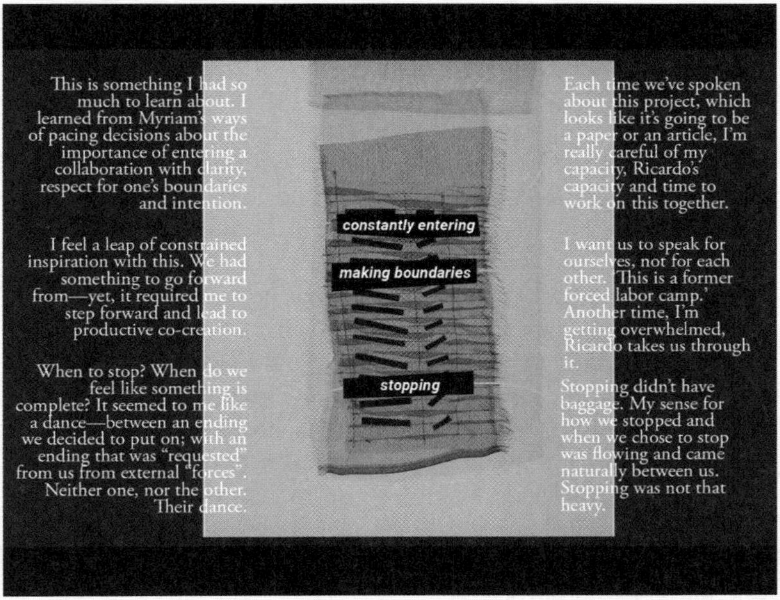

Fig. 18. Excerpt of a collaborative writing project, "Threading Notes."[13]

The vignette in Fig. 17 is from a full paper, "Family of Sensibilities," co-authored with Ricardo Dutra Gonçalves and Lisa Grocott.[14] The two columns presented in Fig. 17 live in the introduction of this paper. It was written at the beginning of the collaboration, when Ricardo and I had started to give shape to the paper. From the beginning, we were thoughtful about how our ideas merged as we collaborated—we chose not to speak as, for, or in place of each other.[15]

13 Myriam D. Diatta and Ricardo Dutra Gonçalves, "Threading Notes_Family of Sensibilities," Department of Art and Media, Monash University, 2020, https://doi.org/10.6084/ m9.figshare.13353374.v2

14 Diatta, Gonçalves, and Grocott, "A Family of Sensibilities."

15 Linda Alcoff, "The Problem of Speaking for Others," Cultural Critique 20 (1991): 5-32, https://doi.org/10.2307/1354221.

This politics and approach to our collaboration was expressed in the paper by changing and mixing our writing voices and our use of two columns in portions of the paper. I resisted speaking in one voice—fragmenting our authorship and making multiple what we bring to the essay. Knowing we were writing for an academic audience, we chose to write in the first person. Over the series of weekly calls we had together to develop the content of the paper, I was constantly considering what it meant to co-author. Whenever I see multiple authors listed in a paper or book, the order of their names suggests something. Who wrote what or, more interestingly, why the authors are writing together and how they managed to present one set of ideas in a paper is often omitted. We maintained our aims when Lisa, one of the co-authors, eventually began collaborating with us. We allowed space for each of our distinct motivations to be unpacked. I did not aim to assert ownership of my respective ideas but sought to resist having them collapsed, with the risk of my positionalities, politics, and background being subsumed into one coherent narrative.

Soon after we wrapped things up and submitted our collaborative paper to a journal, Ricardo and I spent a one-hour call reflecting on our collaboration. We agreed to do so because there was something that "worked" in the year that we had co-written the paper that we wanted to articulate. On the call, I workshopped a reflexive writing exercise with Ricardo. It was a playful iteration on the split columns we had developed in "Family of Sensibilities," but this time, it was not about the content of the paper but about how we worked together. On a casual call with a few other colleagues, the two of us talked about how aware we were of each other's capacity to work on this project over the year. I described that action as "constantly entering" the collaboration week to week—choosing and disclosing what we did and did not have the capacity to work on. We were accountable for our own time and communicated that with each other.

Overall, we named 12 points important to our collaboration. Fig. 18 is an abbreviated version of "Threading Notes" and features a vignette of three of the 12 attributes: "constantly entering," "making boundaries," and "stopping." "Threading Notes," as an exercise between Ricardo and me, shows a transition from my aim to fragment and multiply my authorship to looking back at the self-accountability and values I brought to our collaboration. In our brief two-person writing workshop, I prepared a shared online document with two empty columns and another in the middle containing the 12 attributes of our collaboration. Starting from the first attribute at the top of the middle column, we used this as a prompt, so we each spent a couple of minutes on a call writing whatever surfaced in us. We moved down the column until we had both contributed our remaining impressions from our year of working together.

B. USING REFLEXIVE MODEL MAKING

5. ALIGNING DOUBLE CONSCIOUSNESS AND [WHO MY WORK IS FOR]

FACILITATING A SESSION WITH DESIGNERS

The Main Concerns of this Context

This context—online at a design conference—was concerned with creating situations in which the aims I create are not aligned with my values. Regardless of how prepared or observant a facilitator I may be, this context was concerned with putting myself in situations in which the professional culture is in the way of my and others' relating with one another in ways I care to.

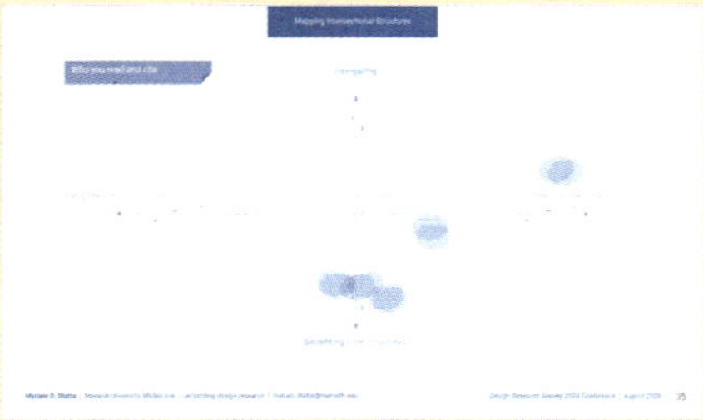

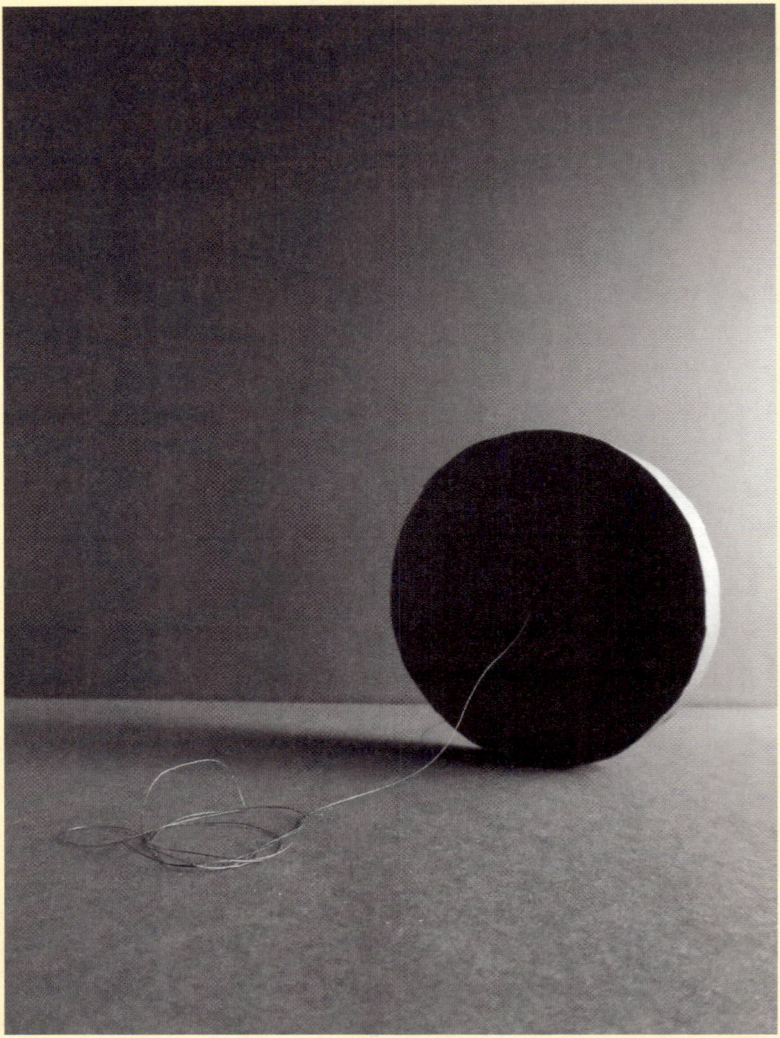

Fig. 19. Image of finished paper model pertaining to facilitating a session with designers.

From the position of being a facilitator of a design workshop, I had a difficult time with this hour session. I was organized and clear in my delivery, I prepared the content well beforehand, and I still stand by the framework I built. But what I had not done so thoughtfully was consider how the participants' experiences of our time together would be out of step with what I value as a facilitator. With the half-day session I had originally planned for, I could allow us to get to know one another, have the time and space I needed to process how things are going, make adjustments based on what the group was ready for, arrange the room in thoughtful ways, and personally check in with each person as they worked. I did not translate these needs into the truncated one-hour version of the workshop or make enough adjustments in the plan for the workshop.

Beyond these social and logistical issues, I had put myself in a situation that replicated the kind of work I had spent years in my studio work transitioning out of: I made detailed strategic plans, scaffolded our time to reach a practical outcome, and geared myself up to lead a group of people. I positioned myself as a design facilitator. As a facilitator, I was offering knowledge about oppressive systems and structures to a mixed audience—all things I was no longer interested in because my practice and politics had shifted dramatically. I set out for this research to be by and for Black, Indigenous, and/or folk of color, but I opened up my work to a notoriously white society of design researchers. I missed connecting in the workshop with the people my work is by and for. Before the workshop, I thought I had my reasoning for submitting a workshop proposal to this conference and for opening it up to an inclusive group of participants, but as soon as I sat down to start the workshop, I sensed the dissonance as a migraine headache came on. My shoulders were tense as I made myself hold these misaligned, moving components in my mind while I facilitated.

I felt flimsy in the structured setting of the conference proceedings, the reputation of the conference, and the culture around design research—in all its formality. At this point, I was still struggling to find the creative home of this PhD research. I felt thin, too easily thrust by the winds and tides of design and academic research. Initially pulled by the standard of presenting at design conferences and publishing in design journals, that thinness extended, getting more and more involved—applying, being accepted, planning, replanning, scripting, designing, and facilitating. After the workshop, looking at where I had led the participants and led myself, I felt my insides drifting further and further away from the fullness I knew to be the core of my work. How flimsy was this, in contrast to the theory I know? How spare were my questions and modes of working? How thin was my relationship with each participant in the hour we had? I could feel something close but off to the side of the flimsy state I was now in. It was the lushness[16] I had come to know about who my work is for, the ethos of the theories I carried with me, and what I bring to the table.

I pulled a long piece of thread from a spool and gauged the proportion of the lushness so that I could cut and build it. Thanks to the model in Fig. 19, I could see what little I had managed to offer participants in comparison to what I know I can in a more intimate, one-to-one, or small group setting by and for Black, Indigenous, and/or folk of color. The contrast in what I did in a formal setting and the way I prefer to show up was stark. Sitting with the impressions left from facilitating the design workshop and materializing it in a paper model affirmed what I was working to transition into: a practice that centers[17] our ways of knowing.

16 "yes. yes I do. have the right to be this lush and neverending" (Waheed, *Nejma*, 27).

17 Angela Davis points out, "We always tend to use, as our standard, those who are at the center of the systems we want to dismantle. And so why would women want to become equal to men? Why would black people and latinos and muslims want to become equal to white people? Why would the LGBTQ community want to become equal in the context of heteropatriarchy?" ("WOW: Angela Davis in Conversation," Southbank Centre, March 11, 2017, 34:38, https://www.youtube.com/watch?v=lBgdzK3jfEg).

6. ALIGNING DOUBLE CONSCIOUSNESS AND [THE COMPANY I KEEP]

BETWEEN CONTEXTS

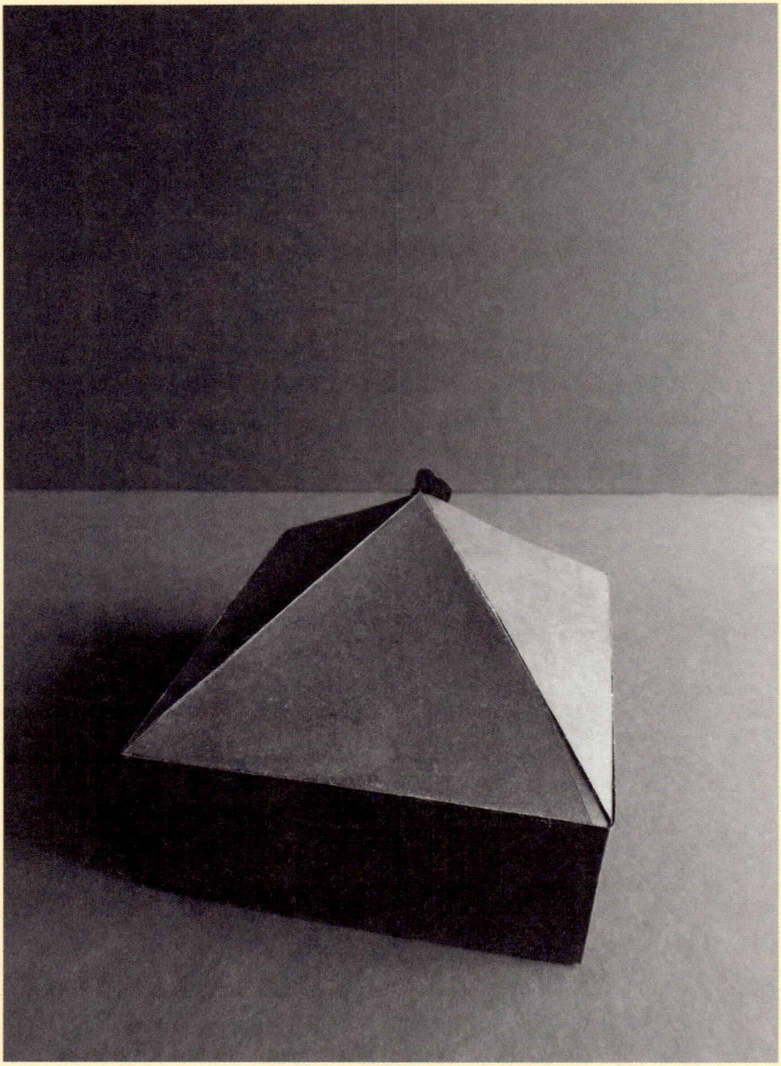

Fig. 20. Image of finished model pertaining to passive influences in the work.

Some of the aligning I did happened outside of the specific contexts summarized in the previous chapter. The aligning consisted of accounting for my movements and temporalities *between* the contexts. I worked on the model pictured in Fig. 20 to investigate negotiations of being between the formal, academic space in which I have done the research and the private, inner experiences with myself and others I work with.

When I sat down to attend to this, the gaze on me while writing my PhD and the gaze on me as I made this model came forward. These gazes are chronically present on me as I write drafts of my dissertation, so I have developed a habit of keeping YouTube videos of talks by beloved artists and theorists who critically engage with Blackness playing up in the top right corner of my laptop screen. I was struggling to keep the company I wanted in my mind's eye as I worked. That effort felt heavy and concentrated right behind my eyes. And that space held an outward and downward movement, accumulating into a large mass over my shoulders, where the company I kept grew a weighty founding to it, becoming sturdier with time. As I started to cut and glue to materialize these precise sensations, I started to see the form come together.

From this vantage point, I could see how the work of Barry Harris, American Artist, or Rian Phin that I was listening to leaked from the corner of my screen, filling up space. The ethos of their work sank deeper down into my consciousness. Because the model externalized this, I could draw the connection: the large mass accumulated over my shoulders as I wrote the paper was sore because thicker, wider paths were being drawn on them, steadily, more frequently, and fluidly navigating among the unwanted gazes, welcomed gazes, private and inner, and formal and academic spaces.

I made the nourishing, safeguarded videos small, tucked in the corner of my screen. Yet from that peripheral[18] place, the ethos of the ideas, intimacies, and debates that made up the content of

18 Boylorn, "Sit With Your Legs Closed."

the videos "grew a weighty founding" in me as I wrote the paper displayed on the same computer screen. This was "particularly significant for people speaking from the periphery"[19]: as I wrote from the outer edge of dominant discourse. This matters because it is this understanding that encouraged me to show up peripherally, between inner and formal spaces, being reflective and opaque as I write about these matters here.

19 Boylorn, "Sit With Your Legs Closed," 174.

7. ALIGNING DOUBLE CONSCIOUSNESS AND [HOW I DECIDE TO DO A PHD]

BEFORE THE CONTEXTS

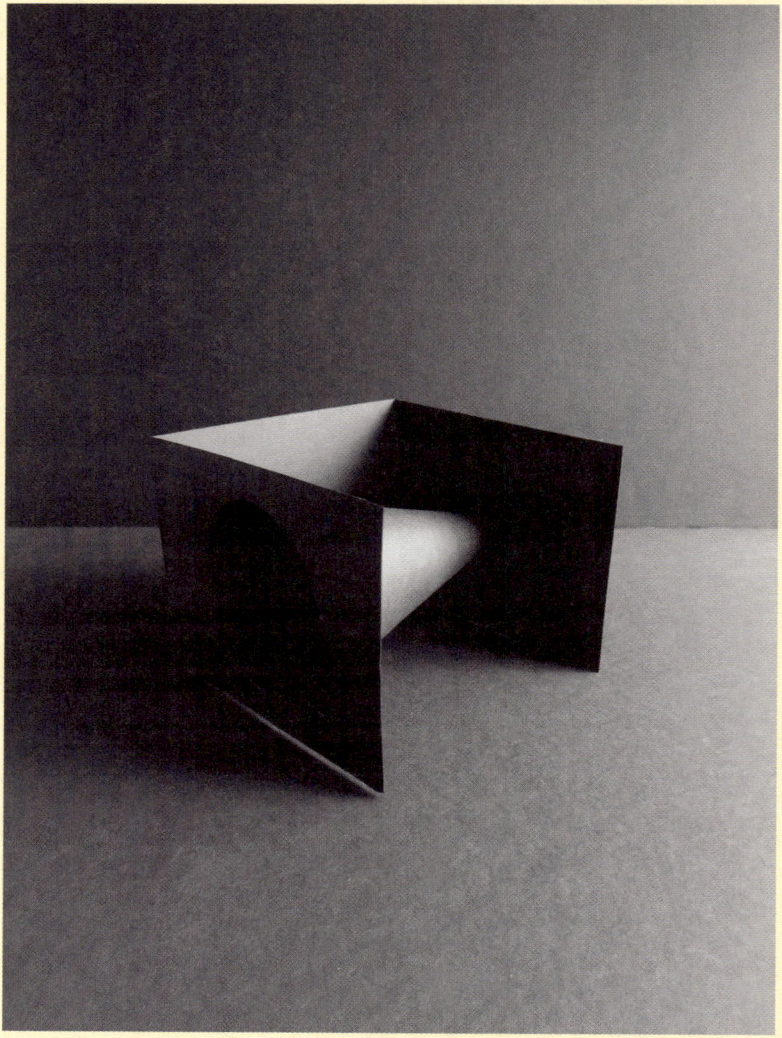

Fig. 21. Image of finished model pertaining to email exchanges before beginning the PhD.

In September 2017, I considered for the first time in my life pursuing a PhD. I knew enough from personal experience to be worried about surviving academia.[20] I had an inkling of a project in mind (i.e., the home tours project called "Our Everyday Forms") and, before considering a PhD, was thinking of pursuing grant funding or a residency or making it a casual personal project one weekend each month. The pursuit of a PhD with this project at the center made the intimacy and interiority of the project complex. I thought the one-to-one, *by us for us* values of "Our Everyday Forms" would become compromised by the values of capitalist knowledge production. Before deciding to take on a doctorate, given the opportunity, the questions asked about it are typically about how to do research and how to get on a path toward becoming "an intellectual in the modern university."[21]

Knowing I needed to be two steps ahead, I studied[22] and sought advice online. I found an article titled, "Living Beyond Survival: 11 Tips for Women of Color in Academia."[23] In it, Karen B. Hanna, the author, affirmed all my worries about being a PhD candidate. The

20 Karen B. Hanna, "Living Beyond Survival: 11 Tips for Women of Color in Academia," This Bridge Called Our Health, October 11, 2016, https://thisbridgecalledourhealth.wordpress.com/2016/10/11/living-beyond-survival-11-tips-for-women-of-color-in-academia.

21 "In the face of these conditions one can only sneak into the university and steal what one can. To abuse its hospitality, to spite its mission, to join its refugee colony, its gypsy encampment, to be in but not of - this is the path of the subversive intellectual in the modern university" (Harney and Moten, *The Undercommons*, 26).

22 "Moten and Harney propose that we prepare now for what will come by entering into study. Study, a mode of thinking with others separate from the thinking that the institution requires of you, prepares us to be embedded in what Harney calls 'the with and for' and allows you to spend less time antagonized and antagonizing" (Jack Halberstam, "The Wild Beyond: With and For the Undercommons," In The *Undercommons: Fugitive Planning & Black Study*, ed. Stefano Harney and Fred Moten [AK Press, 2013], 11).

23 Hanna, "Living Beyond Survival."

article gave concrete suggestions that signaled the need to consider tactics for navigating the university before I went in. I would stay in the periphery of the institution and create deliberate inlets into it for when it was appropriate to be present and involved. I sent her an email with the subject, "PhD Dilemma," to seek her advice.

We had a warm email exchange that left me with important things to consider and, ultimately, more equipped to become a remote, part-time PhD candidate. Those few messages written back and forth over several weeks felt to me like a quiet channel running between us. This channel can be recognized in cone shaped form in Fig. 21. I felt the loneliness[24] of what I was about to take on mellow out, thanks to a bridge connecting me to someone else who had already gone through it. What she offered me was wide. It funneled toward me—a narrow opening only just starting to expand. In the surround of this channel was negative space that reminds me of "what was not created for us."[25] I would have two modes of operating: in the quiet channel and out of the channel.

24 "They accuse us of not 'doing theory' even though a more critical analysis would show that we are creating theory rooted in these lived experiences" (Hanna, "Living Beyond Survival").

25 Hanna, "Living Beyond Survival."

C. USING BOTH REFLEXIVE WRITING AND MODEL-MAKING

8. ALIGNING DOUBLE CONSCIOUSNESS AND [HOW MY BODY MOVES]

SITTING WITH THE SHAPES MY BODY MAKES

The Main Concerns of this Context

This context became concerned with proper, respectable movement and refusing it. It was an exercise in bringing awareness to the tacit and constantly active changes in my body. It resulted in experiments where I physically leaned into everyday physical pain in white-dominated spaces or into the sensation of a desire to scream or get up and leave the room when restricted from doing so with ease.

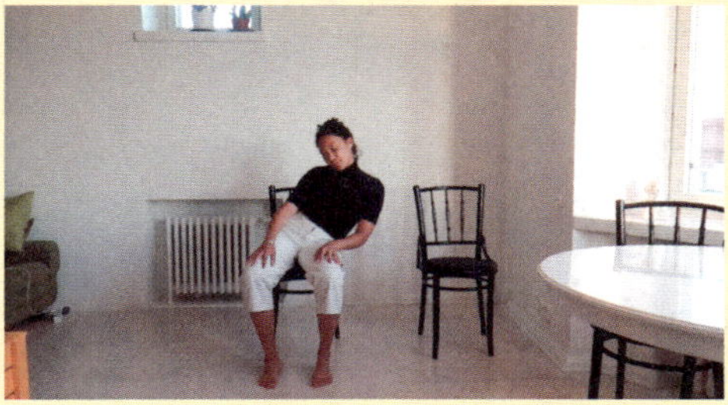

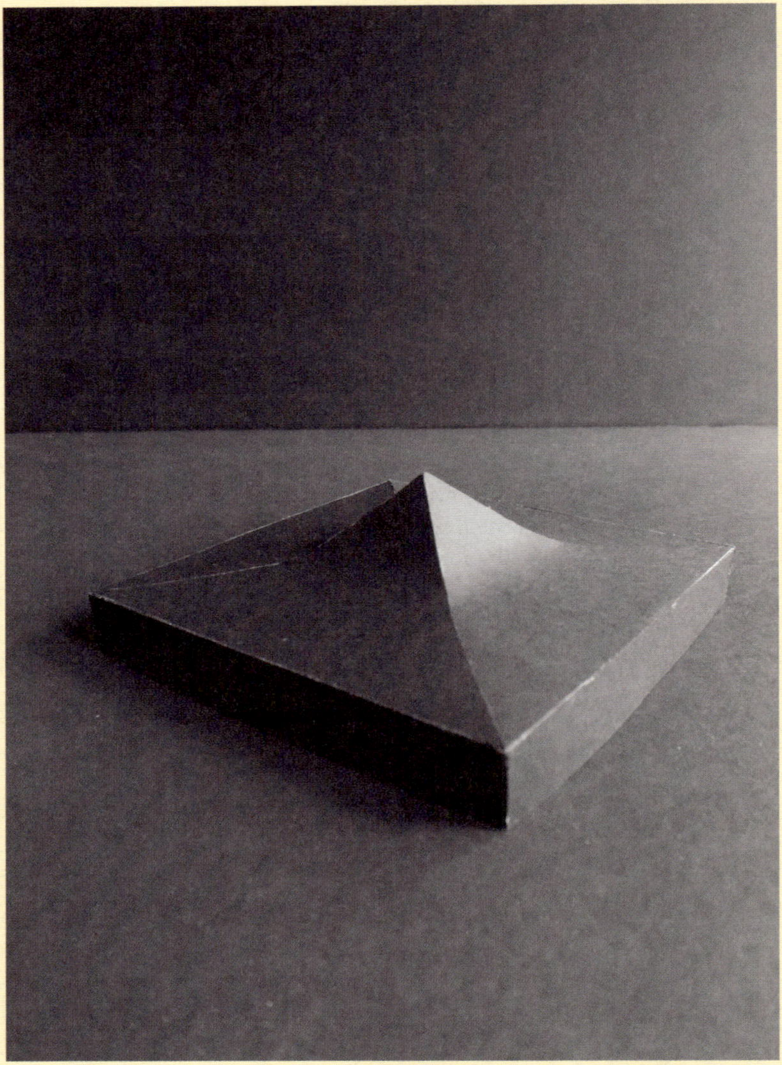

Fig. 23. Image of finished model pertaining to the shapes my body makes.

> *I am heading into a meeting that I have been hyping myself up to go to, building myself up to show up to. I feel tiny but dense and heavy as I walk up the street, into the building, and go up in the elevator. I feel nearly my original size by the time we all arrive and are sitting at the table but a little crooked and bent. I excuse myself to go to the bathroom because I feel a pounding in my head and pressure behind my eyes, and I throw up in the toilet. I feel better and back to full size but with lots of aches from being tiny and crooked. Thick oil was surrounding me back then, but I didn't know it. We start the meeting.*

Fig. 22. An excerpt from an unpublished, stream-of-consciousness essay, "How might you em/body your own becoming?"

When I sat down to attend to this, I let myself try to understand more precisely what was happening in the lead-up to the meeting with my colleagues. I did the sitting experiments every day and the writing experiments six months later. I was not certain at the time, but there seemed to be knowledge behind the embodied exercise I had conceived. When I attempted to explore this, I recalled one of the pieces of writing I had generated about the meeting, excerpted in Fig. 22.

I had written about how it felt to be there, but I revisited it, this time making visible how it felt to name that it happened in the first place. That effort felt like a fine point melting. The melting was not a kind of disarray or ruin, but was of the kind that settles in and spreads out into the foundations. I collected scraps of paper on my desk and sat down to give shape to these sensations. Seeing the model in Fig. 23 come together suggested to me how the point at its tip was the impossibly tight space I was giving myself to process the density, pressure, and aching I often felt leading up to loaded encounters—like that meeting that day. Seeing that sharp tip made visible how I internalize the "narrow, concrete driveway where I am unwelcome, ... a bleached-white, stiff-straight master plan."[26] I reproduced it in the fixed, tight space[27] I often give myself to process all that there is to process. In the context of this work meeting, for instance, the gaze on me flared up my self-awareness—a hyper-awareness of how I *appear* in the meetings as unfocused or tensely aimless.

How did this fine, fixed point come to melt? Naming the aching and pressure reminded me of my habit of suppressing or pushing past the gaze. It was a necessary and always welcome refamiliarizing. Putting the model together let me see what it feels like when I do linger and stay[28] in the aches and quietude.[29] I made visible how it felt to name the details of this event in the first place, and it

26 Bruce, "Mad Is a Place," 352.

27 La Marr Jurelle Bruce "would rather brave the pointy tips of sandspurs than cross a bleached-white, stiff-straight picket fence that pricks and wounds [their] black queer feeling" ("Mad Is a Place," 52).

28 "This loitering queers and signifies upon the legal category of 'vagrancy,' which was enshrined in (anti-) Black Codes throughout the US South after the Civil War. Furthermore, this loitering converges and conspires with Fred Moten's 'fugitivity' (2007), with Tina Campt's 'fugitivity' (2014), with Sarah Cervenak's 'wandering' (2014), with Saidiya Hartman's 'waywardness' (2015), and with my own 'derangement' (Bruce 2017) – all captioning blackness out of (legally and culturally sanctioned) place. Whereas fugitivity, wandering, waywardness, and derangement are modes of motion defying modern mandates for 'proper' movement, loitering is slowness or stillness that violates said mandates. The fugitive goes when told to stay, while the loiterer stays when told to go" ("Mad Is a Place," 353).

29 "What this represents is an ethic of quiet, the sense that the interior can inform a way of being in the world that is not consumed by publicness but that is expressive and dynamic nonetheless. This scene is a rare characterization of a black subject exploring herself and trying to understand what being human means for her beyond the prescriptions of social identities" (Quashie, *The Sovereignty of Quiet*, 52).

grounded me in what I already know: "the *appearance* of aimlessness might conceal a truth of deliberation, strategy, and care."[30]

There are three parts to consider. First is the exploration in meditative sitting that acted as the context. Second is the reflexive writing about moving through a city, up an elevator, and making my way to a meeting. Third, is the reflexive model making that was a meta-reflection on how it was to make visible an incident like the one I wrote about. In each activity, I slowly came to build a thicker understanding of the repeating concerns across all three parts: they are each varying "modes of motion defying mandates for 'proper' movement."[31] Through working in these three ways, I recognized the meditative sitting I did as a small defiance; I had crafted an exercise for myself that let me listen to my body and physically, literally lean into sensations rather than keeping still in them or plowing through them. I storied the tiny, dense, heavy, crooked, bent, purging, aching, and surroundedness to account for all these muted, hidden, private, inner movements present at that time. And lastly, the cutting, gluing, and making I did let me see why and how these modes were "defiance" in the first place.

The description above is part of a previously published essay titled, "A Place to Meet: How Critical Theory Cares for the Everyday in Artistic Practice."[32]

30 Bruce, "Mad Is a Place."

31 Bruce, "Mad Is a Place," 353.

32 Myriam D. Diatta, Stacy H. Jones, and Kate McEntee, "A Place to Meet: How Critical Theory Cares for the Everyday in Artistic Practice," *Research in Arts and Education Journal: Special Issue on Critical Artistic Research as Practices of Care,* December 2021.

9. ALIGNING DOUBLE CONSCIOUSNESS AND [WHOM I WRITE TO]

REMAKING TO WHOM AND HOW I WRITE

The Main Concerns of this Context

This context—an academic paper—analyzed the codes of conduct set by citation manuals and journal templates. This context was concerned with how to take care of multiple aligned and discordant theories and author backgrounds. It was concerned with resisting showing up with an authoritative, static objectivity toward producing knowledge.

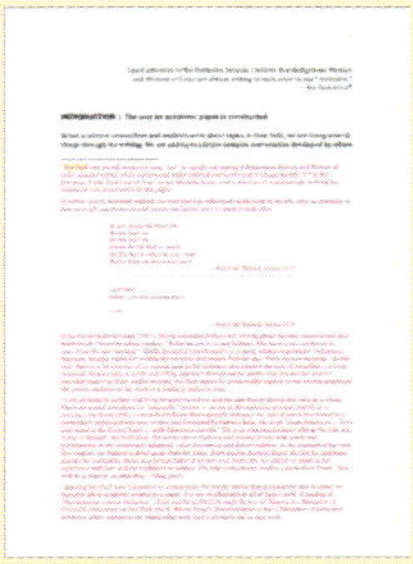

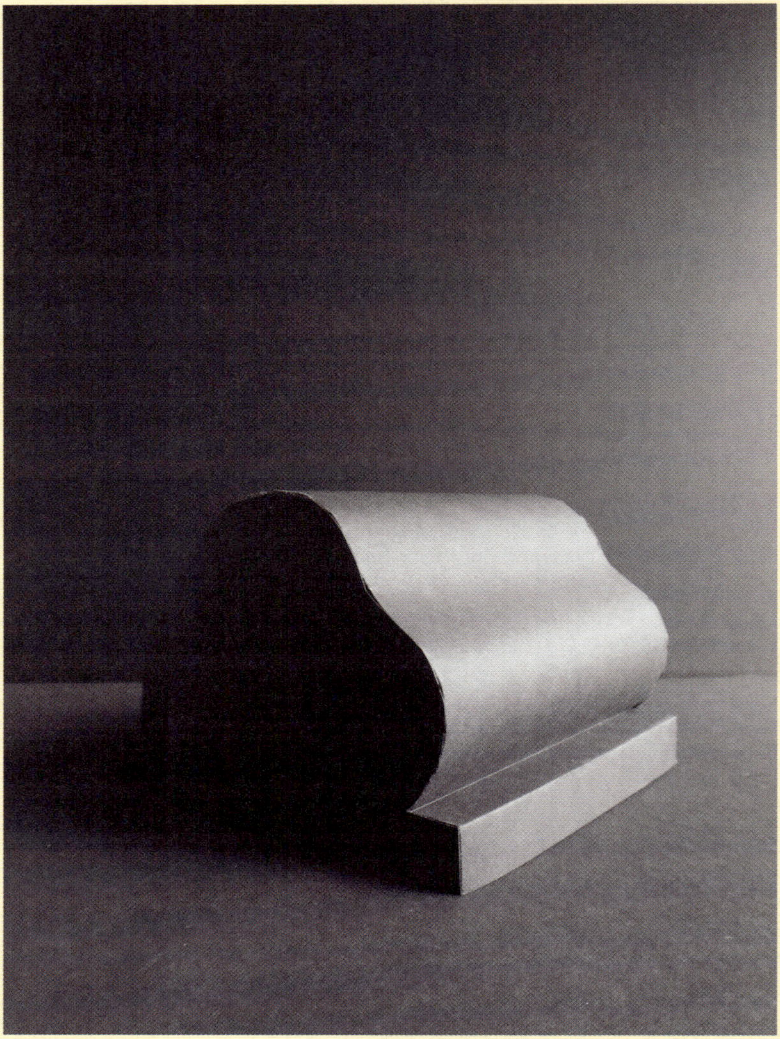

Fig. 24. Image of finished model pertaining to writing the unpublished essay, "I Paid Attention to the Footnotes."

I paid attention to the footnotes because I believe that Indigenous Women and Women of Color are always writing to each other in our[1] footnotes.[2]
— Eve Tuck (The Graduate Center, CUNY 2013)[3]

INTRODUCTION | The way an academic paper is constructed

When academic researchers and students write about topics in their field, we are doing several things through the writing. We are adding to a larger complex conversation developed by others.

....

1. Eve Tuck (2013) uses the plural, possessive case "our" to signify a grouping of Indigenous women and women of color situated within white supremacist settler-colonial patriarchy and to situate herself, "I," in this grouping. I take Tuck's use of "our" as her speaking to me, and this is why I see it as appropriate to bring her statement into conversation in this paper.

In nejma, Nayyirah Waheed (2014), the poet who has influenced more than any other in my life, gives us examples of how we might use pronouns and passive and active voice to speak to each other.

do not choose the lesser life.
do you hear me.
do you hear me.
choose the life that is. yours.
the life that is seducing your lungs.
that is dripping down your chin.
— (Waheed 2014)

Fig. 25. Excerpt from an unpublished essay, "I Paid Attention to the Footnotes."

A quote is used as the epigraph on the first page of my essay, "I Paid Attention To The Footnotes," shown in Fig. 25. To it, I added three superscript numbers that point to footnotes. Those three footnotes overtake three-quarters of the first page of the essay. The contents of the footnotes open a conversation between me, Eve Tuck, and other scholars and artists. It is in the footnotes that I surface why I have brought Tuck with me into this paper. I bring with me the poet Nayyirah Waheed and her use of the first-person voice to address her intended and non-intended readers. I continue by unpacking parts of Tuck's body of work with which I do not align. I used the traditional structure of a research paper to mess with its hierarchies and tone. I considered the footnotes, endnotes, sources, and even ideas and drafts left out as components of an academic paper. This essay was an exercise in taking up space with the colliding, negotiating, and caring for that goes on behind the body of a paper.

I brought Waheed, Tuck, Toni Morrison, Danez Smith, Jenny Boully, and dozens of others with me to the footnotes. Forgoing the convention that "the body" of the text (above ground) is where the most important things happen, I put on a more formal voice in the body and reserved my conversations, dilemmas, and theoretical groundings for the footnotes. Typing out lines from Waheed's poetry into the footnotes situated the conversation I was having with her work. It was a weight at the bottom of my spine. It felt as if it were anchoring me there in the horizontal block at the bottom of the page. This can be seen in Fig. 24. However, the stability I felt and the enclosed space there were only temporary. Slowly, the impressions and echoes of Waheed, Tuck, and others' work seeped through and began to bubble upwards. By looking inwards, I came to understand what the footnotes were doing for me as the author. When I began writing the essay, I was set on making it an exercise in how I preserve our inner conversations while keeping an eye on what is public and exterior. What the model-making process showed me was the movement between things.[33] It brought attention to what I was already doing—*traversing* the body and the footnotes, not simply separating the two.

33 Yoko Akama, "Attuning to Ma (between-ness) in Designing," *Proceedings of the 13th Participatory Design Conference 2* (2014):2124, ACM, https://doi.org/10.1145/2662155.2662179.

CHAPTER FIVE

This chapter comes out of the interiorities of the previous chapter to look back at the meaning this framework has for creative work and our political bodies.

The previous chapter moved from situation to situation, exposing how I used the framework and my methods over a three-year period from 2019 to 2021.

Chapter 5 serves to close the explorations of the framework. I do so by imparting the sensibilities that were necessary for the work. I make plain the numerous ways in which theory and the everyday mutually articulated one another. I restate the social implications I called out at the opening of this book—*What is at stake?*—and underscore what the contents of this book offer to practice-led research.

I close the chapter with a statement on whom this framework is for, acting as a transition into Chapter 6, a comprehensive hands-on guide for critical creative practitioners to start using the framework.

1
WHAT IT TOOK

A surface-level evaluation of what it takes to do this work may have hinged on how well I show mastery over relevant theories and how well I applied theory to my practice. A functionalist approach will have sought to eradicate contradictions and systematically fix misalignments in practice.

Instead, the priority as I developed my *parallel practice* was to design an approach to inquiry that is capable of supporting embodied ways of knowing—like grinning, twirling, and double consciousness. My efforts in using the framework should be evaluated for the ways and extent to which I mess with the notion of thinking with written theory and the doing of everyday life. I assert that *doing theory, thinking practice* is a framework capable of enabling embodied, creative, and critical inquiry. At the end of the Introduction chapter, I named an admiration and wish for practitioners to expose what it takes for them to show up in the way they do, to lift the hood or pull back the curtain. Here, I expose what it took to do this work.

IT TOOK A LATERAL APPROACH

Looking back at what I did, I foreground that I was constantly triangulating theory, my personal experience, and making. By moving laterally while I worked, I was able to engage the three at once. I needed my lateral way of working to build the structure of the framework, to piece together what entails a *parallel practice*, to use the reflexive methods, and to define many more aspects of my practice.

I put forth a working definition that describes the lateral manner in which I worked. With the term "lateral," I refer to an orientation from or to the side. The roots of many plants grow laterally from its primary root, spreading wide. Anatomically, lateral views of the body suggest views from the side, revealing inner structures, depth, thickness, displacements and layers not accessible otherwise. Importantly, the term describes a dynamic relation. This manner of working was not linear or vertical. I did not follow a sequence of pre-planned steps. It was not funneled upwards or downwards toward a single resolution. Nor was it an exercise in free association or open-ended experimentation.

In the midst of making a paper model or composing a piece or writing, I drew conceptual analogies. I linked adjacencies. This is described in Chapter 3, Section 2, and demonstrated in Chapter 4. From an embodied place in practice, I looked to a past experience. From that orientation, I work inwards to access the conflicts and impressions present in my body. These impressions move me back outwards, creating different understandings about my double consciousness. I consider the following: How do I stay with the sensation and move within it? What is familiar? What kind of minor moves might I make to begin turning it outwards, to materialize it? In this outward movement, my experience branches out and is confronted, carried out, and thickened by critical theory.

I attended to my personal experience. I allowed for it to affect and be affected by theory. In the process of making a paper model, for instance, I related its shapes and trajectories to La Marr Jurelle Bruce's notions of "mandates for proper movement."[1] I could only do this by simultaneously attending to the ethos of this notion. The essence of this concept stayed with me from my first reading of Bruce's essay. The forms I made were the vehicle to remember and to think with multiple theories at once. They are what allowed me to work laterally across periods of time and the ethos of theory.

Additionally, it was important that the structure of the

1 Bruce, "Mad Is a Place," 353.

framework inherently encourages this lateral work. In Chapter 2, to establish theoretical grounds that can support what I have done in practice, I drew together cases across methodological influences. This required confidence in working laterally—not only was I influenced by what Stuart Hall, Della Pollock, and Stacy Holman Jones each offer about theory and practice, but I also pulled forward implicit connections across them. I did not pick an established framework off the shelf but traced and then pulled a single methodological throughline across three scholars and fields of study that supported what I was doing in practice. The framework, once I defined it, allowed for the work to maintain simultaneous contact with theory, making, and lived experience.

Finding a relevant and critical conversation to join also required a lateral approach. In Chapter 2, I situated three creative practices together beyond their disciplines and distinct political directions. Across Daria Garina, Torkwase Dyson, and Robin Boylorn, I highlighted the qualities of their work that delineated a relevant home for all that I had made and developed. Connecting their practices contributed to making the case for what I call a *parallel practice*. The lateral qualities of my practice support my non-disciplinary orientation to inquiry. Through this work, I have come to know that the qualities that make my *parallel practice* distinct are its conceptual, analogous, and lateral sensibilities.

IT TOOK A POLITICIZED COMMITMENT AND A SET OF ATTRIBUTES

What have I committed to? I could only start this work by identifying what I aimed to commit to in the first place. Because of the complex, constantly moving conditions of our social lives, this is an ever-changing endeavor.

I committed to double consciousness. To commit to doing

double consciousness and to theories about double consciousness meant being attentive to constant negotiations with the boundaries of what may or may not be aligned with the commitments. These attempts are grounded by naming a collection of attributes or features that make up the commitment. The specificity lets me approach my *parallel practice* with closer attentiveness and provides a vocabulary for understanding how my practice was changing. Along the development of this practice, five attributes of my double consciousness have emerged: illegibility, fragmentation, multiplicity, quiet, and periphery. Below are my personal working definitions of these attributes. Importantly, these commitments below emerged from being in my practice, not from following an external set of values determined by someone else. They were qualities that I repeatedly noticed in my work thanks to using reflexive writing and paper model making. I detail how my practice and theory interpenetrated and mutually influenced one another.

> *Fragmentation* refers to resistance against narrative as something clean, that "makes sense," and connects parts in coherent ways. While we may occasionally squeeze into the shape of a coherent narrative with a beginning, middle, and end, the temporality and shape of our bodies and lives stay fragmented. I felt the relations between the fragmented parts as dissonance. It is Dionne Brand, poet and essayist on Blackness, who makes clear for us, "Narrative contains our demise. ... [The] pressure of that shape on Black life. The bargain of narrative is an exchange of death for less death."[2] The doubling and multiplying of my consciousnesses, our existence, the constitution of my body, our form, and aesthetic are antithetical to the nature of narrative.

2 Dionne Brand, "Dionne Brand: The Shape of Language," 28:25.

Illegibility refers to one of the dimensions of my double consciousness—that of the private realm. For outsiders—and the many ways that may be defined by a person with double consciousnesses: there are thoughts, relationships, expressions, and ways of being in the world that will always be opaque and illegible. It refuses transparency.

Multiplicity refers to the multiple compounding and harmful imaginations, systems, structures, and ideologies we navigate. Multiplicity refers to the corresponding lenses we carry, which Gloria Anzaldúa refers to as "plural modes"[3] and Legacy Russell regards as a splintering, expanded consciousness.[4] We put mechanisms in place that account for these compounding gazes and charges—mechanisms like our two-way mirrors[5] and the use of both serpent and eagle eyes[6] at once.

Periphery is the position of being at the edge and at a distance. It is being peripheral to centralized, dominating positions, which means remaining in a less harmful periphery. It means taking up space, being neverending, and staying tethered to the periphery of dominating, harmful ways of showing up.

Quiet can be synonymous with motionlessness, complicity, or silence. However, this space is not emptiness. It instead describes "a stay against the dominance of the social world."[7] Quiet is the volume at which our dreams, devastations, fights, fears, and vulnerabilities make themselves lived and felt.

3 Anzaldúa, *Borderlands*, 101.

4 Russell, *Glitch Feminism*.

5 Boylorn, *Sweetwater*.

6 Anzaldúa, *Borderlands*.

7 Quashie, *The Sovereign of Quiet*, 6.

This set of attributes was not treated as a checklist, nor does it work like a determined set of workplace values. The attributes emerged from every which way when I sat down for a day of reflexive writing exercises or a morning of model making. It became clear that these attributes were the rich details of my experience with double consciousness and that they would continue to develop.

For instance, when I sat down to read a theoretical book, its contents would remind of the constant opacity and illegibility with which I operated every day. As I made models, I recognized edges and peripheries within them. In the middle of an interview, I recognized my own disorienting multiplicity. I read articles and books through which I sharpened my radar and thickened my understanding of the quiet of my own interior life. I started to remember a kind of incoherence and fragmentation in my experience as a teenager walking down to Roswell Mill.[8] I came to know that there was, in fact, an intentional commitment behind how I told a personal story—sharing it one way with one person, omitting a detail with another, and telling it differently again for another audience. I recognized how incoherent and fragmented it felt looking out from Île de Gorée on my first trip back to my birth city years ago.

At times, I encountered things that did not feel familiar. I had a stable enough footing in my own commitments to challenge theories and think, "We know better." [9] At other times, things did feel familiar, and yet I understood it as inappropriate to fold them into my work. It takes a busy, sprawling tangle of reading, doing, watching, sensing, thinking, making, carrying, linking, and being to arrive at this living collection of commitments.

8 I was an intern at an architecture firm from the age of 16 to 18. The office was housed in a former cotton mill built in Roswell, Georgia, US in 1882.

9 Alexis Gumbs, *Undrowned: Black Feminist Lessons from Marine Mammals* (AK Press, 2020).

IT TOOK MULTIPLE PATHS

There were dozens of footpaths that accumulated while traversing between the textual theory I read and my design practice. The footpaths can be regarded as running between practice that is done and critical theory that is thought about. More specific to my case, the everyday living of double consciousness and abstract written theorizations about double consciousness. When viewed methodologically, the paths could be articulated as running between being and knowing, making and thinking. When viewed onto-epistemologically, everyday acts of grinning, twirling, doubling, loitering, and going-on-living resist the separation of theory and practice from their outset. However, when institutions, publications, and other platforms produce books, lectures, articles, discourse, and texts that separate theory and practice, those of us who engage with the ideas produced in these formats must learn to bridge our actions and these ideas we value. It is when we look to intensify and deliberately practice our values that attending to any separations becomes worthwhile. Below are a series of paths I have found myself taking while moving between reading theoretical texts and doing my practice. My aim was not to complete the task of identifying all possible paths between theory and practice. To know about or be able to convincingly discuss the relationships of theory and practice is one thing—to internalize and embody the relationships is another. The capacity to intentionally deepen the relationship between theory and practice is yet another endeavor.

One Path: Sometimes, ***doing theory*** is not practiced deliberately.

Far more often than not, many of us "do theory" and engage with practice and theory at once without ever hearing the terminology or any of the academics who have theorized, written, published, and popularized the theories. This work does not belong to academia. Often, we merge doing and thinking and are in lockstep with them without any explicit effort to identify, let alone deliberately circulate the two.

Another Path: Sometimes I happen to recognize theory in the practice.

Sometimes, as I sat in someone's living room for an interview or at my keyboard writing about a past experience, I bumped into and recognized the critical theory nestled in that moment. Because of the ideas I had already come to know about the structures and ideologies, I could recognize the quiet or the illegibility in the comment a person made or my understanding of the histories of a place in which we were gathered. I happened to access theories I had already come to know, and which kept me company as I worked to navigate the weight of being in that living room or sitting there, drafting that essay.

Another Path: Sometimes I happen to recognize practice in the theory.

While sitting down to read discussions about a theory in a book or article, or while watching two people have a conversation about theory at an event, I recognize a critique or conviction in the discussion that strikes me and leads me to think about practice. Theory can generate momentum that reactivates my relationship with my practice. Other times, a sentence in a book or a comment made in a theoretical discussion makes me consider my own, the author, or the speaker's everyday political life. Through this process, I came to understand the ways that theory can tug on our internal unrest as we confront the ways we move in the world.

Another Path: Sometimes, I spent time growing a library of critical theories.

I was watching endless videos on the internet, scouring Google Scholar and my university library, bugging scholars to talk to me about their work, downloading zines being passed around, reminding myself of conversations with friends and family, jotting down notes from lectures and seminars, and ordering books on the internet to read. Your theory may be something your grandmother taught you, it may come from literature in a formal field of study, it may take the shape of getting struck while dancing, come from an interview with an artist, or a video essay on the internet recorded on a kitchen floor. Spending time with these critical worldviews in bed, in the shower, through exhaustion, at the keyboard, has shaped not only how I understand systems and structures but my entire conception of how the world is made. It affects how I show up and make meaning of the time I spend with people and in places. By *doing theory, thinking practice*, I have come to develop ways of reading and listening that slow the pace and weight of the sensation of being messed with by critical theories.

Another Path: Sometimes I sat at my desk or on the floor and said, "Ok, I'm now going to exercise my skills for *doing theory, thinking practice*."

I did reflexive model making and reflexive writing with the intent of feeling my way into my political commitments more deeply and to grow a stronger critical reflexivity. This mattered to me, as I thought of the undertaking as a kind of self-preservation and as preparation for collective action. Contemporary American jazz musician Wynton Marsalis tells us, When you feel the swing, you don't just stay there, you swing some more. Intentionally exercising the ways I am *doing theory* is the "swinging some more" that lets me continuously re-understand and re-make my understanding of the structures we navigate.

Another Path: Sometimes I brought the theory with me to shape the practice.

These paths I have taken over and over have come to provide me with a skillset. I am progressively developing an awareness of how I do my practice. For instance, remembering what a family member had said about being illegible 15 years ago, knowing its truth, and practicing this illegibility in a conflict with a colleague. Or hearing the silence of Thelonious Monk's piano in a YouTube video from 1966, watching him get up from his piano as he shuffled towards Charlie Rouse singing on tenor sax, and doing Monk's quiet in a community event I attended. Or doing the two-way mirror that Robin M. Boylorn framed in her writing during a conference call at work. The sensitivity toward the ways I am *doing theory* shows through in the slightest of ways—like where a sentence is placed on a page—and shows through in wide, lateral ways, too—like decisions about who and how to collaborate on a years-long project.

Settling into the political commitment of my practice not only involved having a stack of books on the shelf to pull from, having a folder of documents to reference, or engaging in an inquiry that stacked theory onto theory. I came to recognize my lived experience in written theory. In turn, I recognized theory in my everyday lived experience. This means letting critical theories about our social lives affect me to the degree that it tints the way I see the world, the way I hear what others are saying, and how I attempt to make sense of the things I experience. I problematize the notion that aligning values and actions is limited to a one-way path of aligning my actions to theory or to other abstract concepts like values and principles. I came to know the relationship between theory and practice through my movements traversing them and by recognizing, with precision, where and how they are already interpenetrated. I developed a rhythmic and repetitive relationship with theory and practice.

2
REVISITING WHAT IS AT STAKE

One of the first statements I made in this book was, "In every political act lies a relationship between what is done and what is valued in theory. The ways we show up in a meeting, for a friend, fund a project, or respond to an emergency may be in tension with the politicized commitments with which we may associate." These misalignments have consequences at both intimate and societal scales.

I developed and applied this framework over three years. By 2021, it had materially changed how I work. It reshaped how I position myself in interviews, how I attend to my body under tension, how I read and digest academic literature, and how I define the boundaries of my design practice.

Through this process, I grew into an ease with my quiet, illegible, multiple, peripheral, and fragmented ways of showing up. This ease is not complacent; it is deliberate and self-aware. I am attentive to whom I speak to, when I speak, and where I place my effort—as a researcher, designer, community member, and friend. This has made my actions more centered, more aligned with the worldviews to which I am committed, and more open to challenge without easily becoming destabilized.

This shift also became visible in public settings. One small example of this happened during the question-and-answer portion of a lecture I gave in 2021. In my answer, I spoke directly about why I work the way I do without deferring to established design fields to authorize my practice. Where I used to lean on established disciplines like service design or speculative design to attempt to give myself credibility, I now relate with the discipline of design without depending on its validation.

Between 2020 and 2021, I initiated three communities and working groups aligned with my political commitments. They ranged from an intimate monthly gathering of five to online communities of approximately fifty and two hundred participants. These spaces are not organized around formal theory-making or design exercises, but we made them explicitly reflective, critical, and slow. When I first proposed them, my expertise was not in how to govern or structure our gatherings, but in naming our commitments and building paths to continue radicalizing our critical perspectives.

3
PRACTICE-LED RESEARCH

Similar to the way that other research disciplines—be it sports science or archaeology—study how things work in their disciplines to further understand and advance things with the intention that the published research trickles down to everyday professional practice, the research fields of art, design, performance, and architecture do the same. I've had the chance to come across researchers based in Melbourne, New York, Helsinki, Stockholm, Aarhus, and Copenhagen who are interested in an important meta-perspective. To varying degrees, they are stopping to ask, *How can we study critical creative practice? By third-person observation? By curating after the fact?*

By historical analysis? Is there theory in these practices? What knowledges do they produce? If we're trained as historians, critics, or anthropologists, how do we advise and evaluate the creative practitioner whose project we supervise? My PhD itself was nurtured in a practice-led research lab, WonderLab at Monash University, leading the way in answering these questions.

Redesigning PhD evaluation from inside the academic institution is outside the scope of the aims and audience of this book and my current capacities as an independent scholar. I do argue that the framework, methods, and process presented in this book are one answer to these meta-questions. I respond not in theory but in practice.

WHO SHOULD DO THE THEORIZING AND EVALUATING?

The critical creative practitioner themself is equipped to articulate the goings-on in their own practice. In both an ideological and deeply emotional and convicted way, the process developed here bets on the epistemic depths of critical creative practice. Rather than 'speaking from nowhere'—in which a gigantic gap between thinking and doing is enforced, the practitioner becomes equipped to speak back to theory from their bodies, particular social contexts, and making knowledges.

HOW CAN THE PRACTITIONER "PROVE" THEIR CRITICALITY? WHERE'S THE THEORY?

As critical practitioners who are racialized, gendered, classed, disabled, etc., theory is already being done in our everyday practice. Disability studies, gender studies, Black Studies, etc., are often first lived through a theorist's own body—irrespective of whether it eventually gets written about, published, or reified via the academic institution. We only need to revisit past experiences in our practice, scan the sensations in our bodies, and materialize them in order to locate the theory and 'prove'—to ourselves primarily—that it's present.

IS THE RESEARCH CRITICAL ENOUGH? ARTISTIC OR DESIGNERLY ENOUGH?

Art, design, architecture, and performance educators look to instill self-awareness and professional and academic maturity in their students. Through this framework, the practitioner learns to:

1. locate with precision the theory in their practice;
2. write about the ways it's present in their practice;
3. redefine concepts and theories in terms of their own practice;
4. detail how the theory in their practice speaks back to relevant lineages and schools of thought.

Creative practitioners who are politically engaged negotiate socio-political concepts as we glue, code, weld, cut, twist, etc. I wish for those of us who work with socio-political contexts in conceptual and creative ways to engage with theory spaciously and intensely—approaching it as a space for intimate embodied exploration, radical world-making, and unmaking.

4
BY WHOM, FOR WHOM?

Through this process, I investigated my own experience so that I may bring stronger self-accountability to collective efforts with others. Using the methods was an inquiry into my own ways of knowing the world as someone who lives with double consciousness. Double consciousness is one of many ways of knowing that is specifically politicized, lived-in, and necessary. By this phrase—politicized, lived-in, necessary ways of knowing—I mean it is a particular way of knowing that is a chronic, everyday reality that imparts knowledge about the ways in which the world works. This is a shared type or genre of ways of knowing.

Behind this individual scale lies the question, "What is the scale of our 'individual' experience?" During situations in which you are reflecting on your own lived experiences, it is not necessarily about yourself. Our personal subjectivities are structured by systems of oppression and therefore make the conditions with which a person lives collective in particular ways. This is not to be mistaken with subsuming, universalizing, or generalizing any and all experience. The particular ways that W. E. B. Du Bois, Alice Walker, Robin M. Boylorn, and Legacy Russell each speak to their Black American positionalities and their relationships to whiteness as mirrored, two-way, doubled, and tripled are not identical, but they are shared in subtle and unmistakable ways. There are places or points at which our deeply specific, personal, situated positionalities intersect. This place is where Akeema's boarding school experience meets my Southern American public high school experience. It is where my experience of growing up ten minutes away from a former chattel slave plantation briefly met the workers at the former Spanish slave camp I visited in Mexico. This book has demonstrated methods and paths for entering this shared space.

This book and its framework were created for those of us with politicized, embodied ways of knowing. Outside of the scope of my personal explorations, for you, your knowing may stem from borderlands at which you recognize the multiple consciousnesses of growing up in an anti-Indigenous geopolitical border. It may be Black queerness, where you recognize the fragmentation you live with that defies mandates for proper movement. It may be acculturation, where your state of being has come to be deeply embedded in having to assimilate into dominating Western cultures. You may recognize your politicized, lived-in, necessary way of knowing as double consciousness, as I have, where multiple gazes upon you instill a particular kind of self-awareness. Acculturation, double consciousness, borderlands consciousness, queerness, and many other critical theories are written about but first lived in. They are experienced through oneself, imparting knowledge about ways of showing up in the everyday. Living and thinking in them is what gives shape to ways of remaining critical and armed in dominating social conditions. In this project, the treatment of these ways of knowing was not to fix or eradicate them. It was not to imagine it possible to transcend the fact that you live in a hostile geopolitical border or to replace the self-awareness you use to survive the prongs of whiteness with something else. Like I asserted in Chapter 1, these would be dangerous endeavors. This work is about recognizing your ways of knowing that are required in the oppressive conditions that generate them in the first place. It is to recognize that how you know the world has its own depths and wisdoms to it.

•

While my experience and the descriptions of the framework come to a close here, the final chapter is a liminal space; Part 3, Chapter 6 is designed to transition you out of reading about the approach to using this approach yourself.

Even if you do not plan to use the hands-on guide illustrated in Chapter 6, I recommend reading through it to fully close the loop on how this exploration started with actual experience and professional practice, theorized what happened in practice, and offers a functional guide for doing practice-led research.

PART THREE

CHAPTER SIX

This final chapter is a hands-on guide. It is designed to transition you out of reading about the framework to using the framework yourself.

WHAT IS THIS GUIDE?

This is an introductory guide. It is not necessary to have read the previous chapters of this book before diving in. This chapter should be used as a workbook to learn about the inner workings of your own critical creative practice.

It walks you through how to do so layer by layer:

Preparing
Skill 1: Body Scanning
Skill 2: Materializing
Skill 3: Locating Theory in the Material Record
Skill 4: Recognizing What is Between Theory and Practice
Exiting

Skills & Process
Each of the four distinct skills are a component you will learn to use together. Collectively, the skills will be referred to as "the process."

Exiting
While the section on Exiting is at the very end of the book, I strongly recommend reading about what may be required to wrap up a session before you start using this guide.

Book Jacket
On the inside of the book jacket, you will find the prompts for the four skills summarized. This way, the second, third, and hopefully dozens of times you work with the skills and overall process, you can return to the summary and this in-depth guide for direction.

Demonstrations
Chapter 4 features nine in-depth demonstrations of the process.

WHO IS IT FOR?

1. The prompts in this guide are written and designed primarily for creative practitioners who are politically engaged.

   The process requires the practitioner to have previous experience studying and using socio-political concepts in their work.

   This process is designed for many types of creative work. It asks the practitioner to repurpose their own material know-how: of working both conceptually and technically through painting, writing, playing an instrument, sewing garments, dancing, coding, etc. The guide will show you how to adapt your making skills toward investigating past experiences in your own practice.

   As of 2025, the process has been used by musicians, spatial designers, performers, visual artists, and writers with various educational experiences, including PhD and master's students, and auto-didactic professionals. I continue to teach the process to politically-engaged creative practitioners and encourage you to adapt it to your creative practice.

2. This process can also be used by anyone who works in social or political contexts.

   I developed the earliest variations of this process between 2012 and 2018 through collaborations with clinicians and parents participating in family therapy, K12 educators, cultural workers, public health workers, and librarians. With them, I facilitated reflective exercises in which they used metaphors to materialize intangible components of their professional practice—therapy principles, cognitive science models, community values, harm reduction principles, and workplace values, respectively.

This process will involve identifying and using defined, abstract concepts (referred to here as theories) you already use in your practice. I used prompts similar to the ones in this guide to help participants reflect on past experiences, make the intangible tangible, negotiate their qualities, and practice them more deliberately.

If your political practice does not involve traditional design, performance, or visual art, start by using writing as the creative medium you work with.

WHAT SHOULD I EXPECT?

You will learn four skills that, when used together and repeatedly, allow you to study the inner workings of your practice.

You can find the links between what you make in your studio or rehearsal space and the political ideas you care about. You can mature your understandings of the collective ethos—made up of you, your peers, and your environment. You can give ample space to the fragmented, incoherent, impossible conditions of being in your political body. You can gain language to describe how detailed elements in your practice come together. You can become more accountable to the things you value. Importantly, you can build a thicker understanding of what happens between theory and practice.

This may not feel easy. It can be conceptually challenging. It can be deeply emotionally challenging. I did not translate the organic process I developed into prompts in this guide with ease as the aim; I designed the prompts for clarity. You may find completing a task difficult, understanding the whole process conceptually overwhelming, or you may feel emotionally affected by the personal things that come up as you work with past experiences.

I have carefully laid out notes, tips, and heaps of examples as tender guardrails for you along the way. Take it one step, one prompt at a time.

WHAT WILL BE GENERATED?

The tangible outputs of using the process are

1. Materializations of your inner experience. The materializations take the form of the actual medium(s) of your creative practice.
2. Written entries containing your inner experience—importantly, with theory woven throughout its contents. These pieces of writing may be kept simply as journal entries or incorporated into a practice-led doctoral dissertation or master's thesis.

WHAT DO I NEED TO START?

This guide will help you carve out space and time to study your own practice. A *parallel practice* is a mode of working that is separate yet adjacent to your usual critical creative practice. It is a concentrated time for studying the inner workings of theory and practice.

For more, see Chapter 2, Section 2, Demarcating "Parallel Practice" and Chapter 3, Section 1, Defining My Parallel Practice.

YOU NEED SPACE

This guide is designed for you to crack it open while you are in your creative workspace. You should refer to it as you work. You will need

1. the materials you use in your creative practice
2. access to the critical and political references you usually work with. *E.g. books, films, audio recordings, poems, etc.*

YOU NEED TIME

To complete the Preparing section, you will need approximately half a day.

The time required to complete one full cycle of the process will vary depending on your level of familiarity with the types of prompts given and your proficiency with taking in approaches that are new to you. It may take one day or require several sessions over a few days.

YOU NEED A PLACE TO WRITE

Throughout the guide, you are provided with designated space to write, marked by large rectangles drawn with a thick black line.

You may choose to try the process for the first time by writing your responses directly in the space provided in this book. You may then write in your own notebook when you use the process in the future. Or, you may choose to keep the writing space in this book blank and only write in your own notebook.

Your *parallel practice* is a particular kind of work and may require a designated notebook. Each time you go through the full process, you will need approximately five notebook pages or their equivalent in a digital format to take notes and do the writing exercises.

Stay organized—you'll need to find and refer to your notes as you work through the guide.

YOU NEED A FRAMEWORK

By following the process in this guide, you will start to learn one framework to support your *parallel practice*. That framework is: *doing theory, thinking practice*.

Framework

You will be guided through one layer of the framework at a time. The framework consists of revisiting past experiences you had in your practice, materializing your inner experience, locating the theory in that experience, and naming the relationships between theory and practice.

For more on the theoretical framework, see Chapter 2, Section 3.
For the methods of the framework, see Chapter 3 Sections 1 and 2.

WHEN AND HOW DO I USE THIS?

Start with Preparing. Do all of the preparations first. Then, possibly on another day, move through all four skills over one chunk of time (whether in a day, weekend, series of mornings, etc.).

However, that's just one way to go about it. After Preparing, you can also begin with Skill 1 and practice it many times over weeks or months before moving on to the next skill. You may go through Skill 1 and Skill 2 one weekend, and come back to Skill 3 and 4 weeks later. The point is: go in order, for now. Let the sequence guide when and how you use the process. Let yourself pause at any point.

If you ever get lost in the process, come back to this introduction. Use it to reset, to remember how the parts connect, and to find your footing again.

WHO CAN PARTICIPATE?

This work is an individual task. It is a way to study your own practice.

That doesn't mean you can't do it with friends and peers. It may be done in pairs or in a small group where each of you independently practice each skill and then gather to discuss your experiences learning the skills. Before starting, be sure you have each fully read this introduction. This guide is not equipped to support all that comes with being exposed to others' vulnerable and potentially triggering experiences, their maturity levels in educational settings, or their ability to handle learning new challenging skills without disturbing others' potentially sensitive states.

Always work with your own practice, theories, and materials.

WHAT IS THIS *NOT*?

This guide is designed for autonomous personal use. Do not use this guide as a tool for facilitating others through the process. It's not a manual for teaching or leading a group. There is a breadth of technical, social, pedagogical, political, and emotional skills to master in order to facilitate this process for others. Neither this guide nor this book covers these capabilities and risks.

The purpose of this guide is not to introduce you to political ideas. Use the social and political concepts you have already worked with in the past.

Though you may revisit challenging experiences through this process, this is not a therapy tool. It is your responsibility to know what you have the capacity for, how far you take the process, check yourself, and to stop where needed. Please take the prompts, notes, tips, and examples seriously as I have flagged when and how to pay attention to your capacity.

This guide is not a recipe that guarantees perfect results if followed exactly. This guide is designed to introduce you to four skills that, when used together, equip you to develop your own *parallel practice.*

This simplified guide is not the full scope of *doing theory, thinking practice*—it's a beginning!

EVENTUALLY...

With practice, you will start to gain confidence to use the skills. You'll internalize how each skill builds on the others. You will start to work intuitively with the skills to suit your intentions as you study the inner workings of your practice.

Eventually, you may not need to write anything down. You may no longer need to refer to the skills or steps written here, because you will have memorized and embodied the process. Some parts will always call for writing things down. For others, you may learn that you complete best without words. Eventually, you'll change the order in which you use the skills because you have clarified your own purpose within the framework. You will learn what time of year or day suits you best to enter your *parallel practice*.

Eventually, the process will be yours.

CONTENTS

We gain some insight into what inner investigations and approaches may look like if we imagine what we do behind closed doors. ... There is a politics to the inner dimensions of social life.

CHAPTER 1, SECTION 2

Be sure to read the introduction to this guide before starting.

Before diving into the framework of *doing theory, thinking practice*, there are a few preparations to make the process smoother, clearer, and to set you up for a nourishing experience.

Throughout the guide, you are provided with designated space to write, marked by large rectangles drawn with a thick black line.

What do you hope to gain?

Write

down what you wish to gain from using this process.

The process, including the four skills, can offer you many things. Leave some empty space for you to edit your response later, if needed.

EXAMPLES

I hope to speak with more self-assuredness about my practice.

I hope to gain a stronger connection between the queer theory I read about and the piano I play.

I want the bravery to challenge what my professor says about the correct way to work with theory. Above all, I hope to gain a new relationship with theory that is my own.

Write what you wish to gain in the space provided below.

Check

if your hope is right-sized.

Do you have the capacity to care for what comes with pursuing and achieving this aim? If not, what might you need to find the capacity?—A friend? More time?

Might you benefit from scaling down what you hope to gain so it matches your capacity?

Is your hope appropriate for the purpose of this guide? If you're not sure, revisit the previous section, starting with What Is This Guide?

Edit

what you wrote in the previous page if necessary.

Choose moments

from your

practice to revisit.

Jot down

at least five past moments from your practice in which your actions felt misaligned from your values.

Choose moments that you want to revisit. You should have a sense that each moment has more to teach you or reveal to you—some may feel less interesting or inspiring than others. That's okay, write them down anyways!

Each moment should be concrete and involve a limited time and physical place that you experienced firsthand.

The political aspects of each moment may be explicit or you may sense them implicitly.

You do not need to explain the experiences for now. Note it down in a brief phrase on the following page.

EXAMPLES

A tense conversation I had with colleagues about our work this week

Interviews I did in 2018 for a research project about the design of national borders

Facilitating a workshop at a university last year

Gluing rubber cement on paper to make a sculpture about the politics of refusals this morning

Last autumn, reading an essay about whiteness that was really difficult to get through

Visiting my mother's hometown for 5 days

Examples that are too broad so should **not** be used:

A project I worked on for three months last year

Going to drawing classes throughout my adolescence

The four years I spent studying music at a university

Write at least five past moments in the space below.

Plot

each moment on the safety scale below. Copy the phrase you wrote on the previous page into the scale.

Moments where you experienced:
slow heart rate, feeling regulated and relaxed,
ready to learn, attend, and problem solve

SAFETY

0

1

2

3

4

5

6

7

8

9

10

DANGER

Moments where you experienced:
fast breathing, dissociated panic, freeze, rage,
attack, ready to move away

This scale was adapted from research published on the autonomic nervous system.

CHAPTER SIX

Choose the medium

you will use for this process.

Write

down the mediums of your practice on the following page. Use this format: *Medium / Materials and tools needed.*

For the purposes of this process, "medium" broadly means the stuff you use to make things in your creative practice.

EXAMPLES

Jazz / Double bass, hands, anchor, chair, and endpin

Multimedia / Pen and notebook to write poetry, Blender for 3D rendering, and my body to dance

Performance / My body, Environments to respond to

Architecture / Bristol paper, Foam core board, Exacto knife, Rubber cement, ruler, cutting mat

Writing / Word processor on my computer, notebook, pencil

Photography / Ricoh GR IIIx digital camera, MacBook Pro, Affinity Pro software

Write down the mediums of your practice below.

As you first learn to use the process, the medium you work with should *not* contain content itself—it should be a basic material through which you will generate content.

HINT

Note that the examples named on the previous page generally do not involve ideas or stories themselves. For example, if one of your mediums involves recorded video files that contain recordings of interviews about a particular topic, it should not be used. However, a video or audio recording device itself would be appropriate as a medium to use for this process. Or, for instance, if your medium is writing or poetry, the tool you adapt for this process should be a blank page in a word processing program or a pen and a blank page of a notebook, not your past writings.

As you become more proficient in using the process, you are encouraged to make the process yours and use mediums as you see fit.

Mark

any mediums on the previous page that contain content.

HINT

If you are unsure if a medium contains content, mark it with an "X", leave it for later. Start with what you're certain does not involve content.

Circle one

medium that you will use to adapt to this process. You will need access to the material(s) in order to practice the process.

HINT

With more experience with the process, you may decide to use a different medium. However, to start, you must work with one medium to reduce the number of variables you bring into the mix of what you have to manage. Choose one based on the medium that you both have comfort in using.

Decide

how you will record yourself while you use this medium.

EXAMPLES

If the medium you chose to work with is dance, you will set up a phone camera or a digital camera to record your movements and sound.

If you are working in a program on your computer, take a screenshot or a photo of the monitor itself to record what you make.

If your medium is writing and you are writing in your notebook by hand, take a photo of the writing you have done.

You will not need to record yourself until you use Skill 2: Materialize. You will need to record to revisit and reflect on what you made.

This step may not apply to you if the material you have chosen to work with for this process happens to be a recording device like a camera or audio recorder.

HINTS

It is not recommended to use analog film for the sole purpose of documenting what you make, as you may need instant access to what you recorded.

The simpler the recording device, the better. A fancy high-tech recording device is not necessary to document what you make. If you prefer not to use digital devices, you may draw to capture what you make in detail.

Choose

the critical theories that

you will use for this process.

To use this process, you should have familiarity with specific theories and their key underlying concepts. This framework is not designed to teach you new socio-political theories.

For the purposes of this guide, "critical theory" is a broad term. It refers to defined ideas and frameworks about social, geographical, and political conditions.

Theories about socio- and geo-political conditions may be found in a book, documentation of a political movement, ancestral knowledge, a film, field recordings, an oral story, an essay, a podcast episode, a poem, an interview, a conversation between friends, a workbook, a zine, etc. Formal socio-political theories may include queer theory, ecofeminism, Afropessimism, borderlands, anarchism, decolonization, cyberfeminism, and much, much more.

HINT

For further definition of theory as it relates to this book, start with the Introduction chapter at the beginning of this book.

The following is an exercise to help you name theories and the key concepts within them.

Name three

critical theories you engage through your practice.

List the title of the reference, author(s), format, and key concepts for each reference.

Name at least one text-based source—a published book, essay, poem, article, etc.

For now, it is not necessary for the theories you choose for this exercise to relate to the past moments or mediums you selected.

EXAMPLES

Title: *"your novels" in Nejma (p. 39)*

Author: *Nayyirah Waheed*

Format: *Poem*

Key Concepts: *how my people walk down a street, novels of my mother, novels of my grandparents, classic novels, novels of my world*

Title: *how to build personal style II: conceptual approach / unconventional, Dec 5, 2022*

Author: *Rian Phin*

Format: *YouTube video*

Key Concepts: *fashioning identity, Spatial wRapping, sound and marginalized groups, masculinity, policing sound, bangles, Timberlands, taking up space, intracommunal codes*

Title: *Black Meme*

Author: *Legacy Russell*

Format: *Book*

Key Concepts: *mixed company (p. 40), fractal and rhizomatic transmission of Emmett Till (p. 5), cha-cha-chá (p. 13)*

Turn the page for more examples and guidance on Key Concepts!

TITLE

AUTHOR(S)

FORMAT

KEY CONCEPTS

TITLE

AUTHOR(S)

FORMAT

KEY CONCEPTS

TITLE

AUTHOR(S)

FORMAT

KEY CONCEPTS

HINT

"Key concepts" refer to specific notions and pieces that make up the broader theory. Name the concepts from your chosen reference that are most relevant and inspiring for your creative practice. The more concepts you name, the better.

Key concepts should not be mistaken for general themes. For example, if one critical theory you work with is written about in a book about debt, key concepts may be "mutuality" or "credit," as defined in your reference. However, "socialism" or "capitalism" are too vast and general.

HINT

If narrowing down to three theories feels limiting, choose based on those that have been the most influential and that you have been engaging with recently.

Remind yourself

of the definition of each key concept you listed. If you don't know the definition, look back at the reference itself or through a general search of the term(s). These are theories you should be familiar with. If the reference and concept are unfamiliar to you, this step will require more time, and you may need to take extra notes elsewhere.

Let’s define

your

parallel practice.

Fill

in the table with the details of your *parallel practice*.

For the heading, complete the phrase, "doing theory, thinking..." with the medium you chose.

For Practitioner, write your name.

For Medium, write down the medium and materials you chose earlier.

For Politicized Direction, write three or four words that encapsulate the critical theories you named. Write what feels clearest for you.

EXAMPLES of headings

doing theory, thinking jazz

doing theory, thinking code

doing theory, thinking lighting

doing theory, thinking dance

doing theory, thinking poetry

HINTS

For inspiration and examples of how to fill in this table, refer to the beginning of Chapter 3 or Chapter 2, Section 2.

For more on *doing theory* and *doing theory, thinking practice*, see the beginning of Chapter 2 and Chapter 2, Section 3.

For more on *parallel practices*, see Chapter 2, Section 2, Demarcating "Parallel Practice" and Chapter 3, Section 1, Defining My Parallel Practice.

Parallel Practice

DOING THEORY, THINKING	
PRACTITIONER	
MEDIUM	
FRAMEWORK	*doing theory, thinking practice*
POLITICIZED DIRECTION	

CONTENTS

First, notice your surroundings.
Revisit how your body felt in this past moment.

SKILL 1: BODY SCANNING

In *doing theory* in the everyday,
we have the bodies and flesh we live in
as points of intervention—we can grin,
twirl, loiter, go-on-living.

CHAPTER 2, SECTION 2

Before you start, read about Exiting the process at the end of this guide.

It will help you be proactive for your transition out of the session you have today.

Pick

one moment you plotted between 0 and 2 on the safety scale in the Preparations section. Don't write it down just yet.

HINTS

Once you get the hang of the process, you can work with moments with various levels of safety. Use the scale to gauge what you're ready to handle. It may depend on your current energy and stress levels or the demands of what you have planned before or after your session using this process. Begin with a moment you plotted between 0 and 2 on the safety scale.

It is your responsibility to be aware of what you can handle and take seriously the safety scale provided to you to make this decision.

If you do not have a moment plotted between 0 and 2 on the scale, create one.

Define

a specific time and place within that moment.

You do not need to remember the date or day of the week, but narrow the moment down to something you experienced over a few minutes or hours at most.

Write

one or two sentences to define the moment. Name the specific time and place.

EXAMPLES

Last autumn, I read an essay about whiteness that was really difficult to get through. I read the essay on the 20-minute bus ride on the way to the park to meet my friend.

I had a tense conversation with colleagues about our work this week. The conversation happened on Tuesday over lunch in our office lunchroom.

First, notice

your

surroundings.

Read

these prompts below. Simply read the six questions below, for now.

What is straight ahead of you?

What's behind you?

What's to your right?

What's to your left?

What's above you?

What's below you?

Close

your eyes, imagine yourself back in this past moment, and explore all six prompts on the previous page one by one. The intention is to revisit your surroundings at the time. This may take approximately 30 seconds to a couple of minutes.

Your job now is simply to notice your surroundings using the six prompts.

The six spatial prompts were adapted to this process from Lynda Barry's illustrated book, What It Is.

HINT

If you have a previous somatic practice, this may feel like meditation. However, while you're learning and using this process, do not add other approaches to any of the prompts here until you've practiced the full process of *doing theory, thinking practice* several times.

The steps of the process become increasingly layered and complex from here, so it is important to maintain the clear simplicity here.

CHAPTER SIX

Revisit how your body

felt

in this past moment.

Next, you will scan your body.

Starting from the tip of your head, you will slowly move downwards to the tips of your toes.

While you scan your body, imagine yourself in the past moment you're exploring.

Pay attention to any physical sensations that come up. You might feel warmth, an itch, heaviness, an ache, etc.

Close

your eyes to scan your body for approximately 30 seconds to 5 minutes.

Write

down at least three sensations you felt on your body and their physical locations in your body.

Be specific. Be precise.

HINT

Tactile sensations may include throbbing, itching, tingling, bubbling, poking, etc. *Attributes* may include temperature, weight, texture, scale, volume, taste, etc. *Physical locations* may include places such as behind your ear, in your kidney, on your skin on your shoulder, your lower back, your entire front half, etc.

Moving forward, I will refer to these traits as "physical qualities" and "material qualities."

HINT

If you didn't feel anything physical in your body, that's alright!

Close your eyes and try again, but instead of trying to feel physical sensations, recall what you think you *might* have been feeling in that moment. How do you usually react in these kinds of situations? Do you tense up in your back? Clench your teeth? Feel a flow throughout your torso? Write it down.

EXAMPLES

Tingling in my palm that starts in the center and radiates out

Throbbing heat in a 2 cm area at the top of my head

Loud humming vibration in my right ear

Warmth behind my sleepy eyes and tingling in my eyelids

A sweet and light taste, mainly on the sides of my tongue

Heaviness in my upper thighs, weighted at the back of my legs

CONTENTS

Materialize what you felt in your body.
Explore the material qualities of what you materialized.

SKILL 2: MATERIALIZING

We make based on the embodied things we know through our bodies.

CHAPTER 2, SECTION 3

For this skill, you are going to give actual shape to a physical sensation you felt using a medium from your practice. You'll take this sensation—an impression, feeling, ethos, or inkling from this moment—and make it visible, tangible, or audible.

Materializing
Here, the term "materializing" specifically refers to taking things that are internal or intangible and making them external and tangible.

The phrase "material record" is used in this guide to describe the artifact produced from the materializing process.

HINT

For more on the term "materializing", see Chapter 2, Section 2; Chapter 3, Sections 1 and 2; Matter—Mind Studio's Emotion-Centered Design Lookbook (2018); and Myriam D. Diatta's previous master's thesis, Material Communications (2014).

Pick one

sensation you named in Skill 1 and rewrite it here.

Pick a sensation that you are curious to learn more about or are excited to materialize.

Include its physical qualities and location in your body.

HINT

If this process has been feeling challenging, be gentle with yourself. To start, pick a sensation you think will be the easiest to materialize.

Prepare

the materials you need to use the medium you chose. You will need to use them in a moment.

Set up

the recording device you decided to use earlier. Be prepared to document what you materialize.

HINT

Depending on the medium you picked, you may need to hit record or document as you're materializing, for example, if you will be dancing or singing. Or you may only need to document after you've finished materializing, for example, if you will be making a drawing or sculpting something.

Materialize

what

Materialize

the sensation you chose using the medium you selected. Experiment! Explore!

Refer to the examples on the right.

For now, do not interpret the entire past moment or all the sensations you felt.

you felt in your body.

EXAMPLES

These examples below ask how you might make tangible the [sensations in your body] by using [the medium of your practice].

Your task may be to explore,

How do I use the [sound through my piano keys, pedal, hammer, and string] to convey the [throbbing and aching in my right shoulder]?

How can I convey [the cooling sensation on the back of my neck] through [writing and collaging words together]?

How can [a pinching sensation between my fingers] be materialized using [the light and the negative and positive impressions in my photography]?

How may [the stitches and pleating I sew] reflect [the layers of weight on my chest]?

Save

your documentation for safekeeping. You will need to revisit it for the next step. You also may choose to work with what you materialized again at a later date.

Stellar.

You've materialized what you felt in your body.

You may have created one materialization or several. Both are great.

For simplicity, select one to use for the remainder of the guide.

CHAPTER SIX

Explore the material

qualities of what you materialized.

Observe

the physical qualities of what you materialized. Notice the shadows, curves, volume, its lengths of time, pace, height, weight, tension, softness, rigidity, etc.

Write

at least 10 physical qualities you observe in the space to the right. The more you list, the better.

Be specific. Be precise.

EXAMPLES

a dark corner at the base

a long pause between chaos

a thick, heavy mark in the periphery

From Your Practice

Below, write at least 10 physical qualities you observe in what you materialized.

CONTENTS

SKILL 3: LOCATING THEORY IN THE MATERIAL RECORD

By examining one of these freestanding made objects, it is possible to identify its interior structures and find in it attributes of the human condition.

CHAPTER 2, SECTION 3

Put what you materialized, documented, and noted in Skill 2 to the side for now. Clear your workspace.

You will come back to them later.

HINT

If you are taking notes outside of this book, start Skill 3 on a fresh, new page.

Explore the material qualities of the

theories

you engage with.

Revisit

all the key theoretical concepts you named in your Preparations. Reread what you wrote, considering their definitions and meaning to you.

Copy

10 to 15 key concepts from the Preparations section into the left side of the table here. Copy only the key concepts. Make a list, one concept per row.

Write

down any physical qualities each concept might have. Note them on the right side of the table next to the relevant key concept.

HINT

The physical qualities may include temperature, weight, height, texture, shape, scale, volume, pitch, duration, taste, shape, density, speed, opacity, stability, symmetry, an effect, etc.

Ask yourself, does this concept have any metaphors that suggest physical traits? Does it suggest movement like spinning, direction like a curve, an elevation like 10,000 meters, a shape like a rectangle, a relation like a reflection, an effect like amplification, or a density like thick murky darkness?

EXAMPLE

For examples and more hints, turn the page.

Make loose and playful interpretations!

HINT

Your ideas are for your eyes only unless you choose to share them. This exercise is not about making rigid or factual correlations—you are not expected to prove your interpretations.

From Your Theory

KEY THEORETICAL CONCEPTS	PHYSICAL QUALITIES OF EACH CONCEPT

EXAMPLES

In the Preparations section of this guide, I gave examples for the prompt, "Choose the critical theory from your practice that you will use for this process." The example included a poem by Nayyirah Waheed, a video essay by Rian Phin, and a book by Legacy Russell.

As an example of how to complete the prompt in Skill 3, here, I continue building on these examples. Without needing to know the exact context of the poem and book I refer to, you can see how I came up with the Physical Qualities of Each Concept (right side) from each theoretical concept I listed (left side).

On the left, I copied the key concepts from my example of Nayyirah Waheed's poem. I listed these concepts in the Preparations section of this guide.

KEY THEORETICAL CONCEPTS		PHYSICAL QUALITIES OF EACH CONCEPT
how my people walk down a street	⟷	*upright, winding, open*
novels of my grandparents	⟷	*steady, layered, long legacy*
novels of my world	⟷	*cylindrical, curving, airy*

Here, I use the key concepts in the example I gave of Legacy Russell's *Black Meme* in the Preparations section:

KEY THEORETICAL CONCEPTS		PHYSICAL QUALITIES OF EACH CONCEPT
mixed company	⟷	*mixed*
fractal and rhizomatic transmission	⟷	*fractals, rhizomes*
cha-cha-chá	⟷	*One, two, three footwork pattern*

HINT

What if there are no physical qualities?

If a concept does not appear to carry any physical qualities, look up the definition of each term. Check to see if there are any physical qualities present in the definition of each word. You can use a dictionary or look back to where the term was mentioned in your original reference (in the book, film, etc.) and check how it is defined there.

For instance, the key concept, "cha-cha-chá" used in the second example on the previous page may not immediately appear to have a physical quality. However, upon rereading the paragraph in which the term was used in my reference, I found a description of its historical context and that it is a "footwork pattern ... one, two, three, cha-cha" and "draws its influence from Afro-Cuban dance." Dance, patterns, and rhythm all have or are physical qualities.

If you do find that there is a physical quality suggested in its definition, note it down in the right column next to the respective key concept. If it does not, simply put this key concept on pause and move on to the next key concept. Remember, you are playfully brainstorming here and making loose associations only where you can!

Calibrate theory and

practice with one another.

HINT

For details about "calibrating theory and practice," see the beginning of Chapter 2, Section 3.

Revisit

your theoretical concepts.

Look back at the list of concepts and the physical qualities you identified. You made this list in the previous prompt.

Revisit

what you materialized.

Look back at what you made. Look at the list of its physical qualities you created. You listed them under the final prompt in Skill 2.

Explore

Do any physical qualities from the theory I've read match any physical qualities of what I materialized?

For now, just explore.

In the previous prompts, you listed at least 10 physical qualities of what you materialized and at least 10 physical qualities in the theory you are working with.

Now, your single aim is to see if it is possible to match *one* physical quality of what you materialized and *one* physical quality from a key theoretical concept you named in the previous prompts.

Make casual and playful interpretations! You're not looking for literal or even true connections, but loose connections.

HINTS

For instance, you might find, "Hmm, these little holes and chambers in what I made sort of feel like the idea of 'cells,' in the prison abolition text I'm working with," or "Oh! 'Degradation' from the economic theory I'm interested in kind of remind me of the frayed and loose quality in the fibers I made."

There is no correct sequence for this exploration—you might start with what you materialized and match it to a concept, or start with the theoretical concept and match it to a quality in what you materialized. You might organically match the two at the same time. All these approaches are great.

Write

down one physical quality from materializing and one physical quality from a key theoretical concept that you matched to one another.

EXAMPLE

A practitioner is using photography and light as their media for materializing. At the same time, they are studying "fractal transmissions" from Legacy Russell's book, *Black Meme.*

This practitioner has matched a physical quality from what they materialized [light that is fragmented and reflective] with one from the concept they are studying [fractals, patterns that bounce, spread, or bend].

PHYSICAL QUALITY FROM MATERIALIZING	PHYSICAL QUALITY FROM A THEORETICAL CONCEPT
Fragmented light reflecting through holes	*Fractals*

HINT

If nothing easily comes to mind, you have two options:

Try another

Simply move on and work with another quality. Then see if you can match it with another physical quality.

Open your search

Alternatively, pick one specific quality in what you materialized—like a ripple or a sharp point—and try to think of a theoretical concept you have a hunch relates to it. Then flip through a book, video, poem, lecture, etc., you know talks about these qualities to find words or phrases that connect.

Or, you can start the other way around. You can pick one specific quality you named from a theoretical concept you're working with—like *a steady, layered, long legacy*—and then look at what you materialized and search for steadiness, layeredness, or long-ness in it.

Calibrating Practice and Theory

PHYSICAL QUALITY FROM MATERIALIZING	PHYSICAL QUALITY FROM A THEORETICAL CONCEPT

You may choose to move on after finding one match—great. Or, you may enjoy finding multiple matches—also good. Write them above if you found multiple matches.

Pick

and circle one pairing to continue working with.

You've done a lot of challenging work!
Take a break here or stop for the day, if needed.

Circulate

theory and

practice.

Excellent, you have linked together a theoretical concept and what you materialized!

Now, you can try to make meaning of it.

Revisit

what you materialized.

Briefly look at, watch, or listen to what you materialized.

Remind yourself of the actual past moment you materialized. Remember who, where, when, and what was involved. Remember how your body felt at the time. You have already done this work; just take a moment to remind yourself.

Revisit

what you filled in for the previous writing prompt: "Calibrating Practice and Theory." Reread and revisit the physical qualities you matched to each other. Remind yourself of the relevant key theoretical concept and what it means.

Consider,

is the key theoretical concept you named in the previous writing prompt actually present in the original moment that you materialized?

Just think about it for now.

EXAMPLE

Let's start with this scenario:

> A photographer is using this process to explore a tense experience she had with colleagues at work this week.
>
> She used Skill 1 to scan her body and environment at the time.
>
> She then used Skill 2 to materialize her experience using her camera. To do this, she took an abstract photograph of a decorative mirror reflecting light. She noted that there is "fragmented light reflecting through holes" in the photograph she materialized.
>
> By using Skill 3, she then loosely matched the "fragmented light" in her photograph with the concept of "fractal transmissions" from Legacy Russell's book, *Black Meme*.

To answer the prompt on this page, this photographer would ask herself, Are [fractal transmissions] actually present in the [tense conversation I had with my colleagues this past Tuesday]?

If yes,

where? How? Briefly write your response in two or three sentences in the space provided on the following page.

If not,

that's alright! It's a normal and expected part of this process. You have been playing with connections between theory and practice to see if they might be relevant to the past moment you are working with. Use these hints for ways to keep exploring:

HINT

When I can't easily make a connection, I use these three routes to keep tinkering. And you can too.

Look Again
It might not seem like the concept is actually present in the past experience you had, but could the concept be disguised or found in the details? Revisit the theoretical concepts and definitions you explored in Preparations. Then try using Skill 1 to revisit the same past moment. Scan your body and surroundings and see if you can connect a concept with your past experience.

Switch Pairings
If you noted down more than one pairing for Skill 3: Calibrate theory and practice with one another, pick another pairing and explore the same prompts from there.

Make New Pairings
Flip back to the lists you made in Skill 2 and Skill 3—the two lists have small headings that say, "From Your Practice" and "From Your Theory." Use the physical qualities you named in each of these lists to create new pairings in Skill 3: Calibrate theory and practice with one another. Explore the same prompts from there.

Once you've found a connection, briefly write your response in two or three sentences on the next page.

Is the key theoretical concept actually present in the original moment that you materialized? Where? How?

Once you have written about where and how the key concept is present in the original moment, consider the following:

Consider,

were you embodying the concept in your actions?

If yes,

in what ways—in your speaking, posture, impact, etc.? Write your response in two or three sentences in the space provided on the right hand page.

Who or what was embodying the concept in this past moment? In what ways?

If not,

what effect would the concept have had on you in this past moment? Write your response in two or three sentences in the space provided above.

CONTENTS

Recognize what is between theory and practice.

SKILL 4: RECOGNIZING WHAT IS BETWEEN THEORY AND PRACTICE

Getting to know what happens when we oscillate between what is concrete and what is abstract means we can approach our work with more self-awareness in contemporary socio-political contexts.

CHAPTER 1, SECTION 1

Recognize

what is

between theory and practice.

There are multiple relationships between theory and practice.

Choose

one of the phrases below that applies to you. Or, add your own short phrase to the list describing what was happening between theory and practice.

I now recognize that in the past moment, theory was already present in what I did or made.

I now recognize that practice was already in the theory I was reading, listening to, watching, etc.

I now recognize that in the past moment, I was growing my library of socio-political theory.

I now recognize that in the past moment, I was deliberately working to align theory and practice.

I now recognize that in the past moment, theory and practice were already aligned..

HINT

For inspiration, you can also revisit the artist interviews in the Interlude section of this book. In it, you can read what other critical creative practitioners have said happens for them "Between Theory and Practice." Look for the subheading at the end of each interview.

Write

one of the phrases from the previous page at the top of the space provided here.

Elaborate

on the phrase that you chose. Make loose and playful interpretations!

Use the phrase as the first sentence, writing in the style of a journal entry. Elaborate by defining the relevant key theoretical concept(s) in your own words. Anchor your definition in the specific actions, thoughts, and impressions present in the moment you've reflected on.

Describe exactly the nature, scope, and meaning of the concept(s).

HINT

For nine examples of what I recognized from using this process, see Chapter 4.

In each of the nine examples, the heading, The Focal Concerns of this Context, is the past moment or situation I started with.

For each, you can see the things I materialized in the text with a black background (where I used writing as my medium) or black and white images of sculptures (where I used paper model making as my medium).

The paragraphs that follow are my version of what I recognized about theory and practice in the past experience I started with. Note that though I do not start my writing with "I now recognize," I use that structure for your clarity in this guide.

What is Between Theory and Practice

I NOW RECOGNIZE THAT...

You may keep this piece of writing simply as a journal entry. You may also incorporate it into a thesis or doctoral dissertation: You have precisely articulated how your practice is engaged with ideas about our contemporary realities.

HINT

See Chapter 5, Section 3: Practice-led Research for more on how this process applies to a creative thesis project or dissertation.

You may also continue this writing prompt by reflecting on the question you answered in the beginning of this process: What do you hope to gain?

What has your first attempt in using this process shown you so far? How might you continue to explore your hopes through this process?

EXITING

I use double consciousness as an apparatus, positioned between what is public and oppressive and what is private and interior—a deflective tool to manipulate the boundaries of what is cared for in private and what is exposed to the risk of the public.

CHAPTER 3, SECTION 1

The political direction and theory you work with may not be double consciousness as noted in this quote above, but I highlight the excerpt here to emphasize the importance of the interior, private work that a *parallel practice* requires and the outer, public nature of the professional practice that surrounds it.

Just as you did some preparations to enter your *parallel practice*, each time you exit the space and time you created, it is important that you prepare both your mindset and practical matters for leaving this inner space. To do this, I offer a few options for operating with opacity or transparency:

Canceling plans
Be prepared to send an email or make a phone call to cancel plans you may have had after a session of using the process. You may not be able to predict what arises from revisiting a tough moment or realizing something profound about your relationship with theory. The work of *doing theory, thinking practice* is not always light, and you must respect the effort, labor, and energy you put into it.

Assigning a companion
Let a trusted friend know you're going to be working in your *parallel practice* this weekend, for instance. Even if they do not know the process, let them know you may lean on them to digest what you're working with or to take a walk together to take your mind off the process. Communicate your needs with them: Do you need a listener? Are you looking for advice? Someone to come up with a plan for you? Remind you of something?

Exercise caution for whom you disclose your experience
There may be exciting realizations and overwhelming feelings that come from using this process. Especially if your tendency is to think out loud and process your thoughts with others, be intentional about who you do this with. You may find that you're actually in quite a fragile state, so someone's unassuming comment can deflate something precious you are starting to build. Without realizing it, you may be seeking affirmation from someone, but you're met with blankness or misunderstanding that has a deeper effect than you predicted. Or, you may need to practice listening to yourself and someone may steer you down a road you might not have gone down otherwise. While we are capable of navigating social interactions and there is importance in collaboration, be deliberate about when you invite it in, where you do it, and with whom.

In whatever stage you might be in learning this process, thank you for trusting its potential and my guidance. To close, I echo a message from the Introduction chapter of this book.

This book was written to affirm
what you already know about the world
through your experience.

My hope is that if you are experiencing isolation
as a professional or student among harsh,
dismissive, corporate, state, or institutional
contexts, this book will become a trusted
companion as you navigate, contribute to,
abolish, leverage, refuse, and subvert these spaces.

INTRODUCTION CHAPTER

REFERENCES

Alcoff, Linda. "The Problem of Speaking for Others." *Cultural Crtique* 20 (1991): 5-32. https://doi.org/10.2307/1354221.

Akama, Yoko. "Attuning to Ma (between-ness) in Designing." *Proceedings of the 13th Participatory Design Conference* 2 (2014): 2124. ACM. https://doi.org/10.1145/2662155.2662179.

Anderson, Leon, and Bonnie Glass-Coffin. "Learn by Going." In *Handbook of Autoethnography*, edited by Stacy Holman Jones, Tony E. Adams, and Carolyn Ellis (Left Coast Press, 2013), 57-83.

Angelou, Maya. "The Mask." Thames Television, London, 1987. Television performance.

Anzaldúa, Gloria. *Borderlands: The New Mestiza = La Frontera*. Spinsters/Aunt Lute, 1987.

Barad, Karen. *Meeting the Universe Halfway: Quantum Physics and the Entanglement of Matter and Meaning*. Duke University Press, 2007.

---. "Posthumanist Performativity: Toward an Understanding of How Matter Comes to Matter." *Signs: Journal of Women in Culture and Society* 28, no. 3 (2003): 801-31. https://doi.org/10.1086/345321.

Barnard Center for Research on Women. "What Is Self-Accountability?" September 27, 2018, Video. https://www.youtube.com/watch?v=6a-TfuWyYn8.

---. "What Is Accountability?" July 26, 2019, Video. https://www.youtube.com/watch?v= LjRbj57vBvA.

Barry, Lynda. *What It Is*. Seattle: Drawn & Quarterly, 2008.

Black Rose/Rosa Negra - Anarchist Federation. "Anarchism and Black Struggle: A Panel Discussion." March 23, 2020, Video. https://www.youtube.com/watch?v=2LKvRUe_rZA.

BOMB Magazine. "Portfolio: Tuning by Torkwase Dyson." *BOMB Magazine*. https://bombmagazine.org/authors/torkwase-dyson.

Boughedir, Férid, dir. *Caméra d'Afrique: 20 ans de cinéma africain (Twenty Years of African Cinema)*. Documentary film. 1983.

Boylorn, Robin M. "On Being at Home with Myself: Blackgirl Autoethnography as Research Praxis." *International Review of Qualitative Research* 9, no. 1 (2016): 44-58. https://doi.org/10.1525/ irqr.2016.9.1.44.

---. "'Sit With Your Legs Closed!" And Other Sayin's from My Childhood." *In Handbook of Autoethnography*, edited by Stacy Holman Jones, Tony E Adams, and Carolyn Ellis (Left Coast Press, 2013): 173-85.

---. *Sweetwater: Black Women and Narratives of Resilience*. Peter Lang, 2013.

Boylorn, Robin M. and Mark P Orbe, eds. *Critical Autoethnography: Intersecting*

Cultural Identities in Everyday Life. Taylor & Francis, 2016.

Bruce, La Marr Jurelle. "Mad Is a Place." *American Quarterly* 69, no. 2 (2017): 303-8. https://doi.org/10.1353/aq.2017.0024.

---. "SHORE, UNSURE: Loitering as a Way of Life." *GLQ: A Journal of Lesbian and Gay Studies* 25, no. 2 (2019): 352-61. https://doi.org/10.1215/10642684-7367824.

Campt, Tina. "Black Feminist Futures and the Practice of Fugitivity." Lecture presented at the Helen Pond McIntyre '48 Lecture, Barnard College, October 7, 2014.

Candy, Linda, and Ernest Edmonds. "Practice-Based Research in the Creative Arts: Foundations and Futures from the Front Line." *Leonardo* 51, no. 1 (2018): 63-9. https://doi.org/10.1162/LEON_a_01471.

Carrington, André. "Mike Brown's Body: New Materialism and Black Form." *ASAP Journal* 2, no. 2 (2017): 276-83. https://doi.org/10.1353/asa.2017.0025.

Cervenak, Sarah J. *Wandering: Philosophical Performances of Racial and Sexual Freedom*. Duke University Press, 2014.

Chen, Nancy N. "'Speaking Nearby': A Conversation with Trinh T. Minh-Ha." *Visual Anthropology Review* 8, no. 1 (1992): 82-91. https://doi.org/10.1525/var.1992.8.1.82.

Cole, Teju. "Black Body: Rereading James Baldwin's 'Stranger in the Village.'" *The New Yorker*, August 19, 2014. https://www.newyorker.com/books/page-turner/black-body-rereading-james-baldwins-stranger-village.

Collins, Patricia Hill. *Black Feminist Thought: Knowledge, Consciousness, and the Politics of Empowerment*. Unwin Hyman, 1990.

Crenshaw, Kimberlé. "Demarginalizing the Intersection of Race and Sex: A Black Feminist Critique of Antidiscrimination Doctrine, Feminist Theory and Antiracist Politics." *University of Chicago Legal Forum*, no. 1 (1989): 139-67.

Da Silva, Denise Ferreira. "Toward a Black Feminist Poethics: The Quest(ion) of Blackness Toward the End of the World." *Black Scholar* 44, no. 2 (2014): 81-97. https://doi.org/10.1080/00064246.2014.11413690.

Davis, Angela. "WOW: Angela Davis in Conversation." Southbank Centre, March 11, 2017, Video. https://www.youtube.com/watch?v=lBgdzK3jfEg.

Davis, Angela Y. *Are Prisons Obsolete?* Seven Stories Press, 2003.

Davies, Bronwyn. "Ethics and the New Materialism: A Brief Genealogy of the 'Post' Philosophies in the Social Sciences." *Discourse* 39, no. 1 (2018): 113-27. https://doi.org/10.1080/ 01596306.2016.1234682.

Day, Iyko. "Being or Nothingness: Indigeneity, Antiblackness, and Settler Colonial Critique." *Journal of the Critical Ethnic Studies* 1, no. 2 (2015): 102-21. https://doi.org/10.5749/jcritethnstud.1.2.0102.

Diatta, Myriam D. "Freezing Ontologies: Making Visible the Messiness of Working with Theory." *Text and Performance Quarterly* 42, no. 2 (2022): 97-110. https://doi.org/10.1080/10462937.2022.2058076.

---. "Material Communications." Conference presentation at The Art of Research V Conference, Helsinki, November, 2014.

---. "Our Everyday Forms." Medium, n.d., Online archive. https://medium.com/our-everyday-forms.

---. "Undisciplining Who We Bring to the Academic Table: Practical Tactics to Accompany Critical Creative Inquiry." *Parse*, no. 17 (2023). https://parsejournal.com/ article/undisciplining-who-we-bring-to-the-academic-table/

Diatta, Myriam, D., and Ricardo Dutra Gonçalves. "Threading Notes_Family of Sensibilities." Department of Art and Media, Monash University, 2020. https://doi.org/10.6084/ m9.figshare.13353374.v2

Diatta, Myriam D., Ricardo D. Gonçalves, and Lisa Grocott. "Family of Sensibilities: Toward a Relational Design Practice Grounded in Materiality and Embodiment." *Design and Culture* 14, no. 2(2022): 205-9. https://doi.org/10.1080/17547075.2021.2018539.

Diatta, Myriam D., Stacy H. Jones, and Kate McEntee. "A Place to Meet: How Critical Theory Cares for the Everyday in Artistic Practice." *Research in Arts and Education Journal: Special Issue on Critical Artistic Research as Practices of Care*, December 2021.

Diatta, Myriam, and Lillian Tong. "Emotional Design for Learning." Medium, November 2017. https://medium.com/matter-mindstudio/emotional-design-for-learning-ad2b52c7e97d.

Douglass, Patrice, and Frank Wilderson. "The Violence of Presence: Metaphysics in a Blackened World." *Black Scholar* 43, no. 4 (2013): 117. https://doi.org/10.1080/00064246.2013.11413674.

Du Bois, W. E. B. *The Souls of Black Folk: Essays and Sketches.* Project Gutenberg. A. C. McClurg, 1903.

Dyson, Torkwase. "Torkwase Dyson: Black Compositional Thought and Systems of Spatial Navigation." Columbia University Graduate School of Architecture, Planning and Preservation, 2019. https://www.arch.columbia.edu/media-archive/podcasts/171black-compositional-thought-and-systems-of-spatial-navigation.

Ellis, Carolyn, Tony E. Adams, and Arthur P. Bochner. "Autoethnography: An Overview." *Historical Social Research* 36, no. 4 (2011): 273-90.

Evans-Winters, Venus E. *Black Feminism in Qualitative Inquiry: A Mosaic for Writing Our Daughter's Body*. Routledge, 2019.

Frayling, Christopher. "Research in Art and Design." *Royal College of Art Research Papers* 1, no. 1 (1993): 1-5.

Gamble, Christopher N, Joshua S. Hanan, and Thomas Nail. "What Is New Materialism?" *Angelaki: Journal of Theoretical Humanities* 24, no. 6 (2019): 111-34. https://doi.org/10.1080/ 0969-725X.2019.1684704.

Garba, Tapji, and Sara-Maria Sorentino. "Slavery Is a Metaphor: A CritIcal Commentary on Eve Tuck and K. Wayne Yang's 'Decolonization Is Not a Metaphor.'"*Antipode* 52, no. 3 (220): 764-82. https://doi.org/10.1111/anti.12615.

Garina, Daria. "The Centered Accountability Course." Accountability Mapping. March 3, 2021. https://www.accountabilitymapping.thinkific.com.

Graham Foundation. "Christina Sharpe and Torkwase Dyson in Conversation." June 13, 2018, Livestream. https://www.youtube.com/watch?v=B-mmVQxz2HEg.

---. "Dionne Brand: The Shape of Language." July 21, 2018, Video. https://www.youtube.com/watch?v=r_HdOZ-IFElO.

---. "Wynter-Wells School TORKWASE DYSON. " May 3-July 26, 2018. http://www.grahamfoundation.org/public_exhibitions/5800wynter-wells-school

Grande, Sandy, Stefano Harney, Fred Moten, Jasbir Puar, and Dylan Rodriguez. "A Conversation with Sandy Grande, Stefano Harney, Fred Moten, Jasbir Puar, and Dylan Rodriguez." Strike MoMA, May 28, 2021, Video. https://www.youtube.com/watch?v=V2vzhwnjy4s.

Grocott, Lisa. "Design Research & Reflective Practice: The Facility of Design-Oriented Research to Translate Practitioner Insights into New Understandings of Design." PhD thesis, RMIT University, 2010.

Groth, Camilla. "Making Sense Through Hands: Design and Craft Practice Analysed as Embodied Cognition." PhD thesis, Espoo: Aalto University, 2017.

Gumbs, Alexis P. *Undrowned: Black Feminist Lessons from Marine Mammals*. AK Press, 2020.

Halberstam, Jack. "The Wild Beyond: With and For the Undercommons." In *The Undercommons: Fugitive Planning & Black Study*, edited by Stefano Harney and Fred Moten (AK Press, 2013), 2-13.

Hall, Stuart. 'Constituting an Archive.' *Third Text* 15, no. 54 (2001): 89-92. https://doi.org/10.1080/09528820108576903.

---. "Marx's Notes on Method: A 'Reading' of the '1857 Introduction.'" *Cultural Studies* 17, no. 2 (2003): 113-49. https://doi.org/10.1080/0950238032000114868.

Hanna, Karen B. "Living Beyond Survival: 11 Tips for Women of Color in Academia." This Bridge Called Our Health. October 11, 2016. www.thisbridgecalledourhealth.wordpress.com/ 2016/10/11/living-beyond-survival-11-tips-for-women-of-color-in-academia.

Harney, Stefano, and Fred Moten. *The Undercommons: Fugitive Planning & Black Study*. AK Press, 2013.

Hartman, Saidiya V. "Keynote Address." Black/Queer Ontologies Symposium, Princeton University, October 24, 2015, Video. https://vimeo.com/144305401.

---. *Scenes of Subjection: Terror, Slavery, and Self-Making in Nineteenth-Centu-*

ry America. Oxford University Press, 1997.

Hernandez, K. C., and Faith W. Ngunjiri. "Relationships and Communities in Autoethnography." In *Handbook of Autoethnography*, edited by Stacy Holman Jones, Tony E. Adams, and Carolyn Ellis (Left Coast Press, 2013), 262-80.

Holland, Sharon P. *The Erotic Life of Racism.* Duke University Press, 2012.

hooks, bell. "In Our Glory: Photography and Black Life." In *Art on My Mind: Visual Politics* (The Free Press, 1995), 54-64.

hooks, bell, and Arthur Jafa. "bell hooks and Arthur Jafa Discuss Transgression in Public Spaces at The New School." The New School, October 15, 2014, Video. https://www.youtube.com/ watch?v=fe-7ILSKSog.

Jane, E. "I Am Not an Identity Artist Just Because I Am a Black Artist with Multiple Selves." Tumblr, November 1, 2015. https://www.e-janestudio.tumblr.com/post/132335744305/i-am-not-an-identity-artist-just-because-i-am-a.

Johnson, Dominique. "Beyond Bare Life: Onto-Epistemic Archives, Precarity, and the Praxis of Being Human." PhD thesis, University of Pittsburgh, 2017.

Johnson, E. Patrick. "'Quare' Studies, or (Almost) Everything I Know About Queer Studies I Learned from My Grandmother." *Text and Performance Quarterly* 21, no. 1 (2001): 1-25. https://doi.org/10.1080/10462930128119.

Jones, Stacy H. "Living Bodies of Thought: The 'Critical' in Critical Autoethnography." *Qualitative Inquiry* 22, no. 4 (2016): 228-37. https://doi.org/10.1177/1077800415622509.

Jones, Stacy Holman, Tony E. Adams, and Carolyn Ellis, eds. *Handbook of Autoethnography*. Left Coast Press, 2013.

Karera, Axelle. "Blackness and the Pitfalls of Anthropocene Ethics." *Critical Philosophy of Race* 7, no. 1 (2019): 32-56. https://doi.org/10.5325/critphilrace.7.1.0032.

Küpers, Wendelin. "4/29 - Between Non- and Post-Disciplinarity ?!" *Integral Leadership Review* 14, no. 2 (2014). http://integralleadershipreview.com/11426-non-postdisciplininarity/

Latva-Somppi, Riikka, Maarit Mäkelä, and Ozgu Gündeşlioğlu. "Traces from the Anthropocene: Working with Soil." *RUUKKU Studies in Artistic Research* 14 (2020): 1-26. https://doi.org/10.22501/ruu.697190.

Lees-Maffei, Grace, and Linda Sandino. "Dangerous Liaisons: Relationships Between Design, Craft and Art." *Journal of Design History* 17 (2004). https://doi.org/10.1093/jdh/17.3.207.

Leong, Diana. "The Mattering of Black Lives: Octavia Butler's Hyperempathy and the Promise of the New Materialisms." *Catalyst* 2, no. 2 (2016): 1-35. https://doi.org/10.28968/ cftt.v2i2.28799.

Louisiana Channel. "Sam Gilliam Interview: Artists Are Supposed to Change." May 28, 2020, Video. https://www.youtube.com/watch?v=ciN6ZPDMJV4.

Mäkelä, Maarit. "Knowing Through Making: The Role of the Artefact in Practice-Led Research." *Knowledge, Technology & Policy* 20, no. 3 (2007): 157-63. https://doi.org/10.1007/s12130-007-9028-2.

Marx, Sherry, Julie L. Pennington, and Heewon Chang. "Critical Autoethnography in Pursuit of Educational Equity: Introduction to the IJME Special Issue." *International Journal of Multicultural Education* 19, no. 1 (2017): 1. https://doi.org/10.18251/ijme.v19i1.1393.

Mahtani, Minelle, Ann Morning, and Jared Sexton. "What's Radical About 'Mixed Race?'" APAInstitute, May 18, 2015. Video. https://www.youtube.com/watch?v=jSMQpRzcGpA=.

Messer-Davidow, E., D. R. Shumway, and D. Sylvan. *Knowledges: Historical and Critical Studies in Disciplinarity.* University Press of Virginia, 1993.

Matter-Mind Studio. "NEW INC, Cultural Incubator: Value-Driven Research for Organizational Health." Matter-Mind Studio, 2018. https://www.mattermindstudio.com/workplace.

Mingus, Mia. "Transformative Justice: A Brief Description." Leaving Evidence, January 9, 2019. https://leavingevidence.wordpress.com/2019/01/09/transformative-justice-a-brief-description.

Mitchell, Ellinor R. "The Lincoln Story." National Acupuncture Detoxification Association, n.d. https://www.acudetox.com/thelincoln-story.

Morrison, Toni. *Playing in the Dark: Whiteness and the Literary Imagination.* Harvard University Press, 1992.

Moten, Fred. "Taste Dissonance Flavor: Preface for a Solo by Miles Davis." *Women & Performance* 17, no. 2 (2007): 217-46.

Nash, Jennifer C. "The Political Life of Black Motherhood." *Feminist Studies* 44, no. 3 (2018): 699-712. https://doi.org/10.15767/feministstudies.44.3.0699.

Paul-Emile, Kimani. "Blackness as Disability?" *The Georgetown Law Journal* 106, no. 2 (2018): 293-364.

Pollock, Della. "Performance Trouble." In *The SAGE Handbook of Performance Studies*, edited by D. Soyini Madison and Judith Hamera (Sage Publications, 2005), 1-8.

Prince, Alanna, and Alisa V. Prince. "What's Haunting Black Feminism?" *Invisible Culture*, no. 31 (2020): 1.

Prus, Robert C. *Symbolic Interaction and Ethnographic Research: Intersubjectivity and the Study of Human Lived Experience.* State University of New York Press, 1996.

Quashie, Kevin Everod. *The Sovereignty of Quiet Beyond Resistance in Black Culture.* Rutgers University Press, 2012.

Rogoff, Irit. "Practicing Research: Singularising Knowledge." *MAkuZine* 9 (2010): 37-42.

Russell, Legacy. *Glitch Feminism.* Verso, 2020.

Scarry, Elaine. *The Body in Pain: The Making and Unmaking of The World.* Oxford University Press, 1985.

Schön, Donald A. *The Reflective Practitioner: How Professionals Think in Action.* Basic

Books, 1983.

Sedgwick, Eve Kosofsky, Michelle Alna Barale, Jonathan Goldberg, and Michael Moon. "Paranoid Reading and Reparative Reading, or, You're so Paranoid, You Probably Think This Essay is About You. In *Touching Feeling* (Duke University Press, 2002): 123-51.

Sefotho, Maximus Monaheng. "Basotho Ontology of Disability: An Afrocentric Onto-Epistemology." *Heliyon* 7, no. 3 (2021): 1-8. https://doi.org/10.1016/j.heliyon.2021.e06540.

Sexton, Jared. "People-of-Color-Blindness: A Lecture by Jared Sexton." UC Berkeley Events. October 27, 2011. https://www.youtube.com/watch?v=qNVMI-3oiDaI.

---. "The Vel of Slavery: Tracking the Figure of the Unsovereign." *Critical Sociology* 42, no. 4-5 (2014): 583-97. https://doi.org/10.1177/0896920514552535.

Sharpe, Christina. *In the Wake: On Blackness and Being*. Duke University Press, 2016.

Smith, Andrea. "Heteropatriarchy and the Three Pillars of White Supremacy." In Color of Violence: The INCITE! Anthology, edited by INCITE! Women of Color Against Violence (Duke University Press, 2016), 66-73.

Smith, Linda Tuhiwai, and Eve Tuck. "INQ13: Decolonizing Methodologies." The Graduate Center, CUNY, April 29, 2013, Video. https://www.youtube.com/watch?v=rIZXQC27tvg.

Spalding, Esperanza. "I'm Not the 'Musical Prodigy' I've Been Made Out to Be." Guy Raz, September 10, 2024, Video. https://www.youtube.com/watch?v=uw7piG9vRic&t=2s

Spillers, Hortense J. "Changing the Letter: The Yokes, the Jokes of Discourse, or, Mrs. Stowe, Mr. Reed." In *Black, White, and in Color: Essays on American Literature and Culture*, by Hortense J. Spillers (University of Chicago Press, 2003), 176-202.

Waheed, Nayyirah. *Nejma*. CreateSpace Independent Publishing Platform, 2014.

---. *Salt*. CreateSpace Independent Publishing Platform, 2013.

Walker, Alice. *In Search of Our Mothers' Gardens: Womanist Prose*. Harcourt Brace Jovanovich, 1983.

INDEX

An index of terms, people, and references designed to help readers locate key concepts, frameworks, and contexts discussed throughout.

Set Margins' #91

Doing Creative Work from Your Political Body
A Guide and Process for Practice-led Research
Myriam D. Diatta

ISBN: 978-90-836052-8-9

Graphic design: Toni Wagner
Layout production: Myriam D. Diatta
Proofreader: Doug Lebsack
Printer: Printon, Tallinn, EE
Fonts: Calvino and Acumin Pro
Paper: Munken Lynx

Special thanks to Zakiya Collier, Linda Dounia, Rain Embuscado, Jelsen Lee Innocent, Baseera Khan, Heesoo Kwon, Fei Liu, and AK Wane.

Brief excerpts of this book are reproduced with permission and have previously appeared in the following: Myriam Diatta, "Turning the Body Inside Out," in *Designing Knowledge*, ed. Bonne Zabolotney (London: Bloomsbury Visual Arts, 2024).[1]. And in Myriam D. Diatta, Stacy H. Jones, and Kate McEntee, "A Place to Meet: How Critical Theory Cares for the Everyday in Artistic Practice," *Research in Arts and Education Journal*: Special Issue on Critical Artistic Research as Practices of Care, December 2021. https://doi.org/10.54916/rae.119529.

First edition, 2026

Set Margins'
www.setmargins.press

Made possible in part thanks to support from the Nordic Culture Fund.

NORDISK
KULTURFOND